Biyaki Samani
4th September 1994
London.

The Hill and the Labyrinth

Hercules Gallicus as depicted in Vincenzo Cartari, *Le Imagini de i dei de gli antichi* (1571).

JOHN M. STEADMAN

The Hill and the Labyrinth

Discourse and Certitude in Milton and His Near-Contemporaries

University of California Press

Berkeley / Los Angeles / London

University of California Press
Berkeley and Los Angeles, California

University of California Press, Ltd.
London, England

Printed in the United States of America

1   2   3   4   5   6   7   8   9

Library of Congress Cataloging in Publication Data

Steadman, John M.
    The hill and the labyrinth.

    Bibliography: p.
    Includes index.
    1. English literature—Early modern, 1500–1700—
History and criticism.   2. Philosophy, English—17th cen-
tury.   3. English language—Early modern, 1500–1700—
Style.   4. Knowledge, Theory of—History—17th century.
5. Rhetoric—1500–1800—History.   6. Milton, John, 1608–
1674—Criticism and interpretation.   I. Title.
PR439.P48S72   1984   820'.9'384   83-6934
ISBN 0-520-04877-6

Contents

List of Illustrations

All illustrations are reproduced by kind permission of The Huntington Library, San Marino, California.

Frontis: Hercules Gallicus as depicted in Vincenzo Cartari, *Le Imagini de i dei de gli antichi* (1571).

(following page 136)

Foreword

In reexamining the relationship between style of discourse and epistemological method in seventeenth-century England, I have attempted to bring into focus certain late Renaissance and baroque tensions between conceptions of the role of language as a vehicle for traditional doctrines and accepted dogmas, as a weapon for attack or defense, and as an instrument of inquiry and discovery. Centered primarily on the Seicento, the present work developed out of researches for a Faculty Research Lecture delivered at the University of California at Riverside in April 1977 and for a monograph on earlier Renaissance thought and style entitled *The Lamb and the Elephant: Ideal Imitation and the Context of Renaissance Allegory* (Huntington Library: San Marino, California, 1974). Portions of the Faculty Research Lecture were privately printed by the Academic Senate of the University of California, Riverside, for distribution to faculty members, under the title "The Hill and the Labyrinth: Rhetoric and Certitude in Milton and His Contemporaries."

Complementary to *The Lamb and the Elephant*, this work begins, in a sense, where the latter left off: "In this uncertain and unpredictable climate—a climate of opinions, not of certitudes—the traditional role of rhetoric was, to a certain extent, compromised. It could adorn and embellish Truth, but it could not discover her. Unlike logic, which aimed at certainties through infallible syllogistic demonstrations, it derived its arguments from probabilities or apparent probabilities. It could be useful in persuading the multitude to follow Truth—once she had been discovered and uncaverned—but it could not assist the philosopher to find her out and to exantlate her. This task—the first and primary labor of the intellectual speleologist—devolved upon the logician; and he must first find a reliable spade—an appropriate instrument or *organon*" (pp. 228–229).

If the traditional rhetoric, an instrument of persuasion, was inadequate as a means of discovering the truth, the Ramist reforms subordinating rhetoric to dialectic had reduced the art of eloquence largely to an art of extrinsic ornamentation. The Ramist theory, as Perry Miller observes, "applied rhetoric to the work merely of adding ornaments or embellishing that which logic had invented and arranged, of uttering logical propositions with appropriate tones and gestures. [Ramist theory] still concentrated the art upon persuasion, but took away from it all power to determine for itself to what it should persuade.... Literary style in the Puritan aesthetic [was] 'varnish'" (*The New England Mind* [New York, 1939; rpt. Boston, 1961] pp. 326, 354).

The relationships between epistemological methods and style in the late Renaissance are too complex to explore in detail here; for further discussion one should consult the studies listed in the Bibliography. In particular the varieties of "plain style," their origins and models, and the relationship between theory and practice in authors of this period remain controversial. With some justification, Socratic and Stoic models, the classical "Attic" style as defined by Cicero and exemplified by Caesar and Sallust, and the *genus humile* in classical comedy, satire, and epigram and the epistolary mode as a variety of classical and Renaissance authors (Cicero and Seneca, Erasmus and Vives) conceived it have all been considered instrumental. Other possible influences include Peter Ramus and his followers, René Descartes and his disciples, the plain style cultivated by Port-Royal, the views on style held by René Rapin, the native tradition of "plain" English, and the "natural," unpretentious conversational style of a gentleman. The views of Morris W. Croll and Richard Foster Jones have been formative, though they have subsequently been qualified by scholars such as George Williamson, Robert Adolph, Jackson I. Cope, Harold Fisch, Brian Vickers, Jonas Barish, Barbara K. Lewalski, Joan Webber, and Stanley E. Fish.

Critics have related epistemology to style in various ways. Croll links the periodic Ciceronian style and the curt and loose varieties of Senecanism with epistemological certitude or incertitude, while Jones associates the plain style of the Restoration primarily with the philosophical and scientific needs of the Royal Society of London. In "Style and Certitude" Don Cameron Allen emphasizes the correlation between literary style and epistemology in seventeenth-century prose; and Leonard Nathanson, Vickers, and others apply this approach to specific authors such as Francis Bacon, Thomas Browne, John Donne, John Dryden, and their contemporaries. In linking stylistic modes with epistemologies, one must resist the temptation to press their association too far. The essay styles of Montaigne and Bacon or of Browne and Locke are in some respects worlds apart, as are the meditative modes of Donne, Descartes, and Joseph Hall. There are suggestive analogies between the analytic method and the meditative style as a vehicle of inquiry and discovery described by Croll; but in some respects Croll's "libertine" mode involves an apparent neglect of method or an implicit subversion of method. In associating the development of plain style with epistemological problems, one must also be aware of the epistemological value of other styles, of obscurity, figurative and metaphorical discourse, and shadowy adumbrations of the truth. In this respect, Browne's metaphysical style, with its deliberate cultivation of obscure "types and shadows" and recondite allusion, is the consciously elected correlative of his own epistemological stance and of his concept of reality.

Epistemology and choice of style are closely interlinked in Nathanson's *The Strategy of Truth: A Study of Sir Thomas Browne*, Webber's *The Eloquent "I": Style and Self in Seventeenth-Century Prose*, and Fish's *Surprised by Sin* and *Self-Consuming Artifacts*. But style does not always support epistemological inquiry: for instance, the self-revelatory aspects of the essay style tend to undercut its efficacy as an instrument for the discovery of truth and the exploration of external reality. The "self" projected may be a conscious literary creation, like the persona of a dramatic monologue, lyric, or satire; the rhetoric of inquiry may be much less premeditated and spontaneous than it purports to be. Apparent self-exploration and self-expression may be no less contrived than the soliloquies of the *dramatis personae* of a contemporary tragedy or comedy. The style that pretends to project a true image of the writer's moods and personality may become studiedly whimsical, fantastical, and tetchy. The attempt to render individuality may result in a consciously affected eccentricity and idiosyncrasy, such as the "skittishness" of baroque prose noted by Barish in *Ben Jonson and the Language of Prose Comedy*.

In moving between the period of Montaigne and that of Thomas Sprat, or between the dialectic and rhetoric of Plato and those of Peter Ramus and Milton, one risks oversimplifying the highly complex relationships between stylistic theory and practice in what were, on the whole, quite different historical contexts. The risk, however, is a calculated one; and in this general overview of the connections between seventeenth-century epistemology and rhetoric, I have attempted to do justice to the different intellectual contexts in which classical, patristic, early Renaissance, and post-Restoration theorists evolved their notions of the function and decorum of the various stylistic modes.

In writing this book, I have been indebted to friends and colleagues at the Huntington Library and at the University of California, Riverside, for help and encouragement. Professor Thomas Kranidas, Mrs. Jane Evans, and Mrs. Winifred Freese kindly read the manuscript and offered valuable advice. A fellowship from the John Simon Guggenheim Memorial Foundation and a subsequent sabbatical leave from the University of California at Riverside were helpful in enabling me to reorganize and revise this work. I am also grateful to the readers for the University of California Press, who offered further valuable suggestions for revision. The illustrations in this volume are derived from books in the collections of the Henry E. Huntington Library and are reprinted by permission of the Huntington Library.

Short Titles

In the notes periodicals are cited by the abbreviations used in the *MLA International Bibliography*; full titles are provided in the bibliography. Works frequently cited in the text and notes are referred to by the following short titles and abbreviations:

CP	John Milton, *Complete Poetry and Major Prose*, ed. Merritt Y. Hughes (New York, 1957).
Essay	John Locke, *An Essay Concerning Human Understanding*, ed. Russell Kirk (Chicago, 1956).
L	Thomas Hobbes, *Leviathan, Parts One and Two*, ed. Herbert W. Schneider (Indianapolis and New York, 1958).
Prose	*The Prose of Sir Thomas Browne*, ed. Norman J. Endicott (Garden City, N.Y., 1967).
S	George Williamson, *The Senecan Amble: A Study in Prose Form from Bacon to Collier* (Chicago, 1966).
SC	*Seventeenth-Century English Poetry*, ed. John T. Shawcross and Ronald David Emma (Philadelphia and New York, 1969).
Studies	Richard Foster Jones, et al., *The Seventeenth Century: Studies in the History of English Thought and Literature from Bacon to Pope* (Stanford and London, 1969).

Style   *Style, Rhetoric, and Rhythm: Essays by Morris W. Croll*, ed. J. Max Patrick, et al. (Princeton, 1966).

SW   *Selected Writings of Francis Bacon*, ed. Hugh G. Dick (New York, 1955).

Veritas simplex oratio.

Trouthes tale is simple, he that meaneth good faith,
goeth not about to glose his communicacion with
painted wordes. Plain and homely men call a figge,
a figge, and a spade, a spade. Rhetorike and
coloringe of spech, proved [*sic*] manye times a
mans matter to be naught.

Richard Taverner,
*Proverbes or Adagies, gathered
out of the Chiliades of Erasmus...*
(London, 1569)

Suche force hath the tongue, and such is the
power of eloquence and reason, that most men
are forced even to yelde in that, whiche most
standeth againste their will. And therefore the
Poetes do feyne that Hercules being a man of greate
wisdome, had all men lincked together by the
eares in a chaine, to draw them and leade them
even as he lusted.

Thomas Wilson,
The Arte of Rhetorique,
Preface (London, 1553)

I. Introduction: The Pursuit of Truth

Hard are the ways of truth, and rough to walk,
Smooth on the tongue discourst, pleasing to th' ear,
And tunable as Silvan Pipe or Song.

(*CP*, p. 493)

Perhaps we should distrust this statement, for the speaker was the archetypal Father of Lies. Its earliest readers, like the hero of *Paradise Regained*, would surely have been on their guard. Yet one suspects that many of them would have agreed with Milton's Satan. The ways of truth *were* notoriously hard and rough, even if one possessed the advantage of cloven hoofs: tenderer heels than those of the archliar would be lucky to escape with no more than a bruise. It would seem few periods were more conscious of the difficulties of the way, its pitfalls and its stumbling-blocks, than the seventeenth century. To a society harassed (if not obsessed) by epistemological problems—questions of certitude, method, doubt versus authority, authority versus experiment, experiment versus reason, reason versus faith—to a society also preoccupied with the limitations of human reason and the effects of original sin, Satan's opening gambit might well seem a commonplace, vulgar truism.

To the same audience, however, his remarks on language would have seemed more controversial. On the one hand, they reflected an ideal of eloquence traditionally associated with Renaissance humanism and often extolled by Milton himself. For its apologists, rhetoric was the handmaiden of truth, skilled in employing the niceties of the verbal dressing-table and capable of making the harshest features of philosophy appear smooth and pleasant. On the other hand, as many of Milton's readers were aware, humanistic methods of education were under attack: rhetoric and poetry were once again being challenged as corrupters rather than illuminators of truth, and eloquence itself denounced as a principal obstacle to the advancement of learning. Language was criticized by some as the feeblest of instruments—far more untrustworthy than a silvan pipe—preferably to be dispensed with altogether if possible. Smooth and harmonious cadences, critics insisted, reflected a concern with style rather than sub-

stance, with fine words rather than solid facts; such sensuous allure-
ments could only divert and distract the serious inquirer from his
strenuous pursuit of truth. For these readers, Satan's emphasis on verbal music would have smacked rather too strongly of the "glosing
Rhetoric" that had formerly seduced our first mother Eve and was
still corrupting the discourse of her fallen posterity.

Satan's metaphor was a commonplace of the period; we shall encounter the same *topos* and similar imagery in the works of a future
Dean of St. Paul's, a Lord Chancellor of England, a Norfolk poly-
math, and John Milton himself as we discuss the imagery of the pursuit of true knowledge and the perils of the quest in several representative authors.

> On a huge hill,
> Cragged, and steep, Truth stands, and hee that will
> Reach her, about must, and about must goe;
> And what the hills suddennes resists, winne so.

John Donne, in his "Third Satire," thus exhorts his audience to a dangerous feat of epistemological mountaineering, but nevertheless offers
little practical advice beyond caution and a skeptical traverse: "doubt
wisely."[1] His image appears to be a variant of the well-known moun-
tain-climbing metaphor exploited by both classical and Renaissance
authors. Some variants emphasize the delights of the prospect rather
than the hazards of the climb; others stress the difficulties and labors of
the ascent as well as the ultimate reward.[2] Francis Bacon appropriately

1. *Poetical Works*, ed. Herbert H. C. Grierson (London, Oxford, New York, 1971),
p. 139.
   In an analysis of Donne's "poetry of scepticism," Margaret L. Wiley examines the
imagery of his "Third Satire," with its metaphorical description of "the process of ap-
proaching truth through the devious ways made necessary by man's essential ignorance." In her opinion, this one figure "sets forth vividly the sceptic despair of knowledge, the belief in doubt as a valuable technique, the inevitability of dualism and
paradox, and the conviction that truth will finally be found at the top of a huge and
cragged hill." Similarly, in his verses on the "new Philosophy" in "The First Anniversary," Donne gives poetic expression to "the shattering effect" of the new learning; see
The Subtle Knot: Creative Scepticism in Seventeenth-Century England (London,
1952), pp. 120–136.
2. For analogues and variations on this image, see *A Variorum Commentary on the
Poems of John Milton*, vol. 2, pt. 2, ed. A. S. P. Woodhouse and Douglas Bush (New
York, 1972), p. 381; vol. 4, ed. Walter MacKellar (New York, 1975), pp. 100–101;
John Donne, *The Satires, Epigrams, and Verse Letters*, ed. W. Milgate (Oxford, 1967).
Editors of Milton and Donne note parallels in Holbein's illustrations of the *Table of
Cebes*, in Horace's *Carmina* 3.24.44, in Hesiod's *Works and Days* 287–292, and in
Plato's *Republic* 2.364C and *Laws* 4.718E. Analogies have also been noted in

introduces his "dispersed meditations" with an essay on truth, but cunningly evades the opening question: "What is Truth?" The answer is worth staying for, he suggests, but he himself does not supply it. His essay is an encomium of truth rather than a rigorous inquiry into its nature or the best means of attaining it. Like Donne, Bacon acknowledges "the difficulty and labour which men take in finding out of truth," but characteristically, his primary emphasis falls on the limitations of the human mind and will, on "a natural though corrupt love of the lie itself." In contrast to Milton's archliar, Bacon argues that falsehood gives greater pleasure than truth:

> this same truth is a naked and open daylight, that doth not show the masks and mummeries and triumphs of the world, half so stately and daintily as candlelight.... A mixture of a lie doth ever add pleasure, ... [a Father of the church has] called poesy *vinum daemonum*, because it filleth the imagination; and yet it is but with the shadow of a lie. (*SW*, pp. 7–8)

Although Bacon evokes the image of the commanding hill, he does not like Donne emphasize the dangers and difficulties of ascent. Instead, he prefers to emphasize the elitist pleasures of the view, though he modifies Lucretius's reference to the lofty "fortified sanctuaries

---

Xenophon's account of the Choice of Hercules in *Memorabilia*, in Matthew 7:13–14, in Palingenius's *Zodiac of Life*, and in Thomas Drant's *The Mirror of Majesty*. Commentators also cite Milton's sonnet 9 ("those few ... / That labour up the Hill of heav'nly Truth") and *Paradise Regained* 2.217 ("Seated as on the top of Vertues hill"). In a recent study Paul Sellin argues that Donne's "Third Satire" "might possibly be a late poem, a poem written after Donne took orders," composed "between January 1 and midsummer of 1620." As evidence for this redating of the poem, Sellin adduces "the golden medallion commemorating the Synod of Dort, conferred on Donne by the States General" at the end of December 1619 and depicting a lofty mountain peak in association with the motto "Erunt ut Mons Sion" ("The Proper Dating of Donne's 'Satyre III'," *Huntington Library Quarterly* 43 [1980]: 275–312). In Appendix B, "Sources proposed since Milgate for 'Satyre III,' lines 79–82," Sellin cites Milton's sonnet 9 ("Lady that in the Prime"). Sellin also cites several recent studies, including M. T. Hester, "John Donne's 'Hill of Truth'," *ELN* 14 (1976): 100–105, and H. D. Ousby, "A Senecan Analogue to Donne's 'Huge Hill'," *N&Q*, n.s. 24 (1977): 144–145.

Quoting Donne's "Third Satire," Herschel Baker credits the poet with asserting that "truth is available to man, but through effort and seeking rather than prescription" (*The Wars of Truth: Studies in the Decay of Christian Humanisim in the Earlier Seventeenth Century* [Cambridge, Mass., 1952], p. 159). But Basil Willey, echoing "The First Anniversary," treats Donne as a conservative reactionary. There are always, Willey declares, "those like Donne for whom new philosophy 'puts all in doubt,' for whom ... new explanation explains nothing, but merely causes distress and confusion; and those, like the Fathers of the Inquisition, for whom new philosophy is simply old error" (*The Seventeenth Century Background: Studies in the Thought of the Age in Relation to Poetry and Religion* [London, 1949], p. 5).

serene, built up by the teachings of the wise," by interpolating a gloss or two of his own:

> The poet that beautified the sect that was otherwise inferior to the rest, saith yet excellently well: *It is a pleasure to stand upon the shore, and to see ships tossed upon the sea; a pleasure to stand in the window of a castle, and to see a battle and the adventures thereof below: but no pleasure is comparable to the standing upon the vantage ground of Truth,* (a hill not to be commanded, and where the air is always clear and serene,) *and to see the errors and wanderings, and mists, and tempests, in the vale below:* so always that this prospect be with pity, and not with swelling or pride. (*SW*, pp. 7–8)[3]

Despite this admiration for the Epicurean poet, Bacon elsewhere contemns the pursuit of knowledge for the sake of pleasure rather than utility:

> For men have entered into a desire of learning and knowledge, sometimes upon a natural curiosity and inquisitive appetite; sometimes to entertain

3. Cf. Lucretius, *De Rerum Natura*, tr. W. H. D. Rouse (London and New York, 1924), pp. 84–85, ll. 1–13. Sellin ("The Proper Dating of Donne's 'Satyre III'," p. 309) observes how "cavalierly" Bacon has rendered Lucretius's phrase "munita tenere / edita doctrina sapientium templa serena." Bacon cites the same passage in *The Advancement of Learning* (*S W*, p. 218): "But it is a pleasure incomparable, for the mind of man to be settled, landed, and fortified in the certainty of truth; and from thence to descry and behold the errors, perturbations, labours, and wanderings up and down of other men." Cf. *De Augmentis Scientiarum*, "at nil dulcius est homini, quam mens per doctrinam in arce veritatis collocata, unde aliorum errores et labores dispicere possit" (*The Works of Francis Bacon*, ed. James Spedding, Robert Leslie Ellis, and Douglas Denon Heath [London, 1857], 1:482–483). Bacon employs a similar variant of this image in *The Wisdom of the Ancients*, no. 28 ("Sphinx or Science"): "All knowledge may be regarded as having its station on the heights of mountains; for it is deservedly esteemed a thing sublime and lofty, which looks down upon ignorance as from an eminence, and has moreover a spacious prospect on every side, such as we find on hilltops" (*S W*, p. 419).

In exploring the recurrent images and image-patterns in Bacon's writings, Brian Vickers emphasizes his "tendency to think in images." Imagery "drawn from a journey, on land and sea, . . . is for Bacon a metaphor for the search for knowledge, the pilgrimage for truth." Conversely, of "all the negatives which oppose positive progress" in the group of images associated with the path or road or way, the "most potent for Bacon" is the image of "the place where man gets lost, be it a wood, a maze, or a labyrinth" (*Francis Bacon and Renaissance Prose* [Cambridge, 1968], pp. 175, 179–183; see also pp. 184–200).

According to Alexander Richardson, a logician in the Ramist tradition, "All thinking . . . is 'the running about of our reason for the finding out of truth,' and we run about because we do not always see the truth at once" (quoted in Perry Miller, *The New England Mind: The Seventeenth Century* [1939; rpt. Boston, 1961], p. 135). In "Of Scepticism and Certainty," Joseph Glanvill observes that "*Free Philosophers . . .* continue to seek Truth in the Great Book of Nature" (quoted in Henry G. Van

their minds with variety and delight . . .: as if there were sought in knowledge a couch, whereupon to rest a searching and restless spirit; or a ter-
race, for a wandering and variable mind to walk up and down with a fair
prospect; . . . and not a rich storehouse, for the glory of the Creator and the
relief of man's estate. (*SW*, p. 193)

In his *Epistles* Samuel Daniel evoked the image of the commanding
height of contemplation in poems addressed to Margaret, Countess
of Cumberland and to Lucy, Countess of Bedford. The verse letter to
the Countess of Cumberland applies this imagery to the commonplaces of Christian Stoicism:

> He that of such a height hath built his minde,
> And rear'd the dwelling of his thoughts so strong
> As neither Feare nor Hope can shake the frame
> Of his resolved powres, . . .
>
> . . . .
> What a faire seate hath he from whence hee may
> The boundlesse wastes, and weilds of man survay.
>
> And with how free an eye doth he looke downe,
> Upon these lower Regions of turmoyle,
> Where all these stormes of passions mainely beate
> On flesh and blood. . . .

Similarly, reminding the Countess of Bedford that the "faire course
of knowledge" that she is pursuing is "th'onely certaine way" to
true glory and true happiness, Daniel declares that it will admit her
to that bliss

> That sets you there where you may oversee
> This rowling world, and view it as it is
>
> . . . .

Leeuwen, *The Problem of Certainty in English Thought, 1630–1690*, 2nd ed. [The
Hague, 1970], p. 83).

The metaphor of the path or road is implicit in the Greek word *methodos* (derived
from *meta* and *hodos*, "way"). As Walter J. Ong reminds us, it signified "a following
after or pursuit," requiring the further meaning "pursuit of knowledge, or an investigation, or the mode of prosecuting such inquiry, with the emphasis on logical rather than
physical procedure." In the Socratic tradition this notion was "fused with that of dialogue or dialectical procedure" (*Ramus, Method, and the Decay of Dialogue: From the
Art of Discourse to the Art of Reason* [Cambridge, Mass., 1958], p. 226). The "sense of
systematic arrangement" was "foreign to Greek" and was developed by sixteenth-century logicians (*New English Dictionary*, s.v. "method").

> And though we cannot finde
> The certaine place of truth, yet doe they [books] stay,
> And intertaine us neere about the same.[4]

We shall encounter similar modes of intellectual hedonism and intemperance in Milton's fallen angels, who seek the "pleasing sorcery" of vain wisdom and false philosophy to charm their pain, yet find "no end, in wand'ring mazes lost." Appropriately it is Belial, subsequently described as "the dissolutest Spirit that fell, / The sensuallest, and after *Asmodai* / The fleshliest Incubus," who appeals to the pleasures of the intellect, while counselling "ignoble ease, and peaceful sloth" (*CP*, pp. 245, 497, 235):

> for who would lose,
> Though full of pain, this intellectual being,
> Those thoughts that wander through Eternity? . . .
>   (*CP*, p. 237)

For Bacon's stress on the difficulties of the way of truth, rather than the delights of the commanding view, one must turn to his more ambitious works, such as the *Novum Organum*. Here the pleasures of the prospect are subordinated to utility, and the rewards of the summit indefinitely postponed until the ascent can be made secure by establishing "progressive stages of certainty" (*SW*, p. 456). The pursuit of truth is a path through a maze; before reaching the hilltop one must like Dante force one's way through a *selva oscura*:

> But the universe to the eye of the human understanding is framed like a labyrinth, presenting as it does on every side so many ambiguities of way, such deceitful resemblances of objects and signs, natures so irregular in their lines and so knotted and entangled. (*SW*, p. 433)

For Bacon, as for his intellectual posterity, the "great instauration" of learning seemed an enterprise virtually "above heroic" (though the phrase is Milton's) excelling by far the exploits of the heroes of myth and romance. One is not surprised, therefore, to find his own choice of method described in the imagery of the Pythagorean "Y" and of Hercules' Choice:

> The two ways of contemplation are much like those two of action, so much celebrated, in this—that the one, arduous and difficult in the beginning,

---

4. *Poems and a Defense of Rhyme*, ed. Arthur Colby Sprague (Cambridge, Mass., 1930), pp. 111, 117–118.

leads out at last into the open country; while the other, seeming at first sight easy and free from obstruction, leads to pathless and precipitous places. ("Proemium," *Instauration, SW*, p. 424)[5]

For the Renaissance, Hercules was the supreme exemplar of *Virtus Heroica*. The traditional scientific methods, Bacon argues, resemble

5. For the Pythagorean "Y"—the Greek letter upsilon as a "symbol of the two divergent paths of virtue and of vice," see *The Shorter Oxford English Dictionary*, 3rd ed., s.v. "Pythagorean." For the traditions of the Choice of Hercules and the Dream of Scipio, see Erwin Panofsky, *Hercules am Scheidewege und andere antike Bildstoffe in der neueren Kunst*, Studien der Bibliothek Warburg 18 (Leipzig and Berlin, 1930). In Xenophon's *Memorabilia*, Prodicus's fable of Hercules' choice between Vice (*kakia*) and Virtue (*arete*) is linked with Hesiod's description of the paths of good and evil, or virtue and vice in *Works and Days*. See *Hesiod . . .*, trans. Hugh G. Evelyn-White (London and New York, 1929): "Badness can be got easily and in shoals; the road to her is smooth, and she lives very near us. But between us and Goodness the gods have placed the sweat of our brows: long and steep is the path that leads to her, and it is rough at the first; but when a man has reached the top, then is she easy to reach, though before that she was hard" (pp. 24–25, ll. 287–292).

See also Thomas Browne's adaptation of the "hill" motif from the *Tabula Cebetis* in *Christian Morals*: "Consider where about thou art in *Cebes's* Table, or that old Philosophical Pinax of the Life of Man: whether thou art yet in the Road of uncertainties, whether thou hast yet entred the narrow Gate, got up the Hill and asperous way, which leadeth unto the House of Sanity, or taken that purifying Potion from the hand of sincere Erudition, which may send Thee clear and pure away unto a virtuous and happy Life" (*Prose*, p. 371).

In *Mundus Symbolicus*, Filippo Picinelli discussed at length the figurative significance of labyrinth, mountain, and Pythagorean "Y." The hill or mountain (*mons*) may symbolize Wisdom, the *vita contemplativa*, the Holy Church, the just man, hope in God, or beatitude. It also serves as a figure for merit or reward or dignities, or for such virtues as constancy and humility. Similarly it is closely associated with the arduous way of virtue, with eminence, and with ascent to the highest estate by way of the lowest. The labyrinth variously symbolizes worldly pleasure or lust; the ways of the irresolute, the heretic, and the damned; or the unsearchable ways of God ("Investigabiles viae ejus"). Contrasting the many erroneous paths through the labyrinth taken by heretics with the one true way of salvation provided by the Holy Church and the Catholic faith, Picinelli quoted St. Epiphanius: "Est via regia Sancta Dei Ecclesia, & iter veritatis." See *Mundus Symbolicus*, ed. and trans. August Erath (Cologne, 1694), bk. 2, chap. 31; bk. 16, chap. 11; bk. 19, chap. 14; fac. ed. *The Renaissance and the Gods*, ed. Stephen Orgel (New York and London, 1976). For other examples of the mountain and the labyrinth in Renaissance emblem books, see Arthur Henkel and Albrecht Schöne, eds., *Emblemata: Handbuch zur Sinnbildkunst des XVI. und XVII. Jahrhunderts* (Stuttgart, 1967).

In a late edition of Cesare Ripa's *Iconologia*, the mountain of the Sisyphus myth was interpreted as a symbol of the "*Life* of Man; the Top of it, the *Quietness* and *Tranquillity* of what we aspire to." The "huge Stone" that Sisyphus rolls "to the Top of a mountain, which still falls back again," signifies "the great *Pains* every one takes to come at it" (i.e., the mountain-top of tranquillity), while Sisyphus himself "signifies the *Mind*" (Ripa, *Iconologia: Or, Moral Emblems* [London, 1709], p. 90; fac. ed., Orgel, ed., *The Renaissance and the Gods*).

the easy road of Vice or Pleasure, the path of dalliance that Hercules had firmly rejected. The new and rigorous method of induction corresponds to the rougher path of Virtue, the way elected by the paradigm of Heroic Virtue himself. We shall subsequently encounter a further variation on this motif in *Paradise Regained* (though combined with themes based on the Judgment of Paris) in the temptation ordeal of Milton's Christian Hercules, "born to promote all truth" as the "living Oracle" of the divine will (*CP*, pp. 487, 493).

Although "experience of untruth had made access to truth more difficult," Bacon believed that he had discovered a "clue to the maze," a *filum labyrinthi*, a valid "formula of inquiry." His use of the maze image is characteristic of his exploitation of classical myth as a vehicle for his own ideas. Closely associated with the image of the forest and sometimes with the imagery of the dance, the myth of the labyrinth had already been adapted to a wide variety of concepts—to the deceits of the senses, to the realm of matter, to the disputes of philosophers and theologians, to the subtleties of nature, to the ordeals of mystagogues and lovers, to the course of human life, to Error in general, to the world itself—and it would subsequently acquire a more specialized significance for Bacon's professed followers. In his program for the reform of natural philosophy, Bacon had called for "a calendar of popular errors" (*SW*, p. 266). Thomas Browne (a thoroughly un-Baconian intellect alternately inspired by Hermetic, Stoic, and Baconian philosophy) dutifully undertook this labor in his *Pseudodoxia Epidemica: or, Enquiries into Very many received Tenets And commonly Presumed Truths*; yet he found the task far more arduous than his master had surmised:

> [We] finde no open tract, or constant manuduction in this Labyrinth, [and are thus] oft-times fain to wander in the America and untravelled parts of Truth. ... For questionlesse in knowledge there is no slender difficulty, and truth which wise men say doth lye in a well, is not recoverable but by exantlation. [We no longer possess] a Paradise or unthorny place of knowledge. [With] understandings ... eclipsed [and] tempers infirmed, we must betake our selves to waies of reparation. (*Prose*, pp. 99, 120)

For Abraham Cowley, in contrast, the period of error is all but past, and his optimism is reflected in images of achieved discovery and imminent conquest. Like Moses, Bacon has led us forth at last from "all long errors of the way, In which our wandering predecessors went" and conducted us to the very border of the promised land:

> But life did never to one man allow
> Time to discover worlds, and conquer too;
> Nor can so short a line sufficient be
> To fathom the vast depths of Nature's sea.
>   ("To the Royal Society," *SC*, p. 404)

To complete the conquest, reinstate the true cult of nature, and restore "deposed truth" to her throne is a heroic enterprise destined to be the province of the Royal Society; and Cowley does not hesitate to compare its "glorious fight" to the battles of Joshua and Gideon:

> From you great champions, we expect to get
> These spacious countries but discovered yet;
> Countries where yet instead of Nature, we
> Her images and idols worshipped see.
>   ("Royal Society," *SC*, p. 405)

Thomas Hobbes, more confident still, has not only discovered a new world, but successfully colonized it:

> Thou great Columbus of the golden lands of new philosophies;
>   Thy task was harder much than his,
>   For thy learned America is
>   Not only found out first by thee,
> And rudely left to future industry,
>   But thy eloquence and thy wit
> Has planted, peopled, built, and civilized it.
>   ("To Mr. Hobbes," *SC*, p. 397)

In Milton's *Areopagitica* the labors of truth are presented through images drawn from the playing field, the battlefield, the riverbed, the mining pit, and Egyptian mysteries. "Our faith and knowledge thrives by exercise, as well as our limbs and complexion," Milton maintains. "Truth is compared in scripture to a streaming fountain; if her waters flow not in a perpetual progression, they sicken into a muddy pool of conformity and tradition." Let Truth "and Falsehood grapple; who ever knew Truth put to the worse, in a free and open encounter." "When a man hath been laboring the hardest labor in the deep mines of knowledge, ... [has] drawn forth his reasons as it were a battle ranged, [and called] out his adversary into the plain," only a craven would shirk the combat of argument by ambushes; though to shirk ambush "be valor enough in soldiership," it "is but weakness and cowardice in the wars of Truth" (*CP*, pp. 739, 746–747).

A more violent image is the metaphor of *sparagmos* ("dismemberment") and quest which Milton derived from Plutarch:[6]

> Truth indeed came once into the world with her divine Master, and was a most perfect shape most glorious to look on. But when he ascended, and his apostles after him were laid asleep, then straight arose a wicked race of deceivers, who, as that story goes of the Egyptian Typhon with his conspirators, how they dealt with the good Osiris, took the virgin Truth, hewed her lovely form into a thousand pieces, and scattered them to the four winds. From that time ever since, the sad friends of Truth, such as durst appear, imitating the careful search that Isis made for the mangled body of Osiris, went up and down gathering up limb by limb still as they could find them. We have not found them all, . . . nor ever shall do, till her Master's second coming. (*CP*, p. 742)

But to "be still searching what we know not by what we know, still closing up truth to truth as we find it (for all her body is homogeneal and proportional), this is the golden rule in theology as well as in arithmetic" (*CP*, p. 742).

John Locke's adaptation of the imagery of the voyage of exploration is less heroic and more modest. Less responsive to the challenge of the unknown, he is primarily concerned for the safety of his adventurers: "It is of great use to the sailor to know the length of his line, though he cannot with it fathom all the depths of the ocean; it is well he knows that it is long enough to reach the bottom at such places as are necessary to direct his voyage, and caution him against running upon shoals that may ruin him." Having thus evoked a marine image, Locke promptly converts it into a metaphor of limits: safe waters for sailing or wading, a known horizon. We "let loose our thoughts into the vast ocean of being; as if all that boundless extent were the natural and undoubted possession of our understandings." Extending "their inquiries beyond their capacities," men let "their thoughts wander into those depths where they can find no sure footing," instead of

6. Milton's image of the dismemberment of Truth and the search by her votaries for her scattered members has been adapted from Plutarch's treatise *On Isis and Osiris*. As Ernest Sirluck pointed out, Plutarch had likened the myth of Isis's ritual search for the dismembered god Osiris to "the effort to arrive at the Truth, and especially the truth about the gods" (*The Complete Prose Works of John Milton*, gen. ed. Don M. Wolfe, [New Haven and London, 1959], 2:549n). Cf. Plutarch, *Moralia*, trans. F. C. Babbitt (London and Cambridge, Mass., 1936), 5:9, 11, 29, 45, 87, 121, 131, 141, 183, and passim. See also the discussion of this and similar myths of *sparagmos* (dismemberment) in Edgar Wind, *Pagan Mysteries in the Renaissance* (New Haven, 1938), pp. 114–116.

seeking the horizon "which sets the bounds between the enlightened and dark parts of things" (*Essay*, pp. 14–15).

Locke's cautious and modest approach to the powers of the understanding is reflected in the comparative mildness of his imagery. The imagery of the pursuit of truth extends far beyond the boundaries of the traditional metaphors of hill and labyrinth. Most of his predecessors' metaphors, we have earlier noted, tend to emphasize the perils of the quest for certitude rather than its pleasures. Drawn from warfaring, wayfaring, seafaring, mountaineering, and ritual quest, they are strenuous, violent images, and they reflect the sense of crisis as experienced in a wide variety of disciplines. Though many noted here are commonplaces (and collectively they scarcely do justice to the rich treasury of metaphors exploited by apologists for the new learning or defenders of the old) they are nevertheless representative of learned opinion in England.

The pleasures of discovery in pursuit of truth were also depicted by writers of this period. Metaphors drawn from hunting and falconry were scarcely less frequent than images of the hill and the labyrinth, the battlefield or the voyage. The pursuit of knowledge became, in fact, another variety of blood sport; and even the most sedentary of authors pursued their epistemological quarry with the zest of a country squire. "He that hawks at larks and sparrows," suggested Locke, "has no less sport . . . than he that flies at nobler game." The activity of the Understanding in its "searches after truth" are "a sort of hawking and hunting, wherein the very pursuit makes a great part of the pleasure. Every step the mind takes in its progress towards knowledge makes some discovery, which is not only new, but the best, too, for the time at least" (*Essay*, p. 1). Thomas Hobbes compared the faculty of invention to a spaniel, ranging "the field until he find a scent" (*L*, p. 34). A poet's wit, asserted John Dryden, "is no other than the faculty of imagination in the writer, which, like a nimble spaniel, beats over and ranges through the field of memory till it springs the quarry it hunted after," seeking "the species or ideas of those things which it designs to represent." It is "a faculty so wild and lawless that like a high-ranging spaniel it must have clogs tied to it, lest it outrun the judgment."[7] Abraham Cowley adapted this image to the chemist and the lover, both misled by fallacious hope:

7. *Of Dramatic Poesy and Other Critical Essays*, ed. George Watson (London and New York, 1962), 1: 8, 98; see 1: 9n for other sixteenth- and seventeenth-century examples of this commonplace.

> By thee the one doth changing Nature through
>   Her endlesse Laborinths pursue,
> And th'other chases woman, while she goes
> More wayes, and turnes, then hunted Nature knowes.

And Crashaw, in turn, transfers the venatory image to religion:

> True *Hope's* a glorious Huntresse, and her chase
> The God of Nature in the field of Grace.[8]

Despite their popularity, even among authors who distrusted metaphors, these images are deceptively nonchalant; they obscure the complexity and the seriousness of the chase. The pursuit of earnest was more hazardous and more difficult than the pursuit of game; one required the aid of metaphors reflecting every stage of the chase and every species of prey. The proverbial spaniel was scarcely sufficient; one also needed boar-hounds, deer-hounds, terriers, retrievers, pointers— as well as a brace of falcons for larks and sparrows. One required methods appropriate to each of the arts and sciences, to the discovery of truth or its mode of delivery, to induction or deduction, analysis or synthesis, to the search for certitude or the exploration of probabilities.

Commonplace images were often multivalent and could readily be adapted to different or even contrary senses. Like its variant the dark forest or *selva oscura*, the labyrinth served frequently as a type of the world, a symbol of error and of intellectual or moral perplexity. Often etymologized as *labor intus*, it was associated with difficulty, but it could also on occasion signify pleasure. The image of the crag in turn might alternatively suggest the hardships of the ascent or the delights of the summit.

Truth might be variously compared to a flowing fountain, a light, a martyred virgin, a militant contestant; to *terra incognita* or to a prisoner in a dark cavern or deep pit. She is the daughter of time, and time himself brings her to light. She is proverbially naked (*nuda veritas*); and in the stylistic controversies of the seventeenth century this convention reinforces the demands for a "plain" and "naked" style in philosophical and scientific discourse and in the pulpit.[9] The inquiry

8. Cowley, "On Hope," and Crashaw, "On Hope," in *The Complete Poetry of Richard Crashaw*, ed. George Walton Williams (Garden City, N. Y., 1970), p. 74.

9. For references by various authors to the commonplaces of the unadorned and naked truth, truth as daughter of time, truth hidden in a pit or well, or truth as a daughter of God, see Burton Stevenson, *The Home Book of Proverbs, Maxims, and Familiar Phrases* (New York, 1948), pp. 2384–396. For example, Aeschylus describes the words of truth as

for truth may be depicted as a quest, a hunt, an exantlation, a battle, a voyage of discovery.

Thomas Browne alludes repeatedly to the "exantlation" of the virgin Truth (*Prose*, pp. 120, 392, 460), as well as to the image of the labyrinth (*Prose*, pp. 23, 99, 343). Further inquiries into the "whole volume of nature" should afford "delightful Truths, confirmable by sense and ocular Observation, which seems to me the surest path, to trace the Labyrinth of Truth"—a more effective path than "discursive" inquiry and "rationall conjecture." Intrigued by "the ordinary and open way" of God's providence, Browne is also fascinated by "a more particular and obscure method of his providence," full of "Meanders and Labyrinths . . . : this we call Fortune, that serpentine and crooked line, whereby he drawes those actions his wisedome intends in a more unknowne and secret way" (*Prose*, pp. 23, 343).

Inevitably the question arose as to whether certain knowledge of the truth was possible at all. On this point, as Richard Popkin and Henry Van Leeuwen have observed, writers of the sixteenth and seventeenth centuries sometimes diverged widely. The "destructive" skepticism of Henry Cornelius Agrippa von Nettesheim, Michel de Montaigne, and Montaigne's disciples Pierre Charron and Jean-Pierre Camus attacked both the old and the new science, holding that, in the absence of true and certain knowledge, men must necessarily rely on faith in divine revelation. In contrast to this pessi-

---

"simple" (*hapla*), and Euripides similarly refers to them as "plain" (*haplous*). According to Seneca, speech dealing with truth should be "incomposita . . . et simplex" ("unadorned and plain"); "Veritatis simplex oratio est." For Ammianus Marcellinus, the language of truth is "absolutus . . . ac . . . simplex" ("unadorned and always simple"). According to Robert Bland (*Proverbs*), "Truth needs not the ornament of many words; it is most lovely when it is least adorned." Horace refers to the naked truth ("*nuda Veritas*"), St. Augustine to "aperta veritas," Samuel Butler to "truth naked and unashamed," and Thomas Fuller declares that "Truth's best Ornament is Nakedness." William Horman asserts that "Trewthe nedeth no peynted or colored termes."

The conception of truth as one of the four daughters of God is based on Psalm 84:10; it reappears in John Ray's proverb ("Truth is God's daughter") by way of a Spanish proverb. To Xenophanes was ascribed the statement that no man has ever seen pure truth, and to Democritus the view that we know nothing of truth, for truth lies "in the depths" (*en bythoi*) or (as Francis Bacon expressed it) "in profound pits, and when it was got, it needed much refinement." The *topos* was echoed by Thomas Browne and by Rabelais (who ascribed it to Heraclitus). In a passage that foreshadows the association of truth with height as well as depth, Montaigne denies that truth is "hidden in the deeps of abisse," as Democritus had maintained. Instead it is "rather elevated in infinite height of divine knowledge" ("eslevée en haulteur infinie en la cognoissance divine").

mistic strain in Renaissance fideistic skepticism, the "constructive" skepticism (as Popkin terms it) of certain French and English philosophers maintained that, even though "absolute knowledge" was unattainable, a useful and limited knowledge, which might seem beyond doubt to a reasonable man, was accessible through observation of sense experience and through conclusions based on sense observations. In France this movement, which provided a limited epistemological basis for science, was associated with Francisco Sanchez, Marin Mersenne, and Pierre Gassendi. In England, a "constructive" skeptical tradition, which sought a middle way between the extremes of absolute uncertainty and absolute certitude was developed in the context of theology by William Chillingworth, John Wilkins, John Tillotson, and others; and in the context of science and philosophy by Joseph Glanvill, Robert Boyle, Sir Isaac Newton, and John Locke. Wilkins's thought provided a bridge between religious and scientific conceptions of limited certainty. Chillingworth argued that though man could not achieve absolutely infallible certainty in religious matters, he could nevertheless achieve "moral certainty," a limited certitude acceptable to any reasonable man. Tillotson similarly held that though no man can be "infallible in any thing, but by supernatural assistance," he could possess moral certainty and a kind of certainty based on "immediate sense perception or demonstration." Such views differ significantly from the dogmatic theories of Descartes and his followers, as well as from Bacon's hope for achieving absolute certainty.[10]

Besides the question of whether one can know anything with certainty—and, if so, what—there is the further issue of the kind of truth one is seeking, along with related problems of how it can best be found. In the "Third Satire" Donne is preoccupied by the question of true religion, and he recommends a judicious use of doubt as a means of discovering it. Conversely, in the "First Anniversary" the doubts that vex him are scientific doubts, the challenge presented by the new natural philosophy to the long-accepted dogmas of the traditional physics and astronomy. In *Areopagitica* and in some of his anti-prelatical tracts, Milton is concerned primarily with religious truth; and in *Paradise Lost* the human protagonists are warned that heavenly

10. Tillotson, cited by Van Leeuwen, *The Problem of Certainty in English Thought, 1630–1690*, p. 36; see also Van Leeuwen, "Certainty in Seventeenth-Century Thought," *Dictionary of the History of Ideas: Studies of Selected Pivotal Ideas*, ed. Philip P. Wiener (New York, 1973–74), 1: 304–311; Richard H. Popkin, *The History of Scepticism from Erasmus to Descartes* (Assen, Netherlands, 1960).

matters and indeed astronomy exceed their comprehension; they are exhorted instead to be "lowly wise" and seek the kind of knowledge appropriate to their nature, their condition, and their moral duties and offices. Bacon is seeking a true knowledge of nature by a radical empiricism; Descartes by an equally radical rationalism. Sir Thomas Browne approaches the knowledge of nature through a system of Platonic or Hermetic analogies and correspondences; Hobbes and the followers of Descartes often use quasi-geometrical methods and logical demonstration. For a Ramist divine, in turn, the problem may be one of semantic exegesis and dialectical demonstration—"opening" the text of the infallible word of God, explaining its literal meaning, extracting axioms and doctrines, and inferring "uses" profitable to his congregation.

The kind of certitude or truth one may be seeking may be mathematical or theological; in the sphere of moral, natural, or political philosophy; or in psychology and the knowledge of man. The writer may be seeking to know himself, to understand the world about him, to comprehend as far as possible the will of God; in his inquiry he may explore one or all of the three traditional "books"—the Scriptures, the book of nature, or his own soul.[11] His method of discovery may be inductive or deductive, analytic or synthetic, as loosely organized (in appearance at least) as the essay styles of Montaigne or Browne or as logically structured as a Cartesian treatise. His inquiry may be directed toward concrete facts associated with a particular object or event, toward moral or spiritual inferences that might be drawn from them (as Thomas Browne's treatment of an urn burial and the pattern of the quincunx in the gardens of Cyrus), or toward the underlying structure of reality and the construction of a systematic natural philosophy or a systematic metaphysics.

Significantly, the problem of certitude developed (as Popkin and Van Leeuwen have argued) primarily in a theological context, in Reformation and Counter-Reformation disputes over the "rule of faith" and the proper criterion for religious truth, and was subsequently extended to the area of secular philosophy and science.[12] Controversialists on both sides exploited skeptical arguments, partly based on the recently revived work of Sextus Empiricus, in order to undercut the dogmatic positions in theological doctrine held by their oppo-

11. See Ruth Wallerstein, *Studies in Seventeenth Century Poetic* (Madison, Wis., 1965).
12. See Van Leeuwen, *Problem of Certainty*; Popkin, *History of Scepticism*.

nents. The interdependence of skeptical arguments and fideistic reliance on divine revelation runs through both French and English thought. Underlying the essays of Montaigne and achieving perhaps its most extreme expression in the thought of LaMothe le Vayer, it is apparent, in milder form, both in Browne's *Religio Medici*[13] and in Dryden's *Religio Laici.* In seventeenth-century England the problem of finding a middle way between the extremes of dogmatic claims to absolute certitude, on the one hand, and total skepticism, on the other, confronts the theologian and the scientist alike; significantly, several of the writers who grapple with this problem are either scientists deeply interested in theology, or else churchmen who are also *virtuosi* and apologists for the new science.[14]

13. For the quality of Browne's fideism as reflected in *Religio Medici,* see *Prose,* pp. 11, 14–15, 79. In *Pseudodoxia Epidemica* he warns against dogmatism and extreme skepticism alike. Deploring "any Academicall reservation in matters of easie truth, or rather scepticall infidelity against the evidence of reason and sense," he insists that incredulity can hinder us from enjoying truth, just as credulity (at the other extreme) can be a cause of error. In *Pseudodoxia,* he declares, "We are not Magisteriall in opinions, nor have we Dictator-like obtruded our conceptions; but in the humility of Enquiries or disquisitions, have only proposed them unto more ocular discerners" (*Prose,* p. 119).

14. See Richard S. Westfall, *Science and Religion in Seventeenth-Century England* (New Haven, 1958).

II. Counters and Will o' the Wisps: Rhetoric and Certitude

The controversy over the roles of rhetoric and philosophy is almost as ancient as the arts themselves, and the marriage of eloquence and wisdom has been no less subject to periodic dissension than that of Socrates and Xanthippe. The contradictory attitudes displayed toward the arts of discourse during the seventeenth century, which included advocations of the radical separation of rhetoric and philosophy as well as their indissoluble union, were alike conventional; almost equally traditional were the arguments and the images employed on both sides. Like analogous disputes over the function of poetry, the pro- and anti-rhetorical polemics of the late Renaissance and baroque periods represented yet another battle in a very old war—a renewal of hostilities in a long-standing quarrel of the arts. Like all battles, however, it was conditioned by circumstances of time, place, and the character and strength of the antagonists. For instance, distinguishing this quarrel from the earlier quarrels between humanist poets or rhetoricians and scholastic philosophers was the fact that both literary tastes and concepts of philosophical method were undergoing significant and indeed radical alterations. The opponents of the poet and orator were no longer the despised schoolmen but the partisans of the "new philosophy"—often accomplished stylists themselves. Aside from the political and spiritual tensions of the period, its philosophical crises—in epistemology, in metaphysics, in theology, in cosmology—were rapidly rendering the old "commonplaces" for dialectical and rhetorical debate obsolete. The ideal union between truth and eloquence, or philosophy and rhetoric, could no longer remain the same when philosophy's fundamental principles were being revolutionized, its traditional doctrines subjected to systematic doubt, and truth itself regarded as unattainable, achievable only by laborious and methodical endeavors, or to be accepted on faith as a last resort. The tradi-

tional relation of "word" to "idea" was inevitably compromised by
the growing realization that many traditionally valid "forms" or
"ideas" were indeed *eidola* or chimaeras with no firm basis in concrete reality or in sense experience. The ontological status of universals—and their traditional superiority to particulars—was being
undercut by the greater epistemological uncertainty of the abstract
idea or universal in comparison with sense data.

The arguments summarized here underlie a wide range of criticism. In varying degrees some of them can be found in the writings of
scholars and critics as diverse as Basil Willey and Marjorie Nicolson,
or Arnold Hauser, Morris Croll, and Odette de Mourgues. Not surprisingly, twentieth-century critics have sometimes attributed to the
epistemological crisis of the late Renaissance and to the altered
world-view of this age the primary responsibility for the major differences between Renaissance, mannerist, and baroque styles in art and
literature. In the disintegration of the older cosmology and traditional hierarchy of arts and sciences, they recognize the principal
causes for the vogue of conceits and epigrams, the development of the
"dispersed meditation" or essay, and the preference for natural, informal, spontaneous (or even fortuitous) sequence over formal and premeditated order. Critics point to the conflicting demands of writers
of the age upon language: that it function as an instrument of persuasion or of discovery, or as a vehicle of authoritative dogma and
acknowledged truth or of tentative inquiry. Correlating develop-
ments in style with changing conceptions of metaphysics, they stress
the implications of the crisis in epistemology for logic and rhetoric,
for the relationship between expression and matter or words and
things—*verba* and *res*—and for the theory of ideas and abstract
"forms," all of which were reappraised, revaluated, or reorganized in
response to new views of epistemology.

1

If the fifteenth century could boast (a trifle too confidently) of
a "revival of learning," the seventeenth could point, with perhaps
greater justice, to learning's radical reconstruction: to a sweeping reformation of philosophy and the natural sciences, and to their reestab-
lishment on more substantial, and prophetically modern, foundations. In 1600, as Douglas Bush has suggested, the "mind and world"

of the educated Englishman were still "more than half medieval"; by 1660 they were "more than half modern."[1]

This association of "mind and world" is not fortuitous; like their colleagues in *Geistesgeschichte*, twentieth-century literary historians often regard the two ideas as correlative. They would argue that stylistic modes have altered *pari passu* with modes of conceiving the universe; the sensibility of an age has altered with its notions of methodology. In Marjorie Nicolson's view, major alterations in literary or aesthetic taste can be correlated with changes in cosmology. With the growing obsolescence of the theory of universal analogy and of the belief in detailed correspondences between macrocosm, geocosm, and microcosm, the older vitalistic, quasi-magical image of the cosmos was displaced by a mechanical model: the paradigm of the universe as a soulless machine. This reorientation in cosmology significantly altered the character of poetic imagery. The popularity of metaphors declined with the decline of the concept of the world as metaphor, to be replaced by less imaginative and more rational figures of speech, like the cautious and prosaic simile.[2]

To be replaced, as R. F. Jones has argued, by a still severer style. In seeking an appropriate vehicle for natural philosophy, contemporary savants were already demanding a naked, plain mode of discourse stripped of imagery and ornament. In the philosophical writers of the century—from Francis Bacon through Thomas Hobbes and John Wilkins to Thomas Sprat and other members of the Royal Society— Jones has traced a growing distrust of metaphors, hyperboles, and other rhetorical figures that were held either to distort the truth or to divert the reader's attention from matter to manner, from things to words. To many of these authors, the schemes and tropes of rhetoric, its figures of speech and thought, seemed grossly inappropriate to the rigors of philosophical method. Blurring distinctions between truth and error, rhetoric appealed to the senses and the passions rather than to reason. It made the language of science ambiguous, uncertain, frivolous, and obscure: it was an unreliable instrument for scientific discourse.

Indeed language per se was the source of no little embarrassment, a principal obstacle to the advancement of learning. In comparison

1. *English Literature in the Earlier Seventeenth Century* (Oxford, 1945), p. 1.
2. Nicolson, *The Breaking of the Circle: Studies in the Effect of the "New Science" on Seventeenth Century Poetry*, rev. ed. (New York and London, 1960), pp. 1–10.

with the mathematical sciences, verbal discourse seemed painfully imprecise. Of all the idols and false notions that possess the human understanding and oppose the entry of truth, the "most troublesome," declared Bacon, are the idols of the marketplace, "idols which have crept into the understanding through the alliances of words and names." This alliance "has rendered philosophy and the sciences sophistical and inactive," imposing the names of "things which do not exist"—such as Fortune, Prime Mover, Planetary Orbits, Element of Fire—or the names of "things which exist, but are yet confused and ill-defined, and hastily and irregularly derived from realities" by "faulty and unskilful abstraction," like the word *humid* (*Novum Organum, SW*, pp. 469, 477–479).

For Bacon and his successors, incertitude and imprecision were pathological symptoms, resulting from the diseases of learning. The latter were not incurable, however, and their remedies were to be sought in the panaceas of methodology. Like contemporary doctors prescribing lenses for bad eyesight or a course of mineral waters for dyspepsia, the new philosophers set about curing the myopia of the understanding and the ventosities and tumors of style with all the confidence of a Paracelsan physician: a plain diet of facts unadulterated by rhetorical sauces and condiments, a purge of the language, corrective spectacles, and a course of mathematics.

As a corrective to the idols or false appearances imposed by words, Bacon suggested, philosophy might profitably emulate the method of mathematics: "yet certain it is that words, as a Tartar's bow, do shoot back upon the understanding of the wisest, and mightily entangle and pervert the judgment; so as it is almost necessary in all controversies and disputations to imitate the wisdom of the Mathematicians, in setting down in the very beginning the definitions of our words and terms, that others may know how we accept and understand them, and whether they concur with us or no" (*Advancement of Learning, SW*, p. 297).

Thomas Hobbes insisted:

> [The] light of human minds is perspicuous words, but by exact definitions first snuffed and purged from ambiguity. . . . And, on the contrary, metaphors and senseless and ambiguous words are like *ignes fatui*; and reasoning upon them is wandering among innumerable absurdities. [Since] truth consists in the right ordering of names in our affirmations, a man that seeks precise truth had need to remember what every name he uses stands for and to place it accordingly, or else he will find himself entangled in

words as a bird in lime twigs, the more he struggles the more belimed. [In] the right definition of names lies the first use of speech, which is the acquisition of science; and in wrong or no definitions lies the first abuse, from which proceed all false and senseless tenets which make those men that take their instruction from the authority of books, and not from their own meditation, to be as much below the condition of ignorant men as men endowed with true science are above it.... For words are but wise men's counters, they do but reckon by them; but they are the money of fools that value them by the authority of an Aristotle, a Cicero, or a Thomas, or any other doctor whatsoever, if but a man. (*L* pp. 41–42, 50; cf. pp. 6–8, 19, 37–49)

The use of words, asserted Locke, is to stand as "sensible marks of *ideas*"; nevertheless, language is an imperfect instrument and

he that shall well consider the *errors* and obscurity, the mistakes and confusion, that are *spread in the world by an ill use of words*, will find some reason to doubt, whether language, as it has been employed has contributed more to the improvement or hindrance of knowledge amongst mankind. And here I desire it may be considered, and carefully examined whether the greatest part of the disputes in the world are not merely verbal, and about the signification of words; and whether if the terms they are made in, were defined, and reduced in their signification . . . to determined collections of simple *ideas* they do or should stand for, those disputes would not end of themselves, and immediately vanish. (*Essay*, pp. 202–207)

When I began to examine the extent and certainty of our knowledge, I found it had so near a connection with words, that unless their force and manner of signification were first well served, there could be very little said clearly and pertinently concerning knowledge.... [For words] interpose themselves so much between our understandings, and the truth . . . that like the *medium* through which visible objects pass, their obscurity and disorder does not seldom cast a mist before our eyes, and impose upon our understandings. (*Essay*, pp. 137, 175–176, 204–207)[3]

2

Aware of the unreliability of words in general and of scholastic terminology in particular, these writers envied the certitude and precision of mathematics. The success of mathematics, they believed,

---

3. Cf. *Essay*, pp. 148–203, on the natural imperfection of language and on the abuses of words resulting from "*wilful faults and neglects.*"

could be attributed not only to its rigorous methods of demonstration but also to its exact definitions and reduction of concepts to nonverbal signs. The natural philosophy of the Greeks, protested Hobbes, "was rather a dream than science, and set forth in senseless and insignificant language, which cannot be avoided by those that will teach philosophy without having first attained great knowledge in geometry." In geometry, "which is the only science that it has pleased God hitherto to bestow on mankind, men begin at settling the significations of their words, which settling of significations they call *definitions*, and place them in the beginning of their reasoning" (*L*, pp. 6, 41).

Reason itself is a sort of arithmetic, for when a man reasons, "he does nothing else but conceive a sum total from *addition* of parcels, or conceive a remainder from *subtraction* of one sum from another; which, if it be done by words, is conceiving of the consequence of the names of all the parts to the name of the whole, or from the names of the whole and one part to the name of the other part. . . . These operations are not incident to numbers only, but to all manner of things that can be added together and taken one out of another." They apply no less to geometry and logic, politics and law than to arithmetic: "in what matter soever there is place for *addition* and *subtraction*, there also is place for *reason*; and where these have no place, there *reason* has nothing at all to do" (*L*, p. 45).

Locke, in turn, countered the popular opinion that mathematics alone could achieve demonstrative certitude by arguing that "the precise real essence of the things moral words stand for may be perfectly known"; hence morality is likewise "capable of demonstration." Some of its disadvantages can be remedied by definitions; and "what methods algebra or something of that kind may hereafter suggest, to remove the other difficulties, it is not easy to foretell." If "men would in the same method and with the same indifferency search after moral as they do mathematical truths, they would find them to have a stronger connection one with another, and a more necessary consequence from our clear and distinct ideas, and to come nearer perfect demonstration than is commonly imagined." In discovering the relations between abstract ideas one must learn the stages of method from the mathematicians, "who from very plain and easy beginnings, by gentle degrees and a continued chain of reasonings, proceed to the discovery and demonstration of truths, that appear at first sight beyond human capacity" (*Essay*, pp. 213, 257, 320).

Moreover, mathematics possesses the further advantage of avoiding the inconvenience of words, "abstracting their thoughts from names, and accustoming themselves to set before their minds the ideas themselves that they would consider, and not sounds instead of them." Mathematicians have thereby avoided "a great part of that perplexity, puddering, and confusion, which has so much hindered men's progress in other parts of knowledge. For whilst they stick in words of undetermined and uncertain signification, they are unable to distinguish true from false, certain from probable, consistent from inconsistent, in their own opinions." Truth itself, Locke added, is nothing other than "the joining or separating of signs, as the things signified by them do agree or disagree with one another"; and he draws a sharp distinction between mental and verbal propositions ("truth of thought, and truth of words") and between "two sorts of signs . . . , viz, ideas and words" (*Essay*, pp. 237, 267, 279–280).

Throughout the seventeenth century the certitude of mathematics provided an enviable contrast to the uncertainties and controversies that seemed endemic to other branches of learning. Under the influence of Descartes there were numerous attempts by Continental thinkers to "Euclidize" philosophy by applying the methods of geometry to problems of ethics and metaphysics.[4] Though Hobbes and Henry More were influenced by this mode of demonstration, the majority of their "Bacon-faced" colleagues preferred to stress the inade-

---

4. Mathematical certainty was proverbial, even for authors who did not, like the followers of Descartes, attempt to impose geometrical methods on philosophy by proceeding systematically from definitions and axioms to the demonstration of propositions and their corollaries. Milton extolled Selden's "volume of natural and national laws" for its "exquisite reasons and theorems almost mathematically demonstrative" (*Areopagitica*, p. 727). Descartes considered the demonstrations in his *Meditations* "to be equal or even superior to the geometrical in certitude and evidence." In the Second Meditation "it was my aim to write nothing of which I could not give exact demonstration, and . . . I therefore felt myself obliged to adopt an order similar to that in use among the geometers, viz., to premise all upon which the proposition in question depends, before coming to any conclusion respecting it" (*The Meditations . . . of René Descartes*, trans. John Veitch [La Salle, Ill., 1968], pp. 4, 15). Spinoza followed a geometrical method of demonstration in his *Ethics* as well as in his *Principles of Cartesian Philosophy*; one encounters similar exploitations of this method in Leibniz and other philosophers of the century. For the resolutive-compositive method (i.e., analysis and synthesis) of Zabarella and other Italian Aristotelians and its influence on Galileo, Harvey, Descartes, and Hobbes, see W. von Leyden, *Seventeenth-Century Metaphysics: An Examination of Some Main Concepts and Theories* (New York, 1968), pp. 39, 203–204; Leo Strauss, *The Political Philosophy of Hobbes: Its Basis and Its Genesis*, trans. Elsa M. Sinclair (Chicago and London, 1963), pp. 2, 6; and S. V. Keeling, *Descartes* (London, Oxford, New York, 1968), p. 257.

quacies of philosophical terminology in comparison with mathematical signs. They were seeking, in effect, either a substitute for words or, ideally, a one-to-one correspondence between word and thing or between word and idea. Thomas Blount observed that Seneca would have preferred to converse by signs in order to avoid all affectations of speech (*S*, p. 219). John Wilkins attempted to dispense with "the many impostures and cheats that are put upon men, under the disguise of affected insignificant Phrases" by inventing a "real character" and "philosophical language," a universal language of "symbols so constructed as to indicate the exact nature of things." Though in his studies of the period R. F. Jones has deplored this degradation of language, this reduction of speech to "the dead symbols of mathematical equations," Wilkins himself regarded his labor as nobler than the compilation of dictionaries: "it being as much to be preferred before that, as *things* are better than *words*, as *real knowledge* is beyond *elegance of speech* (*Studies*, p. 156). The members of the Royal Society, wrote Thomas Sprat, are determined "to reject all amplifications, digressions, and swellings of style; to return back to the primitive purity and shortness, when men deliver'd so many *things* almost in an equal number of *words*. They have exacted from all their members a close, naked, natural way of speaking, positive expressions, clear senses, a native easiness, bringing all things as near the Mathematical plainness as they can" (*S*, p. 286).

Even poets could express such attitudes to the elegancies of style — at least when their subject happened to be the corruption and reformation of philosophy. In his ode to the Royal Society, Cowley protested that the former guardians and tutors of philosophy had treated it like a pampered heir in his nonage, corrupting their ward with "the sports of wanton wit," "the deserts of poetry," and "the pleasant labyrinths of ever fresh discourse":

> Instead of carrying him to see
> The riches which do hoarded for him lie
> In Nature's endless treasury,
> They chose his eye to entertain
>
> . . . .
> With painted scenes, and pageants of the brain.

Bacon, the Society's precursor, had reformed philosophy, suggests Cowley, by converting it from shows to realities, from words, "which are but pictures of the thought," to things, "the mind's right object." Sprat, the Society's historian, had reformed the language of philosophy, purging it of modern follies. His "candid style" possessed all the beauties of nature, "and all the comely dress without the paint of art" (*SC*, pp. 402–406). Similar attacks were launched against the rhetoric of the pulpit in the name of evangelical plainness and the majestic but unaffected style of Scripture. Jones has recognized the decisive role of the new science in the long-standing quarrel between ancients and moderns—a dispute which lasted throughout the century[5]; the new science compelled a fresh revaluation of classical and contemporary learning and a reexamination of stereotypes of progress or decadence in terms of particular arts and sciences.

3

In the anti-Ciceronian movements of the late Renaissance, Morris Croll detects a distrust of rhetoric and a concern for things (*res*) rather than words (*verba*). Many writers, in seeking a soberer and weightier style appropriate for the philosopher's private study or the meditative essayist rather than the public forum or the persuasive orator, deliberately eschewed the qualities assiduously cultivated by Renaissance humanists. For copiousness they substituted brevity; for symmetry, asymmetry; for facility, difficulty; for harmony, deliberate dismemberment,[6] a kind of syntactic *sparagmos* in which Cicero replaced Orpheus as ritual victim. To the resonant verbal schemes of the earlier humanists, designed to please and lull the ear, they preferred figures of thought calculated to tease the mind into activity. (In this respect they differed from their remote posterity, the fellows of the Royal Society, who frequently condemned *figurae sententiae*, or figures of thought, and *schemata verborum*, or verbal ornaments, alike.)

In the eloquence of the humanists Bacon diagnosed the "first distemper of learning," the subordination of things to words: "Men began to hunt more after words than matter; and more after the choiceness of the phrase, and the round and clean composition of the sentence, and the sweet falling of the clauses, and the varying and illustration of their works with tropes and figures, than after the weight of matter, worth of subject, soundness of argument, life of

5. See Richard Foster Jones, *Ancients and Moderns: A Study of the Rise of the Scientific Movement in Seventeenth Century England*, 2nd ed. (Berkeley and Los Angeles, 1965).

6. Compare the "fragmentation" or "dismemberment" of the Ciceronian period (in the view of Croll and his followers), anatomized and resolved into its colons, semicolons, and commas; its members and parts of members.

invention, or depth of judgment." The "whole inclination and bent of those times were rather towards copie than weight" (*Advancement of Learning*, pp. 181–182).

In Croll's survey of the anti-Ciceronian movement the most striking departures from humanist eloquence appeared in the conscious rejection of its artificial syntax. The formal architectonics of the Ciceronian period was in itself suspect. Like its verbal ornaments and its prolixity (*copia verborum*), its careful construction seemed to betray an excessive concern with the style and form of discourse rather than with the substance of discourse. More significant, however, was the tendency of Ciceronian discourse to compel assent rather than to evoke doubts or stimulate thought. With its premeditated harmonies, its carefully turned phrases and clauses, its studied articulation of members and parts of members into an integrated whole, it presented the formal (and, in a sense, retrospective) elaboration of a thought rather than the raw materials or actual process of thinking. For all its effectiveness in public persuasion, such discourse was manifestly inappropriate for private reflection, logical demonstration, or inference from experience. Tailored to the generous dimensions of the public orator, it hung idly, ridiculously, on the leaner torso of the scholar. Inured to a sparser diet unsweetened by candied phrases, the scholar required a tighter, more economical garment, a coat of severer cut.

The response of the anti-Ciceronians was fragmentation or, to use a kinder term, analysis, disintegrating the members of the Ciceronian period and presenting them paratactically.[7] Instead of troubling themselves about an architectural design, the anti-Ciceronians preferred to leave the building materials scattered about the lawn where the carters had dumped them. Alternatively, they built at random, as fancy struck them, adding a room here, a fireplace there without premeditation, or reducing porticos, thresholds, hallways, staircases to an absolute minimum. In short, as Croll has argued, they chose either "the concise, serried, abrupt *stile coupé*" or "curt style" associated with Senecan and Stoic thought or "the informal, meditative, and 'natural' loose style" often employed by "libertine" or skeptical writers of the late Renaissance (*Style*, p. 229 and passim). Intermingling frequently even in the same work, these anti-Ciceronian modes represented "two sides of the seventeenth-century mind: its sententiousness, its penetrating wit, its Stoic intensity, on the one hand, and its

7. See *Style*, p. 232, on the relationship between anti-Ciceronianism and the disintegration of style.

dislike of formalism, its roving and self-exploring curiosity . . . , its skeptical tendency, on the other" (*Style*, p. 230).

In both these styles, but particularly in the latter, Croll recognizes an attempt to render the actual process of reflection: "to portray, not a thought, but a mind thinking." The anti-Ciceronians "knew that an idea separated from the act of experiencing it is not the idea that was experienced. The ardor of its conception in the mind is not a necessary part of its truth; and unless it can be conveyed to another mind in something of the form of its occurrence, either it has changed into some other idea or it has ceased to be an idea, to have any existence whatever except a verbal one." Preferring "to present the truth of experience in a less concocted form," the anti-Ciceronians "deliberately chose as the moment of expression that in which the idea first clearly objectifies itself in the mind, in which . . . each of its parts still preserves its own peculiar emphasis and independent vigor of its own— in brief, the moment in which truth is still *imagined*" (*Style*, pp. 184, 209–210). Similar tendencies were characteristic of baroque art; it preferred "the motions of souls, not their states of rest, . . . forms that express the energy and labor of minds seeking the truth, not without dust and heat, to the forms that express a contented sense of the enjoyment and possession of it" (*Style*, p. 208).

In Bacon's contrast between the "Magistral" method of delivery and the method of "Probation" or discovery appropriate to "induced knowledge," Croll identifies "the philosophy in which Anti-Ciceronian prose has its origin and motive" (*Style*, p. 220). As "knowledges are now delivered," Bacon had protested,

> there is a kind of contract of error between the deliverer and the receiver: for he that delivereth knowledge desireth to deliver it in such form as may be best believed, and not as may be best examined. . . . [Knowledge] that is delivered as a thread to be spun on ought to be delivered and intimated, if it were possible, *in the same method wherein it was invented*; and so it is possible of knowledge induced. But in this same anticipated and prevented knowledge, no man knoweth how he came to the knowledge which he hath obtained. . . . So the delivery of knowledges (as it is now used) is as of fair bodies of trees without the roots; good for the carpenter, but not for the planter; but if you will have sciences grow, it is less matter for the shaft or body of the tree, so you look well to the taking up of the roots. Of which kind of delivery the method of the mathematiques, in that subject, hath some shadow; but generally I see it neither put in use nor put in inquisition, and therefore note it for deficient. (*Advancement of Learning, SW*, p. 304)

4

Bacon was not concerned with style or rhetoric in the passage above, still less with curt or loose periods; he was preoccupied instead with problems of method on a far greater scale. However, he was himself an accomplished rhetorician; rhetorical terms or concepts were deeply embedded in his thought, even in his views on the art of discovery or invention; and Croll is probably justified in perceiving a relationship between Bacon's "probative" method and anti-Ciceronian style. The attacks on rhetoric mounted throughout the century by scientists and clergymen, and the alternate praise or censure accorded individual members of these professions on grounds of style, can hardly be dissociated from contemporary ideas of method or from seventeenth-century criteria of probability and certitude.

As several critics have noted, Bacon's ideas on methodology led him to favor "the delivery of knowledge in Aphorisms" rather than in a more methodical form. Since aphorisms, on the one hand, "cannot be made but of the pith and heart of the sciences," no man can attempt them "but he that is sound and grounded"; in methods, on the other hand, thanks to arrangement, connection, and juncture of parts, "a man shall make a great shew of an art, which if it were disjointed would come to little." Moreover, methods "are fit to win consent or belief, but less fit to point to action," for they depend on circular reasoning; "but particulars, being dispersed, do best agree with dispersed directions." Finally, aphorisms represent "a knowledge broken" and thus "invite men to enquire farther; whereas Methods, carrying the shew of a total, do secure men, as if they were at furthest" (*Advancement*, SW, pp. 304–306).

This attack on "methods" by the champion and propagandist of the inductive method is less paradoxical than it may seem at first glance. Bacon is referring primarily not to methodology but to the contemporary manuals, digests, and compendia that presented the essentials of an art or science in systematic form, as a closed system, or provided an inventory of commonplaces for practical exploitation. Based as they were on knowledge already discovered and reduced to system, they were vulnerable to the objections that he raises elsewhere against the "magistral" or dogmatic method of delivery.

His attitude toward aphorisms is more complex, since it also involves his assessment of the Senecan style. His preference for "a knowledge broken" is reflected not only in his exploitation of the aphoristic mode in the first book of the *Novum Organum* and in the *Essays* ("certain brief notes, set down rather significantly than curiously") but also in his distrust of philosophical systems and in the disjunctive character of the *Essays* themselves; for they are, in essence, merely "dispersed meditations." Significantly he cites Seneca's epistles to Lucilius as the classical prototype of this genre (*SW*, p. 6); but he subsequently displays a more critical attitude toward the Senecan style. Though somewhat sounder than the copious style of Renaissance Ciceronians, the curt and pointed style that succeeded it was "not altogether exempt from vanity." The Senecan style's preoccupation with brevity, point, and compression ("aculeate" words, concise sentences, "the whole contexture . . . rounding into it selfe") made every passage seem "more witty and waighty than indeed it is." Like the Ciceronian style, it is "nothing else but a hunting after words, and fine placing of them," and hence "may be set down as a *distemper of Learning*" (*S*, p. 112).

George Williamson observes that Plutarch attacked the partisans of Attic style as well as "those who 'mind nothing but words and jingle', for both prefer expression to philosophy" (*S*, p. 25). In the latter part of the seventeenth century one encounters a similar tendency to condemn the excesses of the Senecan style along with the verbal ornaments and copiousness of its rival. Williamson associates Plutarch and Seneca respectively with "loose" and "curt" styles. Both served as "ancient models" for Montaigne, Williamson maintains, and both attracted the attention of the essayists Sir William Cornwallis and John Dryden. When "the curt style was rejected, Plutarch remained a proper authority for anti-Ciceronian style" (*S*, p. 225).

5

In these seventeenth-century tiffs between scientists and rhetoricians, theologians and rhetoricians, rhetoricians and rhetoricians, there is much that would have seemed familiar to a classical observer. Through its early association with the oratory of law courts, political assemblies, and public competitions, rhetoric had acquired an ambiguous reputation. Expedient, lucrative, even necessary, it could easily be abused, or deployed with equal facility on either side of a question. More damaging in the eyes of classical philosophers and theologians was its exploitation by the early Sophists and subsequently by the Second Sophistic. Plato condemned as ridiculous rhetoric based on mere appearances rather than on solid truth.[8] Aristotle, who regarded rhetoric as "an offshoot of dialectic and also of ethical studies," nevertheless found it necessary to counter the pejorative connotations of this art and the accusations raised against it. The term *rhetorician* commonly denoted the speaker's moral purpose as well as his knowledge of his art. Yet the abuse of this art does not compromise its potential value for ethics and politics: "If it be objected that one who uses such power of speech unjustly might do great harm, *that* is a charge which may be made in common against all good things except virtue, and above all against the things that are most useful, as strength, health, wealth, generalship. A man can confer the greatest of benefits by a right use of these, and inflict the greatest of injuries by using them wrongly."[9]

Later discussions of the merits or demerits of eloquence and its affinities with ethics and dialectic were apt to be less dispassionate than Aristotle's. For the most part, later discussions were not objective inquiries but rhetorical or dialectical briefs in a dispute that (as many of the contestants recognized) might be endlessly debated pro and con without achieving a definitive answer. Ironically enough, the issue was precisely the kind of controversial question appropriate to rhetoric: "No other of the arts," Aristotle observed, "draws opposite conclusions: dialectic and rhetoric alone do this. Both these arts draw opposite conclusions impartially."[10] Not surprisingly, arguments over the function of rhetoric often became polarized, centered on its use and abuse.[11] In these debates over the role of eloquence, the arts

8. *The Works of Plato*, trans. B. Jowett (New York, [1937]), 3:421–425, 439.

9. *The Basic Works of Aristotle*, ed. Richard McKeon (New York, 1941), pp. 1328–330.

10. Ibid., p. 1328.

11. This tendency toward polarization in controversy should not obscure the diversity of attitudes toward or theories of rhetoric in classical and medieval tradition as well as in the Renaissance. See Donald Lemen Clark, *John Milton at St. Paul's School* (New York, 1948) and *Rhetoric and Poetry in the Renaissance* (New York, 1922); Richard McKeon, "Rhetoric in the Middle Ages," in *Critics and Criticism, Ancient and Modern*, ed. R. S. Crane (Chicago, 1952), pp. 260–296; Jerrold E. Seigel, *Rhetoric and Philosophy in Renaissance Humanism: The Union of Eloquence and Wisdom, Petrarch to Valla* (Princeton, 1968); Marcia L. Colish, *The Mirror of Language: A Study in the Medieval Theory of Knowledge* (New Haven and London, 1968); Hanna H. Gray, "Renaissance Humanism: The Pursuit of Eloquence," in *Renaissance Essays*, ed. Paul O. Kristeller and Philip P. Wiener (New York and Evanston, 1968); Ruth Wallerstein, *Studies in Seventeenth Century Poetic* (rpt. Madison, 1965); Wilbur S. Howell, *Logic and Rhetoric in England, 1500–1700* (Princeton, 1956); Sister Miriam Joseph, *Shakespeare's Use of the Arts of Language* (New York, 1947); and James J. Murphy,

poetical and rhetorical were often linked, acquiring guilt or merit by association. The arguments commonly urged for or against rhetoric frequently recurred in controversies over the philosophical or theological utility of poetry—and vice versa—and in debates among poets or rhetoricians concerning the various levels, modes, and characters of style.

6

The seminal views of Morris W. Croll and Richard Foster Jones on the evolution of English seventeenth-century prose style have been qualified or challenged by later scholars: it may be helpful to summarize briefly the principal issues in these controversies. Croll approaches changes in prose style primarily in terms of classical categories (Attic vs. Asiatic, *genus humile* vs. *genus grande*) and against the background of Renaissance controversies over the imitation of Cicero. He also views them more narrowly in the context of French or Flemish anti-Ciceronianism, noting the influence of Seneca and other Silver Age Latin authors on neo-Latin writers such as Muret and Justus Lipsius and on French vernacular authors. He designates the "new style" (*novum dicendi genus*) by a variety of terms: Attic, anti-Ciceronian, Senecan, *genus humile* or *genus subtile*, baroque. He also describes it as a philosophical or essay style, contrasting it with the oratorical style; he differentiates two kinds of the new style, the curt and the loose, associating them respectively with the Stoic and the libertine aspects of "the seventeenth-century mind." Justus Lipsius exemplified the Stoic style, while Montaigne excelled in the libertine style as a master of "the informal, meditative, and 'natural' loose style" (*Style*, pp. 54, 62, 79, 111, 123–124, 229–230).

According to R. F. Jones, however, "the sudden and decided change that came over English prose in the third quarter of the seventeenth century" substituted "a plain, direct unadorned style for the elaborate and musical style of the Commonwealth" constituting a deliberate "stylistic revolution" of which the "age was quite conscious, and for which many stoutly battled." Before the Restoration, and

especially in the third and fourth decades of the century, the predominating style of preaching was characterized by affectations, fanciful conceits,

Rhetoric in the Middle Ages: A History of Rhetorical Theory from St. Augustine to the Renaissance (Berkeley, 1974).

metaphors, similes, plays upon words, antitheses, paradoxes, and the pedantic display of Greek and Latin quotations. After 1660 the scientific ideal of style—plainness, directness, clearness—steadily gained ascendancy over the older manner of expression. This change was materially assisted by the determined efforts of numerous stylistic reformers, the first of which appeared, as we would expect, in scientific quarters. As early as 1646, John Wilkins, in *Ecclesiastes*, ... had advocated a plain, natural, and clear way of preaching. (*Studies*, pp. 111–113)

Jones further notes that the "reformation of pulpit eloquence" had begun earlier in France than in England and "continued until late in the century." Balzac "frowned upon the use of rhetoric in religious observances," and Port-Royal had "developed a style proper to Christian humility" and "free from ornamentation." The "most important channel" of French influence, however, was René Rapin's *Réflexions sur l'Usage de l'Eloquence de ce Temps* (1672), "which was translated the same year into English" (*Studies*, pp. 138–139).

To a certain extent the controversy between followers of Croll and Jones has been complicated by the ambiguity and indeed the anachronistic character of Renaissance labels for style. Aside from the ambiguity of Attic and Asiatic styles in antiquity, it is often difficult to apply these terms satisfactorily to Renaissance works. Anti-Ciceronian or anti-Senecan labels (and their contraries) are subject to analogous difficulties, and many present-day scholars agree that sixteenth- and seventeenth-century notions of plain style are often highly relative, variable, and in some instances polemical. The variously labeled style that Croll regards as the ancestor of modern prose and associates with the classical *genus humile* is precisely the style that later advocates of the plain style condemned as metaphorical, metaphysical, affected, fantastic, and obscure. The majority of later scholars would agree with R. F. Jones's critique of Croll's conception of this style as the parent of Restoration style and ultimately of modern prose.

Whereas Croll attempts to explain seventeenth-century prose style in terms of classical categories or in terms of the sixteenth-century Ciceronian controversy, Jones emphasizes the linguistic ideals of the Royal Society of London as the decisive factor in the change in English prose style during the third quarter of the seventeenth century.[12] Croll con-

---

12. The degree to which the stylistic ideals of the Royal Society of London for scientific prose actually influenced the style of poetry, the nature of this influence, and the effects of the new science in general on creative literature are still controversial. In *Newton Demands the Muse* (Princeton, 1946), *The Breaking of the Circle* (Evanston,

trasts the philosophical or essay style, inspired by Socratic dialectic and the Senecan style, with the oratorical style, which he associates with the Ciceronian tradition; Jones stresses the stylistic requirements of the new science and its hostility to the figured and witty style associated with the English Senecan tradition. Both contrast a philosophical style with rhetoric, but the kind of philosophy involved and the particular rhetorical features condemned differ significantly. Croll's philosophical style emphasizes self-exploration, self-knowledge, and self-revelation. Taking Montaigne as well as Seneca for his models, he finds the essence of this style in the act of thinking and in spontaneity; the Senecan stylist endeavors to portray not so much a complete and well-turned thought as a mind thinking. The philosophical style as he conceives it is in large part a mimesis of inquiry, an image of the thinking self in meditative action, rather than a systematic logical demonstration of a doctrine already espoused or an insight formerly attained and painstakingly confirmed. Such a style may be admirably adapted to Stoicism or to the skeptical doubts and reasonings of the libertine thinker, but it is less fitted for rigorous logical demonstration or for quasi-mathematical proofs. The kind of discourse that scientists of the Royal Society—or rather, *some* of them—were seeking required quasi-

---

1950; rev. ed., New York, 1960), and other studies, Marjorie Hope Nicolson examines the influence of the new science on the imagery employed by poets in the late seventeenth and early eighteenth centuries, as well as the literary impact of the substitution of a Copernican for a Ptolemaic cosmology. In particular, she stresses the shift in emphasis from finite to infinite space, along with the replacement of a quasi-magical universe, subject to the operation of unseen spiritual forces and an underlying system of hidden analogies and correspondences, by a Newtonian cosmos comprehensible primarily in mathematical terms and the principles of mechanics.

More recently, the problem has been reexamined from a different angle by William H. Youngren. In "Generality, Science, and Poetic Language in the Restoration," *ELH* 35 (1968): 158–187, Youngren disputes the widespread assumptions that the ideals advanced for prose style by spokesmen of the Royal Society were intended to be binding for poetry as well and that Dryden and his contemporaries made "little or no distinction between poetry and prose." Though Restoration critics frequently demand that "poetry be clear or plain," they also insist on its traditional function as moral teacher and assume "that sensuously immediate and concentrated language is more suitable for communicating moral knowledge than flat and colorless language." In "Generality in Augustan Satire," Youngren maintains that the "generality demanded by neoclassical critics" and the "particularity we value in Pope and Dryden" and Samuel Johnson are "not opposed qualities" but are "rather two complementary aspects of a single characteristic use of language" (in *In Defense of Reading*, Reuben A. Brower and Richard Poirier, ed. [New York, 1962], pp. 206–234). Later, in "Conceptualism and Neoclassic Generality," *ELH* 47 (1980): 705–740, Youngren emphasizes the "effortless fusion of general and particular" in the best Restoration and eighteenth-century poetry in the light of "relations between conceptualism and neoclassic criticism."

mathematical plainness largely as a corollary to their admiration for the certainty of mathematical demonstrations in comparison with the methods of other arts and sciences.

Writing with the Ciceronian controversy in mind, Croll emphasizes syntax, contrasting the curt and loose styles of the Senecans with the rounded and balanced Ciceronian period, and the opposition between figures of sound and figures of thought. Jones, viewing the background of post-Restoration science and its linguistic program, places less emphasis on syntactical patterns than on plain diction and the avoidance of metaphors and other tropical expressions in scientific discourse. Where Croll stresses the asymmetry of the Senecan style, Jones stresses the "naked"[13] plainness of the style that the Royal Society advocated in reaction against the metaphorical and rhetorical excesses of the Senecan mode.

In emphasizing the scientific program of the Royal Society as the major factor in its advocacy of plain style, Jones tends to understress the role of religion and especially of the Puritans in the reform of prose style. The studies of Jackson Cope in the case of the Anglicans, and those of Harold Fisch, Perry Miller, William Haller, and Lawrence Sasek in the case of the Puritans, have helped to correct this imbalance. Robert Adolph's study of seventeenth-century style in the context of the evolution of modern prose shows a marked preference for Jones's views over those of Croll. Recognizing both religious and scientific influences in the triumph of plain style, Adolph nevertheless stresses utilitarianism as the most important factor in its development.

Croll's categories of style, it is generally agreed, have proved better

13. For discussion of the "naked" style, see *Studies*, pp. 77ff., 82ff., 102, 114ff., 134, 139.

Juan Luis Vives praised a "speech devoid of 'colors'" as that of Aristotle and Tranquillus, *naked and without ornaments*, as Cicero says the Commentaries of Caesar are, bare, direct, pleasing, stripped of all decorations of oratory as if of clothes." Like Cicero in his "description of the Attic style," Vives and Justus Lipsius compared the epistolary style to "a woman simply dressed." Lipsius also stressed the importance of spontaneity; as in "conversations we love the spontaneous and the artless: so here [in epistles]." See Wesley Trimpi, *Ben Jonson's Poems: A Study of the Plain Style* [Stanford, 1962], pp. 57, 63–65.

Richard Sibbes associated a bare style in preaching with the notion of *nuda veritas*: "Truth feareth nothing so much as concealment, and desireth nothing so much as clearly to be laid open to the view of all: When it is most naked, it is most lovely and powerful." Satan, in contrast, is a "cunning rhetorician" who "enlargeth the fancy, to apprehend things bigger than they are." The "majestie and plainness" of the style of the Scriptures impressed John Preston as characteristic of the style that the Holy Ghost Himself had designed. See William Haller, *The Rise of Puritanism* (New York, 1938), pp. 140, 160, 171.

suited to the earlier seventeenth century than to the Restoration period. As the studies of Wesley Trimpi and Jonas Barish indicate, his conceptions of Attic style and Senecan style may, with qualifications, be effectively applied to Ben Jonson's poetry and prose.[14]

7

Contrasts between Puritan and Anglican attitudes toward style have been exaggerated by recent scholars; some such exaggeration is apparent even in the admirable work of the late Joan Webber. The ideal of a naked style had appeared long before in Cicero's *Orator* as a mark of the Attic style; the correlation between a naked style and the naked truth recurs throughout the seventeenth century—in the writings of the Senecan stylist and Anglican bishop Joseph Hall, in the work of the Puritan nonconformist Richard Baxter,[15] and with

14. Even for the late sixteenth century, some qualification of Croll's views has been necessary. Brian Vickers has challenged Croll's identification of Francis Bacon as a Senecan; but, on the other hand, Jonas Barish has effectively explored the Senecan elements in the prose style of Ben Jonson. In the speech of Ben Jonson's dramatic characters, Barish observes characteristic features of both the curt and loose varieties of anti-Ciceronian or Senecan style noted by Morris Croll, and in the structure of Jonson's *Discoveries* he found resemblances to curt and loose periods; see his *Ben Jonson and the Language of Prose Comedy* (Cambridge, Mass., 1960), pp. 61, 77. In *Ben Jonson's Poems: A Study of the Plain Style* (Stanford, 1962), Wesley Trimpi similarly applies Croll's categories of style to Jonson's poetry in the plain style. Placing Jonson in the antirhetorical tradition of the so-called anti-Ciceronians, Trimpi identifies Jonson's style as Attic, emphasizing the traditional association of the plain style with four literary genres in particular—comedy, satire, epigram, epistle—and analyzing the role of the epistolary style as a medium for self-examination and self-revelation.

Alvin Vos has reexamined and reassessed the Ciceronian style of Roger Ascham and other English humanists of the earlier sixteenth century. In "Form and Function in Roger Ascham's Prose," *PQ* 55 (1976): 305 –322, Vos stresses the functional rather than the ornamental character of the so-called Gorgian figures in Ascham's prose writings. These so-called figures of sound are addressed primarily to the mind and only incidentally to the ear. Ascham utilized the resources of rhetoric not so much to adorn truth as to "organize it more efficiently." In "'Good Matter and Good Utterance': The Character of English Ciceronianism," *SEL* 19 (1979): 3 –18, Vos reexamines Ascham's ideas on the relationship between philosophy and eloquence and between matter and style against the background of Croll's preference for an anti-Ciceronian prose style and Francis Bacon's censure of Ciceronianism. Noting significant differences between English Ciceronianism and Cicero's own doctrine, Vos stresses the "more strict, moralistic, and anxious" views of Roger Ascham and Johann Sturm. For both of these humanists, the relationship between philosophy and rhetoric is a "*necessary* relationship," and "the welfare of one is inseparable" from that of the other.

15. According to Richard Baxter, the Reformed pastor ought to place his primary emphasis on matter rather than manner and to make his teaching as plain and evident as possible, speaking to the capacity of his hearers. "Truth loves the light," he declared, "and is most Beautiful when most naked." Like "the Painted Glass in the Windows that

modifications in Thomas Sprat's *History* of the Royal Society. On the
one hand, there are recognized affinities between John Wilkins's
ideas on plain language and a "real character" as a medium for scientific or philosophical discourse and the views expressed by Sprat. On
the other hand, literary historians find significant resemblances
among the kind of plain but powerful speech that the Puritan William
Perkins favored as a vehicle for preaching the Word of God,[16] the
treatises by John Wilkins and Richard Baxter on sermon oratory, and
post-Reformation Anglican views on plain style. These late Anglican
attacks on rhetorical ornament and metaphorical discourse in pulpit
oratory are often directed against either the earlier metaphysical
styles once fashionable in the Anglican pulpit or the metaphors cur-
rently employed by dissenters and sectaries.

Paradoxically, the attacks frequently recapitulate the kind of objections that an earlier generation of Puritan divines had raised against
the witty and eloquent sermons of Jacobean and Caroline Anglicans.
The metaphysical wit, ornate prose, metaphorical subtlety, and
"dark expressions" and polyglot phrases of the Jacobean and Caroline divines, associated with the policies and tastes of Archbishop
William Laud, the Cavaliers, and the royal court, seemed to the Puritans a "carnall eloquence" based on "words of mens wisdom." The
Puritan preachers, from the Elizabethans Lawrence Chaderton and
William Perkins down to Richard Baxter, demanded a plain and simple pulpit style consistent with St. Paul's apparently antirhetorical

---

keeps out the Light," "painted obscure Sermons" are often the marks of painted hypo-
crites. See Harold Fisch, "The Puritans and the Reform of Prose Style," *ELH* 19 (1952):
229–248.

16. In *The Rise of Puritanism*, Haller cites William Perkins's *Treatise of the Duties
and Dignities of the Ministrie* on the preacher's obligation to observe "an admirable
plainnesse and an admirable powerfulnesse." In *The Arte of Prophecying* Perkins ad-
vises the minister to frame his preaching in such a way that all who hear him "may
judge that it is not so much he that speaketh, as the Spirit of God in him and by him."
He should make his speech "spirituall and gracious," "simple and perspicuous, fit both
for the peoples understanding, and to expresse the Majestie of the Spirit." In preparing
the sermon, according to Perkins, the preacher should have at his command the "arts,
Philosophy, and variety of reading," but in preaching it all "Humane wisdome must be
concealed" and he must avoid "Greek and Latine phrases and quirkes" (*Rise*, pp. 130–
131); Barbara Lewalski comments that Perkins expected that "such plain preaching,
concerned to display God's Word unadorned, would achieve the most powerfully moving effect upon the hearers because of the power resident in the Word itself. The
preacher becomes the vehicle of that power precisely *as* he avoids any display of rhetoric" (*Protestant Poetics and the Seventeenth-Century Religious Lyric* [Princeton,
1979], p. 225).

stance and his reliance on the power of the Word and the Spirit:[17]
"And I, brethren, when I came to you, came not with excellency of
speech or of wisdom, declaring unto you the testimony of God. . . .
And my speech and my preaching were not with enticing words of
man's wisdom, but in demonstrations of the Spirit and of power: That
your faith should not stand in the wisdom of men, but in the power of
God" (1 Corinthians 2:1–5). Elsewhere the Apostle had claimed to
"use great plainness of speech; And not as Moses, who put a veil over
his face" (2 Corinthians 3:12–13).

Differences between Anglican and Puritan sermons have been subjected to extensive discussion and revaluation by W. Fraser Mitchell,
Perry Miller, Joan Webber, and, more recently, Barbara K. Lewalski
and Stanley E. Fish. Before 1640, Miller observes, the "two opposed
theories of the form, style, and function of the sermon" were identified with the Puritan and Anglican parties. To the witty, metaphysical style of their opponents the Puritans opposed their own "plain
and profitable way of doctrine, reasons, and uses," which "perfectly
reflected" their mentality "in form and style as well as in substance."
This opposition "between the metaphysical and the Puritan sermon
was a matter both of form and style" (*New England Mind*, pp. 332).
Joan Webber's study *The Eloquent "I": Style and Self in Seventeenth-
Century Prose* approaches the conventional distinction between Anglican and Puritan from a different angle: that of the author's "literary self-consciousness," his "crucial and unremitting awareness that
he is the subject of his own prose, whether or not he is literally writing
autobiography." Examining representative works by "conservative
Anglicans" and "radical Puritans," she finds that these two categories
summarize "major contrasts in styles of selfhood." With its emphasis
on the correlation between style and self, her approach is partly influenced by Croll's discussion of "meditative style as a type of seventeenth-century prose" and of the "shift from a public and oratorical
to a private and meditational prose." Webber's primary concern,
however, is "less with that shift than with the existence in the seventeenth century of both public and private kinds of self-conscious

---

17. See Haller, *Rise of Puritanism*, pp. 128–172; 386–389; Miller, *New England
Mind*, pp. 331–362; Horton Davies, *The Worship of the English Puritans* (Westminster, London, 1948); Fisch, "The Puritans and the Reform of Prose Style," pp. 229–
248; and Lawrence A. Sasek, *The Literary Temper of the English Puritans* (Baton
Rouge, 1961).

prose." Both the "existence of choices among styles, and the revival of the meditational Senecan mode of discourse accompany and encourage individual styles and personal prose" (*Eloquent "I"*, pp. 4–5, 260, 270).

Distinctions between Puritan and Anglican styles can, however, be pressed too far. As Haller and Miller observe, Puritan divines could exploit the resources of metaphor and other tropes and figures while condemning their Anglican opponents or some of the left-wing sectaries for doing so. Their homiletic theory, moreover, made provision for a rhetorical appeal to the affections of their hearers in the final portion of their sermons, the "uses" or "application." Haller and Miller warn us against taking too literally Puritan claims to naked plainness. (Brian Vickers similarly observes that many of the seventeenth-century scientists and philosophers who denounced rhetorical ornament and the use of metaphors in scientific discourse felt free to exploit the resources of rhetoric and figurative speech in other contexts, including, on occasion, their use to heighten the force of philosophical or scientific arguments.) Other critics stress the danger of taking at face value what Anglicans or Puritans say about themselves or about their opponents. Furthermore, as W. Fraser Mitchell and Perry Miller have noted, "there were Anglicans like Ussher who preached in a mode very similar to the Puritans, and there were moderate Puritans like Henry Smith or Thomas Adams whose works seem to us almost 'metaphysical'" (*New England Mind*, p. 332).

Lewalski also has challenged the validity of the Anglican-Puritan dichotomy. Seventeenth-century stylistic distinctions

> in theory and practice are by no means a simple matter of Anglican and Puritan—a witty, ornate, learned, and allusive Anglican style filled with metaphysical conceits, elaborate wordplay, and quotations in foreign tongues, contrasted with an unadorned, unallusive dialectical Puritan 'plain' style. [The] varieties of sermon structures and styles cannot be neatly matched to ecclesiastical parties. (*Protestant Poetics*, p. 214)

Nevertheless, one can still "identify certain dominant and characteristic stylistic habits or traits with particular seventeenth-century theological postures." Thus in *Five Sermons, in Five Several Styles; or Waies of Preaching*, Abraham Wright includes two Anglican sermons in the manner of Bishop Lancelot Andrewes and Bishop Joseph Hall, respectively, along with parodic sermons in the "manner of Thomas Cartwright and Jasper Mayne," in the "manner of the Presbyterians," and in "the Independent vein" (*Protestant Poetics*, pp. 214–215).[18]

Of the five sermons in Wright's book, four had been previously preached: the sermon in Bishop Andrews's way had been delivered "before the late King upon the first day of Lent"; that in Bishop Hall's way, "before the Clergie at the Author's own Ordination in Christ-Church, Oxford; the third "in Dr Maine's and Mr Cartwright's Way," before the University at St. Mary's, Oxford; and the sermon in the Presbyterian way, before the City at St. Paul's Cathedral, London. In his Epistle "To the Christian Reader," Wright disavows his ability "to pen either like that incomparable *Pair of Bishops*, or the other incomparable *Pair of Students*, who were the *Prime Masters* of this Nation in their several Waies of Preaching." His chief aim in printing these sermons is "to shew the difference between *Universitie* and *Citie-breeding* up of *Preachers*" and to demonstrate to the people that "any one that hath been bred a *Scholar* is able to preach any way to the capacitie and content of any *Auditorie*: And *secondly* that none can do this but they onely that have had such Education." It is "clear and evident" that all men "will not be brought by the same way of preaching to heaven; some are well satisfied with the plain easie way of *Doctrine* and *Use*; others are not taken with any Sermon, but what is filled with depth of Matter, height of Fancie, and good Language." It would be well if all preachers in the Church of England were likewise scholars, "able to deliver themselves upon any occasion, any way, to take every ear, and prevail upon every minde and fancie."

In these sermons, Wright informs his "Christian Reader," it is "not so much the *Doctrine* . . . as the *Style* and *manner* of them" that is "offered to thy view." Intending to teach his reader "the necessitie of that knowne distinction between a *Scholar* and a *Preacher*," and "to shew thee what a *Scholar* may do more than a meer *Preacher*," he emphasizes the "vaste difference between *Shop-board-breeding* and the *Universities*." To be a preacher, "as Preachers are now adaies," is slight, easy, and contemptible.

According to Anthony à Wood, Wright was "ordained priest by Dr. Bancroft bishop of Oxon in Ch[rist] Ch[urch] cathedral; at which time he preached the sermon, which was afterward printed with 4

18. For further discussion of Wright's sermons and parodies of pulpit oratory, see W. Fraser Mitchell, *English Pulpit Oratory from Andrewes to Tillotson: A Study of Its Literary Aspects* (London, New York, Toronto, 1932), pp. 365–367; Miller, *New England Mind*, pp. 333–335, 337. Quotations in following paragraphs are from Abraham Wright, *Five Sermons* (London, 1656), prefatory epistle, "To the Christian Readder."

more; . . . and thereupon he [was] accounted an elegant preacher" and "did frequently appear in S. Mary's pulpit in Oxon, and before the city of London at S. Paul's, and before King Charles I when he resided in Oxon, in the time of the grand rebellion."[19]

In Lewalski's view both Puritan and Anglican poets of the seventeenth century shared a "broad Protestant consensus . . . in regard to doctrine and the spiritual life, grounded upon belief in the absolute priority and certainty of scripture and upon paradigms afforded by the Pauline epistles." Overarching "the Anglican-Puritan divide," this consensus held "great significance for religious poetry" and provided the basis for a "biblical poetics" which underlay the work of George Herbert, John Donne, John Milton, and other Protestant writers of the period (*Protestant Poetics*, p. ix).

Puritans and Anglicans alike might, in diverse contexts, praise the plainness and perspicuity of the Bible, its metaphysical wit, and its majesty. John Donne invokes its divine author as "a *figurative*, a *metaphoricall* God" (Webber, *The Eloquent "I"*, pp. 49–50). As Lawrence Sasek observes in *The Literary Temper of the English Puritans*, Puritan rhetoricians also turned to the Bible "for illustrations of types and other rhetorical devices"; John Smith's *The Mysterie of Rhetorique Unvail'd* (1657) is essentially "a handbook of rhetoric using the Bible, along with Sidney's prose, as a source of examples" (p. 67). When rhetoric is "reduced to a blessed subordination and conformity to the teachings of the Spirit of Truth," Smith maintained, it is "a good gift of God" and may be "very conducent" to understanding the "Figurative and Tropical Elegancies" of Scripture, which abounds with "most excellent and divinest eloquence" (Miller, *New England Mind*, p. 311). As Sasek points out, the "stylistic merits of scriptural writings had various implications for the puritan theory of style." While some Puritans endeavored to follow the example of Scripture and "urged a grave and sober eloquence," others regarded "all human rhetoric" as vain in comparison with biblical artistry and maintained that "it was best to write and speak plainly, leaving a monopoly of eloquence to the Holy Spirit" (Sasek, *Literary Temper*, p. 65).

19. Anthony à Wood, *Athenae Oxonienses . . .*, ed. Philip Blass (London, 1820) 4: cols. 275–278. A colleague of mine at the Huntington Library has suggested that Wright's reference in the third sermon may have been to William Cartwright rather than Thomas Cartwright. Like Jasper Mayne, William Cartwright was a student of Christ Church, Oxford and, according to Wood, he "became the most florid and seraphical preacher in the university," while Mayne became a "quaint preacher and noted poet" (3: cols. 69–72, 671–673).

The Scriptures could serve as a model not only for plainness and simplicity but also for figurative and metaphorical discourse. The chief issue in seventeenth-century controversies over the Bible as "source and model for the presentation of sacred truth as art" concerned "the unique character of the sacred matter" and its "implications for the rhetorician's art" (Lewalski, *Protestant Poetics*, pp. 1, 216). Observing that St. Augustine's *De Doctrina Christiana* was "the starting point for discussion of sermon theory, method, and style throughout the sixteenth and seventeenth centuries," Lewalski finds that the "ambiguity about rhetoric apparent in Augustine characterized many of the Renaissance and seventeenth-century *artes concionandi* influential for Protestant sermon theory" (pp. 216–224). Augustine "refers the preacher to the perfect conjunction of wisdom and eloquence in the 'plain' sermons of the Apostle Paul, and also in the more figured" and more highly ornamented sermons of the prophets (p. 217).[20]

---

20. See Augustine, *On Christian Doctrine*, trans. D. W. Robertson, Jr. (Indianapolis and New York, 1958). Augustine distinguishes between a way of discovery and a way of teaching—but in relation to the wisdom of Scripture rather than to the knowledge of nature (p. 7). He regards the "rules of eloquence" as "very true" in themselves, but acknowledges that they may be used "to make falsehoods more persuasive" (p. 71). But the fact that rhetoric can be abused should not deter the Christian from using it, "for since by the art of rhetoric both truth and falsehood are urged, who would dare to say that truth should stand in the person of its defenders unarmed against lying?" (p. 118).

Quoting Cicero's statement (*De inventione*) that "wisdom without eloquence is of small benefit to states; but eloquence without wisdom is often extremely injurious and profits no one," Augustine argues that "a man speaks more or less wisely to the extent that he has become more or less proficient in the Holy Scriptures." If the heathen teachers of eloquence, who were ignorant of the "true wisdom" which descends from God, thus recognized the danger of eloquence without wisdom, "how much more ought we, who are the sons and ministers of this wisdom, to think in no other way" (pp. 121–122).

Regarding true eloquence as an obedient servant and follower of true wisdom, Augustine praises the eloquence of Scripture, whose words "were poured forth from the divine mind both wisely and eloquently not in such a way that wisdom was directed toward eloquence, but in such a way that eloquence did not abandon wisdom" (p. 132). There is, he maintains, "a kind of eloquence fitting for men most worthy of the highest authority and clearly inspired by God. Our authors speak with eloquence of this kind, nor does any other kind become them" (p. 123). The very obscurity of the divine writings "was a part of a kind of eloquence through which our understandings should be benefited not only by the discovery of what lies hidden but also by exercise" (p. 123). Thus in the "eloquence of the Prophets . . . many things are obscured by tropes" (p. 124).

In Augustine's doctrine, seventeenth-century Puritans and Anglicans might find sanction both for the plain style and for a figured, obscure, and metaphorical style.

8

According to Perry Miller, the differences between the witty, meta-physical sermon and the plain sermon style favored by the Puritans may have been influenced by divergences between Aristotelian and Ramist traditions in logic, rhetoric, and homiletics. Rudolph Kecker-mann's treatise *Rhetoricae Ecclesiasticae* was, in Miller's opinion, "probably the most influential Aristotelian treatise among English Protestants," and, noting Fraser Mitchell's view, the "pattern of most metaphysical sermons" (and of John Donne's sermons in particular) "was taken from Keckermann" (*New England Mind*, pp. 336–337). Miller regards the "metaphysical sermon" as the expression of "men who remained loyal to scholasticism, not merely in physics, as did the Puritans, but in logic and rhetoric as well." For such men, Ramist reforms of these arts were "impious and ignorant"; they couched their own homiletic theory in Aristotelian terms, regarding the ser-mon "as a particular species in the genus of oratory." There were, he believes, "deep affinities between the Aristotelian way of thinking and religious beliefs of the Anglican party, as can be seen in the meth-ods and arguments of Richard Hooker" (p. 337). The opposing style, he suggests tentatively, "the Puritan form with its doctrine, reasons, and uses," was "a consequence of the Puritan adherence" to the Ra-mist reform of rhetoric and dialectic (p. 337).

Ramist logic was "not a reform of philosophy but of pedagogy and rhetoric."[21] In England it established itself at Cambridge and became

21. Miller, *New England Mind*, p. 494. For Ramism and Renaissance concepts of method, see Ong, *Ramus*; Neal W. Gilbert, *Renaissance Concepts of Method* (New York, 1960); Peter A. Schouls, *The Imposition of Method: A Study of Descartes and Locke* (Oxford, 1980); John Webster, "Oration and Method in Sidney's *Apology*: A Contemporary's Account," *MP* 79 (1981): 1–15.

Method, as Ong points out, was Peter Ramus's term for "orderly pedagogical pre-sentation of any subject by reputedly scientific descent from 'general principles' to 'specials' by means of definition and bipartite division" (*Ramus*, p. 30). Gilbert divides the "entire discussion of method" into discussions of "*artistic* method" and those con-cerned with "*scientific* method." Besides tracing the history of method as a philosophi-cal term, his book contains an appendix on "Methodus in Titles of Books in the Late Renaissance." Schouls discusses the distinctions and interplay between analytic and synthetic method, or resolution and composition, in the sixteenth and seventeenth centuries. In *Francis Bacon: Discovery and the Art of Discourse* (Cambridge, 1974), Lisa Jardine reexamines Bacon's writings in the context of sixteenth-century concep-tions of methodology and dialectic; and in *Francis Bacon and the Style of Science* (Chicago and London, 1975), James Stephens discusses Bacon's "philosophical meth-ods," with particular emphasis on his theory of "philosophical style" and his use of the aphoristic manner and the method of emblems and hieroglyphs. In "Francis Bacon and Method: Theory and Practice," *Speech Monographs*, 40, no. 4 (1973): 243–272, Karl

R. Wallace explores Bacon's understanding of the concept *method* and his exploitation of method in his speeches and writings. Pointing out that Bacon "describes seven kinds of methods and alludes by name to five others," Wallace stresses the distinction between the "magistral" and "initiative" methods, as well as Bacon's views on "the delivery of knowledge in *aphorisms*, or in *methods*." In his opinion, Bacon was critical of the current fashion—"probably learned from the Rameans"—of "taking a few 'axioms,' or basic propositions in any subject, deducing a chain of related propositions from these, and illustrating them with examples" (pp. 243–272).

John Webster, in "Oration and Method," analyzes the influence of Ramist ideas concerning method and discourse upon Sir Philip Sidney's secretary, Sir William Temple, and Temple's conception of Sidney's expository prose, emphasizing distinctions between "oratorical" and "methodical" discourse oriented toward persuasion and understanding, respectively. In Melanchthon's view, according to Webster, the "didascalic" discourse, or "method of teaching" pertained to dialectic and could be of "great use in churches."

In England, as Wilbur S. Howell recognized, Ramism was the "central route over which the Ciceronian rhetorical tradition and the scholastic tradition" moved in "reorienting themselves for the modern world" (Ong, *Ramus*, p. 7). Though its influence on Puritan homiletics is generally acknowledged, the extent of its influence on poetry is still controversial. Ong has revised and qualified Rosemond Tuve's view in *Elizabethan and Metaphysical Imagery* that the Ramist reforms heightened the "prestige of logic, both in poetry and elsewhere," accelerating the "development of wit at the expense of purely 'decorative' poetic objectives" and "implementing metaphysical poetry in general" (*Ramus*, p. 6). In Ong's opinion "Ramism assimilated logic to imagery and imagery to logic by reducing intelligence itself, more or less unconsciously, in terms of rather exclusively visual, spatial analogies" (p. 286). See also Rosemond Tuve, "Imagery and Logic: Ramus and Metaphysical Poetics," *JHI* 3 (1942): 365–400; Norman E. Nelson, *Peter Ramus and the Confusion of Logic, Rhetoric, and Poetry*, University of Michigan Contributions in Modern Philology no. 2 (1947); P. Albert Duhamel, "The Logic and Rhetoric of Peter Ramus," *MP* 46 (1949): 163–171; Duhamel, "Milton's Alleged Ramism," *PMLA* 67 (1952): 1035–53; A. J. Smith, "An Examination of Some Claims Made for Ramism," *RES*, n.s., 7 (1956): 348–359; George Watson, "Ramus, Miss Tuve, and the New Petromachia," *MP* 55 (1958): 259–262. Both Duhamel and Smith challenge the claims for Ramus's "literary influence" made by Tuve and other scholars, such as Hardin Craig and Perry Miller. Watson argues that "so far as the English were concerned," Ramism was essentially "a quick handbook for logic with Cambridge and Puritan associations"; in his view, it is "still not clear that there is any need to seek a connection between Ramism and English poetry."

From its "earliest appearance in the Ramist works," Ong points out, "the notion of ornament tends to dominate the other terms and to reduce the auditory element, the resonance of rhetoric, ... to, in effect, a nonrhetorical style. ... Plain style, which is really nonrhetorical style, alone is acceptable to reasonable man" (p. 284). When Melanchthon acknowledged, says Ong, that "dialectic and rhetoric differed in that the former presented things in a naked state, whereas the latter clothed them with ornament," he was partly concerned "with the age of his pupils." In Ramism, however, the concept of ornamentation "undergoes a significant change"; and in its final stage "Ramist rhetoric relies more on ornamentation theory than perhaps any other rhetoric ever has." The basic reason, Ong suggests, is "its restriction of rhetoric to *elocutio*, which meant the use of tropes and figures, commonly considered the 'ornaments'" (p. 277). For Talon, the terms *exornatio* and *elocutio* are "not complementary opposites but synonyms: "'Just as wisdom treats of the knowledge of things,' Talon states in 1545, 'so rhetoric treats of ornamentation and striking expression'" (p. 277).

closely identified with Puritanism, "principally through the work of the great commentators," Sir William Temple, George Downame, and Alexander Richardson (Miller, *New England Mind*, pp. 499–500). Puritan divines in both Old and New England depended heavily on Ramist dialectics for the first two parts of their sermons (doctrine and arguments, or "reasons") and on Ramist rhetoric for the third part (application, or "uses") (pp. 346–347). In Miller's view, Ramist influence may also have been partly responsible for Puritan emphasis on plain style. Puritan manuals insist that style should be "kept wholly subordinate to the Bible," making a "plaine delivery of the Word without the painted eloquence of mens wisdome."[22]

To Puritan pastors the "learned and highly ornate sermons" of the "Laudians" among the Anglican clergy seemed merely "the 'carnall eloquence' of a 'blubber-lipt Ministery.'" Their "Metaphysical high flown Notions," their "Words of Mens Wisdom," their "Clattering" of "Latin, Greek or Hebrew Sentences," and their "obscure phrases, Exotick Words" and "dark expressions" seemed immoral to their Puritan contemporaries—not only because they "blasphemously pol-

---

22. Miller, *New England Mind*, pp. 349. In *Worship of the English Puritans*, Davies observes that, in contrast to "the sermons of Caroline Anglican divines, . . . which were weighted down with classical and patristic quotations, the sermons of the Puritans were restricted almost entirely to Biblical citations" (p. 197). In "opening" the text, the Puritan sermon explicates the literal meaning and thereby enables the spiritual meaning to operate in the minds and hearts of the congregation. For Thomas Goodwin it was not so much the letter of the word as the spiritual meaning of the word that converts the heart and turns it to God. "There is the letter," he declares, "the husk; and there is the spirit, the kernel; and when we by expounding the word do open the husk, out drops the kernel" (p. 188).

In Miller's opinion, Ramistic rhetoric, along with Ramistic dialectic, contributed to the literalization of scriptural imagery by Puritan speakers and writers. If the biblical text "happened to be . . . some figure of speech, some metaphor or hyperbole," the explicator must make the sense plain by stripping the text of its figurative expression and thus making the logical axiom visible. Talon's rhetoric was "ideally suited to just this 'stripping' of figures from the logical sense, for it made tropes and schemes the secondary and subsequent wrappings of a plain speech." Thus it provided a "tool with which Puritans could plane off the colors of speech from Scriptural utterances, leaving the smooth white surface of 'that one entire and naturall sense'"(*New England Mind*, pp. 301–302).

Ong regards the "Ramist plain style" as "the verbal counterpart of the coming visualist universe of 'objects,' voiceless and by that fact depersonalized, which would soon recommend to the Royal Society . . . 'a close, naked, natural way of speaking,' as near the 'mathematical' as possible." Preferring the "straightforward technique of 'opening' a text by analysis" to the "topical" way of preaching practiced by Anglican divines such as Donne, the Puritan advocates of plain style "wanted preaching with method and certainty, giving 'doctrine' and 'reasons' from 'axioms.'" Since axioms were a "part of dialectic," this procedure involved "a retreat from rhetoric back into a pure dialectic" (*Ramus*, pp. 213, 283–284).

ished God's altar and adulterated the Word of God, 'like as Paint doth marble, or as honey and wine in childrens milke,' but also because their sermons could never become a means of grace to common men" (Miller, *New England Mind*, pp. 301–302).

For the Puritans, Miller has argued, rhetoric was subordinate and ancillary to dialectic (or logic); it was sometimes untrustworthy and subject to abuse, but judiciously employed it could serve the cause of truth. Peter Ramus, author of the *Dialectica*, and "his *alter ego*" Omer Talon, author of the *Rhetorica*, "had wrought as important a revolution in rhetoric as in logic, and Ramists could not give allegiance to the one without fully embracing the other" (*New England Mind*, p. 305). Like all humanists,

> The Puritans [were committed] to using rhetoric as a bait for the emotions, but they too had to be on their guard lest rhetoric become an instrument of seduction rather than a means of grace, lest it betray even the truth by bringing men to it through a sinful violation of the order of nature. . . . Just as the Puritans, starting from the Christian doctrine of the fall, came to venerate logic as an instrument of their recovery, so they reached an equally profound respect for rhetoric as the divinely given science for making sermons powerful means of regeneration, [whose rhetoric] worked upon the rational and particularly upon the sensible souls of men. (pp. 308–309)

Whenever Puritans discuss the sermon itself, "they give the preponderant attention to arousing affection" (p. 300).

> Style in the service of reason and the good, of logic and theology, was the teaching which Puritans found in the rhetoric of Ramus and Talon, and they adopted it as their own because it merged perfectly with their theory of the arts, with the doctrinal opposition to the metaphysical style, . . . and above all with their temperamental hostility to any point of view that finds problems of technique as fascinating as problems of sense. The rhetoric, in short, . . . exemplifies the spirit of the Puritan aesthetic, its dislike of any rule of beauty cherished apart from the rule of truth, its profound antipathy to every disposition that can see charms in a movement of words without first being able to say precisely what the words mean. (p. 328)

By separating invention, disposition, and memory from rhetoric, the Ramist reforms had left only style (*elocutio*) and delivery to rhetoric; and style itself was frequently regarded as ornamentation. As the Puritans saw it, the Ramist theory "applied rhetoric to the work merely of adding ornaments or embellishing that which logic had invented and arranged, of uttering logical propositions with appro-

priate tones and gestures." Although Ramist theory continued to concentrate the art upon persuasion, it "took away from it all power to
determine for itself to what it should persuade." For George
Downame, rhetoric was to dialectic "as the moon to the sun"; it
shone with a borrowed and reflected light. Invention and disposition
were like Hercules; eloquence and delivery "merely the Hydra and
the skin of eloquence." Dialectic "affords as it were the body of oratory, rhetoric the clothing."[23]

9

For Stanley Fish, the paired terms favored by earlier critics—"Anglican–Puritan, Painted–Plain, Ciceronian–Senecan, Scientific–
Rhetorical, Utilitarian–Frivolous, Commonwealth–Restoration"—
seem inadequate. He prefers a new pair: *Self-Satisfying* and *Self-
Consuming*. For a "political, social, or religious opposition" he sub-
stitutes "an opposition of epistemologies," which "finds its expression in two kinds of reading experiences." There has been, in fact, "an
epistemological shift that cuts across party lines," and the "triumph
of the plain style" is essentially a "triumph of epistemology."[24]

Seventeenth-century attitudes toward the traditional distinction
between matter and manner, or content and style (*res et verba*) have
also been subjected to revaluation, as have the definitions of the essay
and of the so-called essay style.[25] As the studies of Roger Ascham by

23. Miller, *New England Mind*, p. 326. In Miller's view, the "Puritan style" was far
"removed from the unadorned simplicity and spontaneity of common speech." Among
"orthodox" Puritans, "hostility to the metaphysical style never became . . . hostility to
stylistic cultivation or to the constant use of figures and tropes." Though they might on
occasion "call eloquence a carnal deceit," they were "sufficiently of their times to believe that the faithful preaching which was to enfold the grace of God should be constructed with all possible 'humane help'" (p. 304). Believing that the art of rhetoric was
"completely embodied in the tropes and figures of the Bible," Puritans frequently argued that "since Scripture is eloquent, ministers must study eloquence, first in order to
expound divinity by it, and second to use it as a sanctified help in their own orations"
(p. 310). Thus in *The Mysterie of Rhetorick Unveil'd* John Smith maintained that "all
Science, and particularly, Rhetorique, where it is reduced to a blessed subordination
and conformity to the teachings of the Spirit of Truth, is a good gift of God . . . and
very conducent to the unfolding and right understanding of the Figurative and Tropical Elegancies of the blessed Book, which abounds with most excellent and divinest
eloquence." Quoted in Miller, *New England Mind*, (p. 311).

24. Fish, *Self-Consuming Artifacts: The Experience of Seventeenth-Century Literature* (Berkeley, Los Angeles, London, 1972), pp. 374–382.

25. In "Not Being, But Passing: Defining the Early English Essay," *SLI* 10, no. 2
(1977): 17–27, Ted-Larry Pebworth observes that "the essay as a distinguishable

Alvin Vos and those of Francis Bacon by Brian Vickers have indicated, seemingly contradictory Renaissance statements concerning the relative importance of matter and manner, or words and things, are not as incompatible as they might appear to be at first glance. As Vos has maintained, Ascham regarded excellence in content and style as inseparable, associating wholesome doctrine with excellence of style, and barbarous language with corrupt and unsound doctrines. Bacon himself recognized the expediency of exploiting the resources of rhetoric and adding "reason to imagination" in order to win the understanding and approval of a learned readership for his program for the reformation of learning. As studies by Paolo Rossi, Karl Wallace, and other scholars have shown, Bacon's ideas on methodology were strongly influenced by rhetorical theory. In addition to employing the conventional senses of rhetorical or logical terms like *invention* and *disposition, disposition* and *method, matter* or *things (res)*, he adapts these terms to the study of nature itself and to scientific methods for the discovery of reality. *Invention* now means more than the selection of logical proofs; and *method* means more than the arrangement of arguments in proving or persuading. *Matter* and *things* signify more than the content or subject matter that a dialectician or orator might utilize for discourse and that a schoolboy would classify under convenient topical headings in a commonplace book, in accordance with the humanist educator's notebook-and-headings method and the tradition of Erasmus's distinction between copiousness in content and in diction, *copia rerum* and *copia verborum*. *Matter* can mean not merely the matter of discourse but actual physical

---

genre emerged concurrently with the anti-Ciceronian movements in prose style in the late sixteenth century" and that "the early essayists, both in France and in England, were all anti-Ciceronians of one kind or another." Citing Croll's view on the intent of the anti-Ciceronians "to portray, not a thought, but a mind thinking," Pebworth comments "more cautiously" that these anti-Ciceronians "sought to give the impression, often achieved through diligent revision, that they were essentially the secretaries of their minds in motion" and that the genres that they utilized reflect the same impulse: "lengthy and overtly rhetorical forms gave way to briefer, more loosely constructed ones, the essay among them." Nevertheless "a mind can think in two directions: it can move toward a predetermined, albeit vague or general, goal; or it can wander at will. The first kind of thinking is discoverable in most prose genres of the late Renaissance. The latter freedom defines the essay." Essentially reflective, the essay is "designed to give the impression of a mind thinking on a subject with no predetermined goal or formulaic conclusion toward which it need aim," the "record of a mind apparently roaming freely." Although it uses such devices as "definition, partition, contrast, antithesis, illustration, and example," it calls upon them "as they naturally suggest themselves in a free association of ideas."

reality, the material stuff of the universe; and *things* may signify not simply the conceptual content of discourse but concrete objects themselves, corporeal things existing in material reality.

In both classical and Renaissance rhetorical theory, the distinction between *res* and *verba* is often used to illustrate the distinctions between wisdom and eloquence, philosophy and rhetoric, dialectic and rhetoric, and the like—though these pairs of terms do not have identical meanings. In the Baconian tradition of the seventeenth century, the demand for a "philosophical" style was frequently associated with the ideal of a "real" character, which would form the foundation of a system of notation based (like hieroglyphics) on things (*res*) existing in nature. Such a real character was one of the continuing interests of Bishop John Wilkins (along with the ideal of the plain style in preaching, and the concept of a limited kind of certainty intermediate between absolute certitude and absolute skepticism) and it would be eventually ridiculed and carried to a *reductio ad absurdum* by Jonathan Swift.

The kind of philosophical style sought by scientists of the Royal Society is by no means the same kind of philosophical style that Croll associates with Stoic and libertine prose and with the Socratic dialogues, the epistles of Seneca, and the essays of Montaigne. The impersonality of scientific discourse and the self-revelatory character of the essay style, as Croll conceived it, are at odds. The concept of an essay style, moreover, tends to blur the significant differences between the essays of writers like Bacon and Montaigne.[26] At the same

26. Ronald S. Crane, "The Relation of Bacon's *Essays* to His Program for the Advancement of Learning" (in *Essential Articles for the Study of Francis Bacon*, ed. Brian Vickers [Hamden, Conn., 1968]), accepts as plausible the views of Pierre Villey concerning the relationship of Bacon's essays to those of Montaigne. As Crane explains, according to Pierre Villey, *Montaigne et François Bacon* (Paris, 1913), "the *Essays* of 1597 were conceived, not as essays in the sense which Montaigne had already given to the term, but as collections of maxims or 'sentences'." In composing them, Bacon "utilized to a great extent collections of generalized maxims, both original and borrowed, already recorded in his note-books." He subsequently continued this practice in "a number of the later essays, several of which are demonstrably little more than rearrangements of 'sentences' which by his own acknowledgment he had had by him since his youth." Crane himself maintains, however, that Villey overlooked an equally important factor in explaining Bacon's continued use of the method of aphorisms in 1612 and 1625: "his clearly formulated belief, expressed in 1605 and reaffirmed without change in 1623, that for certain purposes 'writing in aphorisms' is to be preferred to a more methodical and fully developed type of composition" (pp. 272–292). See also Steven Randall, "The Rhetoric of Montaigne's Self-Portrait: Speaker and Subject," *SP* 73 (1976):285–301.

Robert Adolph has contrasted Bacon's philosophical writings both with "the Montaignesque monologue" and with the "Platonic tradition of the classical style." Adolph

time, reflective discourse and self-exploratory poetry and prose comprise a significantly broader tradition than the essay and cannot be limited strictly to Senecan or anti-Ciceronian modes. The various kinds of meditative discourse explored by Louis L. Martz and Barbara K. Lewalski, for instance, are usually far more indebted, ultimately, to writers like St. Augustine than to Seneca or Montaigne.[27] The essay as a genre, can (as in the case of Montaigne, and to a lesser extent the case of Sir Thomas Browne) approximate "the painting of thought" or the picture of a mind thinking.[28] In other instances, however, it may approximate the *copia rerum* of a commonplace book;

---

finds that Bacon utilized "austere aphorisms or, more commonly, the formal 'Methods' of the 'Magistral' style." Moreover, the "impersonality" of Bacon's plain style distinguished him "most obviously from the classical plain style." Unlike the theoreticians of the latter, Bacon "means by 'things' objective physical reality and its causes, existing before and after the writer's perception and independent of him." In the classical plain style, in contrast, "'things' are intellectual and subjective, not physical and objective" (*The Rise of Modern Prose Style* [Cambridge, Mass., and London, 1968], pp. 166–168.

27. See Lewalski, *Protestant Poetics*, p. 13, on "the classic Protestant paradigm of sin and salvation" and its relationship to "the painstaking analysis of the personal religious life" in seventeenth-century poetry and prose.

28. In *The Strategy of Truth: A Study of Sir Thomas Browne* (Chicago and London, 1967), Leonard Nathanson observes that the "problem of truth absorbs Browne's attention more than any other issue" (p. 60). Yet he "was less absorbed than either Montaigne or Bacon in the utilitarian value of truth. Even in his most practical . . . efforts . . . he threads his way through the 'Labyrinth of Truth' and the swamps of mere fact with eager curiosity, but in a disinterested spirit and with little immediate concern for application" (p. 4). Emphasizing Browne's "loosely associative conduct of discourse," often "innocent of apparent organization," Nathanson regards the *Religio Medici* as "a meditative essay" on faith and charity; as such, "its stance is not that of an objective disquisition, but reflects a particular man's contours of response" (pp. 69, 80–81). "[The] Platonic epistemology to which Browne subscribed, with its hierarchical valuation of custom, nature, and Idea encompassing all experience and knowledge, required no overt presentation" (p. 91). Nathanson also emphasizes the contrast between the essays of Montaigne and those of Bacon. In the former, "discursive self-exploration finds expression in the loose Senecan style with its suggestion of tentative probing." Bacon, in contrast, was less interested in "the curve and process of mental exploration than in the hits a discovering mind could make," and accordingly "cultivated the form of Senecan prose that goes under the label 'curt style.'" Their "differing aims and methods" are reflected in their styles (p. 80).

Observing that as an essayist Browne was "closer to the continental tradition of Montaigne than to Bacon, "Adolph comments that, though Browne "repeats Montaigne's desire that language follow mental associations," Browne also "holds that *rhetoric* best illustrates his special intention, which is self-revelation rather than reasoned exposition." What distinguishes him principally from Restoration theorists, in Adolph's opinion, is the high value that Browne "places on 'things' delivered Rhetorically to illustrate his private conceptions." Rather than explanation, he seeks "a series of impressions or associations, closer to the way in which mental experience actually takes place" (*Rise of Modern Prose Style*, pp. 153–155).

this is partly the case with some of Bacon's earlier essays. It may on occasion be very loosely structured, in appearance at least; or, alternatively, it may be tightly and closely reasoned. In some instances the self-revelatory aspects of discourse may involve deliberate eccentricity, and the appearance of personal idiosyncracies, in so extreme a degree that the quirks and whimsies of the authorial persona and his personal style interfere with the rational development of the argument; thus in Burton's *Anatomy of Melancholy* the eccentricities of the "mad" author are intimately associated with the overt medical subject of his treatise (the varieties of melancholy, and their causes and cure) and with the implicit moral and satiric subject of the work (the universal madness of all classes of human society, and of mankind in general).[29]

Moreover, Ben Jonson's use of the Senecan style differs significantly from that of many of his near contemporaries. Quoting Coleridge's description of Senecan style as a series of thoughts "strung together like beads, without any causation or progression," Jonas Barish, in *Ben Jonson and the Language of Prose Comedy*, has observed that the "baroque" or "libertine" writers analyzed by Croll "intended to be wanton as the mind is wanton, to transcribe the process of thought onto the page instead of stifling it ... within prescribed logical schemes. [They] assumed that regularity was artful, irregularity natural and spontaneous, and they wrote accordingly" (p. 65). Jonson's prose is "irregular on principle, and the irregularity transmits itself from the largest phenomena of style down to the smallest" (p. 76). The structure of his *Discoveries* "resembles that of

29. Adolph, *Rise of Modern Prose Style*, emphasizes the "paradoxical tendency of the 'plain' style to evolve into mannerisms, associationism, queerness, and obscurity." What Robert Burton produces in *The Anatomy of Melancholy* is "not the urbane, familiar utterance of the classical plain style but one of the queerest and most private works of the age. The demand of 'libertines' like Montaigne and Burton for complete freedom of subject matter is, to be sure, an extension of the theory of *res et verba* of the classical plain style"; but their "libertine associationism" is not "really in the tradition of the classical plain style, even though that style is its point of departure" (p. 150).

Richard Whitlock's *Zootomia* (1654) illustrates, for instance, "how self-conscious, mannered, obscure, and private libertine prose could become." Though Whitlock "admires all the libertine favorites, including Seneca, Plutarch, Montaigne, and Hall," he "insists that he does not *imitate* them" and that he is endeavoring "to write in his own distinctive way, even for himself alone." The "most readable style reproduces the contours of thought," and in this respect Whitlock acknowledges Montaigne as his master: "'As Montaigne *saith of himselfe*, Tracts *of a* continued Thread are tedious *to most* fancies, *which of it selfe indeed is of that* desultory *nature, that it is pleased with* Writings *like* Irish Bogs, *that it may* leap *from one* variety *to another, than* tread *any* beaten Path'" (Adolph, *Modern Prose*, pp. 151–152).

the curt and loose periods. Like Donne's *Devotions*, Selden's *Table Talk*, and Traherne's *Centuries of Meditations*, the *Discoveries* belong to a genre: . . . the *pensées*, a disconnected series of jottings that explores a few dominant themes in as many ways as the writer chooses. . . . Truth is presented in fragments, in scattered glimpses, rather than steadily and whole" (p. 77).

The "restlessness of baroque style," Barish suggests, "expresses some restlessness within the writer, some inner conflict or war with the world at large." Thus

> it lends itself admirably to the needs of authors like Donne, Browne, Milton, Burton, Montaigne, and Pascal. . . . The common denominator among these writers seems to be an intense, sometimes rebellious subjectivity, for which the skittishness of baroque prose provides an ideal instrument. But when we approach Jonson with similar expectations, we seem to run into a blank wall. . . . What distinguishes the *Discoveries* from the *Devotions*, the *Pensées*, the *Table Talk*, and the *Centuries of Meditations* is precisely the suppression of all doubt and personal revelation. . . . [Where] the other baroque writers explicitly dramatize their tensions, in Jonson, the tensions remain buried.[30]

30. Barish, *Ben Jonson*, pp. 65, 76–87. In *Ben Jonson's Poems*, Wesley Trimpi emphasizes the associations of the epistle both with the process of self-examination and with the use of the plain or conversational style (the classical *sermo*). Montaigne's "detailed descriptions of his own style" exhibit characteristic features of the "epistolary style," in Trimpi's opinion. Montaigne praises Seneca's epistles by contrasting their style with that eloquence "which leaves us with a desire of it, and not of things." Words ought to serve matter in such a way that one does not notice them. "The rhetorical 'outward garment and cloake may be borrowed,' Montaigne declares, 'but never the sinews and strength of the bodie!' The style of his *Essais* is like that of his own conversation: 'a comical and familier stile . . . altogether close, broken, and particular'" (Trimpi, *Ben Jonson's Poems*, p. 35).

The "Socratic and Stoic attitudes" toward experience "and the literary analysis and expression of personal experience in the *sermo*" remain the same, Trimpi argues, "for Jonson and Vives as for the Senecans." Nevertheless the Senecans, "especially those of the Libertine movement, tended more and more to use the *sermo* to express personal idiosyncrasy until the plain style itself became eccentrically mannered." Vives and Jonson, however, "retained, as an ideal, the *sermo* as described by Cicero in his discussion of the Attic orator" (p. 53). Vives describes the style that, in Trimpi's opinion is "closest to Jonson's": "'speech devoid of "colors" as that of Aristotle and Tranquillus, *naked and without ornaments*, as Cicero says the Commentaries of Caesar are, bare, direct, pleasing, stripped of all decorations of oratory as if of clothes'" (p. 57).

In associating Jonson's stylistic theory and practice with his epistemology, Trimpi maintains that for Jonson, as for Bacon, classicism was "a habit of discovery, a constant re-evaluation of epistemological methods as well as the accumulation and mastery of ancient knowledge." "'Truth lyes open to all, it is no mans *severall*,'" Jonson believed; and it was "continually necessary to 'gently stirre the mould about the root of the Question.' . . . To do this the inquiring mind must employ a style that can itself achieve

Style can be the utilitarian instrument or the decorative garment of thought. Seventeenth-century writers vary in their attitudes toward style as functional instrument or as ornament, in their subjective or objective emphasis, and in their attitudes toward "natural" and "artificial" discourse. In some of them one finds not only a tension between content and style (*res et verba*), but also a tension between the content of discourse and the real or apparent personality of the author. Some writers appear to be primarily concerned with the finished structures of thought and only secondarily interested in achieving a mimesis of the act of thinking, while others place greater emphasis on the process of thinking and on the authorial persona as thinker, presenting the act of thinking as an act of self-dramatization or self-projection: the thoughts presented are portrayed as correlatives of the mind and personality of the author and of the meditative process itself.

---

the necessary flexibility in its own structure to fulfill the purposes of such investigations. Epistemologically, this is the most 'classical' reason . . . for Jonson's adoption of the Attic style" (pp. 144–145). Trimpi also emphasizes the distinction between Jonson's plain style, based on the "Attic style" and the plain style of "the native English tradition" (p. 114).

III. Meretrix or Daughter of Truth: The Moral Ambiguities of Rhetoric

The seventeenth-century disputes over the value of rhetoric and poetic and the embellishment or purification of discourse were essentially a renewal of a long-standing conflict begun in classical times
and marked by occasional truces, embassies, and attempts at media-
tion. Though the lines of battle had shifted somewhat, the contestants
continued to employ the strategies and tactics of earlier campaigns.
Many of the arguments and much of the imagery of earlier debates
had survived intact throughout the Renaissance; they had become
commonplaces, and writers proficient in both arts—such as Herbert
and Milton—could apply them to poetry as others were applying
them to prose. Indeed, wrote George Herbert,

> When first my lines of heavenly joys made mention
> Such was their luster, they did so excel,
> That I sought out quaint words, and trim invention;
> My thoughts began to burnish, sprout, and swell,
> Curling with metaphors a plain intention,
> Decking the sense, as if it were to sell.
> ("Jordan [II]," SC, p. 225)

Or, as Herbert wrote in an earlier poem:

> Who says that fictions only and false hair
> Become a verse? Is there in truth no beauty?
> Is all good structure in a winding stair?
> May no lines pass, except they do their duty
>   Not to a true, but painted chair?
>
> . . . .
> Must all be veiled, while he that reads, divines,
>   Catching the sense at two removes?
> ("Jordan [I]," SC, p. 213)[1]

1. Lewalski, *Protestant Poetics*, observes Herbert's commitment in this poem to a
specifically Protestant (and biblical) poetics. He eschews the "notions of poetry as

53

Though Herbert was concerned specifically with poetic discourse, similar arguments were frequently advanced by some of his contemporaries on behalf of the plain style in philosophy and religion. The naked truth demanded a clear and naked mode of writing or speaking (*Studies*, pp. 77, 86, 91n). Truth required no other ornament than her own native beauty; to deck her out in schemes and tropes was to make her indistinguishable from a harlot. At best the embellishments of rhetoric were, like gilding the lily, a vain and tasteless affectation.

---

pointing by means of fictions to philosophical truth, or shadowy revelation, or the platonic ideas." The poetics implied in the final line of his poem "proposes instead a direct recourse to the Bible as repository of truth." The speaker "calls upon biblical models and biblical/poetic resources, ... and associates himself straightforwardly with the Psalmist in heartfelt and uncontrived (plain) utterance." Like those who "renounced human arts in sermons as inappropriate to sacred matter," Herbert renounces "many of the ornaments of secular poetry— 'fictions and false hair'; stock pastoral imagery, riddling allegory. Instead he announces a new ideal of plainness ... akin to that centrist Protestant recognition of scripture as the model for art as well as truth. ... To the question posed in 'Jordan (I),' 'Is there in truth no beautie?' the clearly expected answer is, 'Yes, of course there is, they are inextricably linked'—even as Augustine thought" (pp. 3–4, 227).

In lines 9–10 of this poem ("Must all ... at two removes?") F. E. Hutchinson finds an expression of Herbert's attraction to "a simpler manner of expression than the intellectual subtleties affected by Donne"; and in commenting on line 5 ("Not ... painted chair?") the same editor observed that Henry Vaughan "has the same antithesis of *true* and *painted* in *The Mount of Olives*" (in *The Works of George Herbert*, ed. F. E. Hutchinson [Oxford, 1941], p. 495). Helen Vendler comments: "Mystification is no part of Herbert's allegories; like many other allegories, they exist to be deciphered easily, but they are not concerned to keep up a consistent fictional existence" (*The Poetry of George Herbert* [Cambridge, Mass., and London, 1975], p. 60). In discussing Herbert's "art of plainness," Arnold Stein suggests that "Herbert seems to take the ... Platonic line, rejecting 'fictions' and ornaments and wittily charging poems with idolatrous reverence for pretty, imitative objects." Though the "substance of his challenge may lie in the Platonic emphasis of his rebuke to the conventional love poets, his argument also depends on the charge that their poetry celebrates the wrong subjects in an unsuitable manner" (*George Herbert's Lyrics* [Baltimore, 1968], pp. 11–12). Rosemond Tuve relates Herbert's imagery to "Plato's discussion of the artist's mere 'imitation' of the true in a painted table or bed, &c., in *Republic* X," and observes that Herbert means to "declare in his verses his allegiance to majesty itself, and not the image of it, to the true and not the painted throne" (*A Reading of George Herbert* [London, 1952], p. 187). Mary Ellen Rickey, in *Utmost Art: Complexity in the Verse of George Herbert* (Lexington, Ky., 1966), similarly detects an allusion to Plato's charge that the painter and the poet are "thrice removed from the king and from the truth." "Drawing upon this famous illustration of imitation," Herbert arraigns the poets of his own time. "All poets whose inspiration derives from Helicon, who write of human love, have chosen a subject removed from the truth, which is God Himself; but those who, like the painter, imitate what other people have made, have become even more involved with fiction and falsity. For Herbert, whose wellspring is Jordan, and who will try to write of truth, not fable, the most beautiful words are *My God, My King*" (pp. 28–33).

Both the argument and the imagery (*nuda veritas*) were conventional and no less a commonplace in iconography than in literature. Accusations of deceit against orators were equally traditional. Through devices of amplification or diminution, pleasing schemes and delusive tropes, or merely through ingenious argumentation, the orator, it was thought, could make error look like truth, the worse appear the better reason. Originally applied to the sophist, this *topos* serves to characterize Belial, the most dissolute but also the most polished orator in Milton's Hell; it is significant, perhaps that Belial's traits are foreshadowed by the sensual rhetorician in *Comus*:

> this Juggler [declares the Lady]
> Would think to charm my judgment, as mine eyes,
> Obtruding false rules prankt in reason's garb.
> I hate when vice can bolt her arguments,
> And virtue has no tongue to check her pride.
> . . . .
> Enjoy your dear Wit and gay Rhetoric
> That hath so well been taught her dazzling fence,
> Thou art not fit to hear thyself convinc't.
> (*CP*; lines 757–761, 790–792)

Under the disguise of the false shepherd the Lady has recognized the sophistic orator; the tempter has already exposed himself as such, though his words (like Belial's) reflect his characteristic vice no less than his rhetorical skill:

> I under fair pretense of friendly ends
> And well-plac't words of glozing courtesy,
> Baited with reasons not unplausible,
> Wind me into the easy-hearted man,
> And hug him into snares.
> (*CP*, lines 160–164)

To tempt Eve in *Paradise Lost*, Satan assumes the manner of "some Orator renown'd / In *Athens* or free *Rome*," pretending "Zeal and Love / To Man, and indignation at his wrong." His "persuasive words," replete with guile, seem pregnant with reason and truth. Nor is it insignificant that his deception centers primarily on the fallacy of miraculous speech: the tree whose taste "Gave elocution to the mute, and taught / The Tongue not made for Speech to speak thy praise." To the same category belong the "persuasive Rhetoric" of the tempter in *Paradise Regained* and the "warbling charms" and "sorceries" of Milton's Dalila. A similar emphasis on the deceits of eloquence ap-

pears in Henry Vaughan. In "Idle Verse" he denounces his earlier
erotic poetry as mere "cobwebs," "quaint follies, sugared sin":

> Blind, desperate fits, that study how
> To dress and trim our shame;
> That gild rank poison, and allow
> Vice in a fairer name.
>
> (*SC*, p. 489)

Traditional also were comparisons between rhetoric and delusive
magic, cosmetic paints, spiced cookery, or jingling bells. Of the eloquence of ancient Greece, the hero of *Paradise Regained* speaks with
reserved scorn. In "thir majestic unaffected style" the Old Testament
prophets have taught the rules of politics more plainly and more easily "Than all the Oratory of *Greece* and *Rome*" (4:353–364). As for
the poets

> Remove their swelling Epithets thick laid
> As varnish on a Harlot's cheek, the rest,
> Thin sown with aught of profit or delight,
> Will far be found unworthy to compare
> With *Sion's* songs. . . .
>
> (*Paradise Regained* 4:343–347,
> *CP*, pp. 523–524)

The allusion to varnish was frequently utilized not only by opponents
of rhetoric but also by rhetoricians themselves in criticizing the excesses of the "gorgeous" Asiatic style. Classical authors had compared rhetorical schemes to rouge. As Milton was well aware, the
Latin equivalent (*fucus*) could also imply disguise and deceit. In his
own works *varnish* often carries a similar connotation: "close ambi-
tion varnisht o'er with zeal."[2]

In emphasizing the unaffected majesty of the Scriptures, Milton
may have recalled Longinus's praise of Genesis for achieving the true
sublime: "Let there be light, and there was light. Let there be earth,
and there was earth."[3] Closer parallels, however, occur in contemporary attacks on pulpit eloquence. It "will not become the Majesty of a

---

2. Compare Locke's application of the same image to moral philosophy: "The desire
of esteem, riches, or power makes men espouse the well-endowed opinions in fashion,
and then seek arguments either to make good their beauty, or varnish over and cover their
deformity: nothing being so beautiful to the eye as truth is to the mind, nothing so de-
formed and irreconcilable to the understanding as a lie" (*Essay*, pp. 257–258).

3. See Longinus, "On the Sublime," in *Literary Criticism: Plato to Dryden*, ed.
Allan H. Gilbert (Detroit, 1962), p. 157; cf. Genesis 1:3, 9.

Divine Embassage," declared John Wilkins, "to be garnished out with flaunting affected eloquence." The "grand subject" of the apostles, asserted Robert South, "was truth," which needs no "petty arts and poor additions," and appears at best advantage "just as it is. For there is a certain majesty in plainness; as the proclamation of a prince never frisks it in tropes or fine conceits, in numerous and well turned periods, but commands in sober, natural expressions" (*Studies*, pp. 78, 115). Such a style might seem doubly appropriate to the Second Adam, paralleling as it does the "naked Majesty" of the First Adam and the "lowliness Majestic" of Eve. The quality of plainness had been so frequently associated with the *stilus humilis* or low style, that the paradox of ascribing majesty to it might seem to epitomize other, more powerful paradoxes associated with the kingdom and person of Christ: the voluntary humiliation undertaken in exercising his mediatorial office, the paradox of the Incarnation, and the "Courtly Stable" of the nativity.

These contemptuous poetic dismissals of rhetoric by the author of *Areopagitica* and the two *Defenses of the English People* are neither inconsistent nor paradoxical. Milton's criticism is aimed, of course, not against the *ars rhetorica* as such, but against its corruption. Although he employs arguments that many of his contemporaries were directing against rhetoric as an art, his target is not eloquence per se but the abuse of eloquence. Moreover, his objections have been conditioned by thematic and narrative contexts and by the exigencies of poetic fiction. They are accommodated to specific dramatic situations—to the character of the speaker, the kind of temptation he is facing, and the nature of his antagonist: it would be misleading to dissociate them from the poetic contexts into which they have been so closely integrated. The sensuous and deceptive rhetoric of Comus is morally symbolic: a fitting vehicle for sensual folly and the seductive pleasures of the flesh. In other contexts Milton could extol, rather than condemn, the passionate and sensuous qualities of poetry and oratory.

Similarly the objections Milton raised against Hellenic eloquence in *Paradise Regained* are fully intelligible only in the light of his conception of the Logos. To interpret them as a response to the antirhetorical movement, or as a reflection of alleged tensions between humanist and Puritan sympathies in the poet himself, as some have done, is at best to raise considerations tangential to the unique nature of the hero as the Word made flesh. For the divine wisdom, or divine voice, arts of logic and rhetoric are superfluous; such arts are largely

58   *The Hill and the Labyrinth*

irrelevant to the *internal* operations of the Word within the human soul, to spiritual illumination and persuasion. Complementing the lure of Greek philosophy, the bait of pagan eloquence, elsewhere praised, serves here as a foil to illustrate the superior wisdom and higher persuasive efficacy of the divine Word.

The massive rebuttals in the temptation of Athens are based, in fact, on the venerable ideal of the harmony between truth and eloquence. They support, rather than undercut, Milton's commitment to the idealistic conception of rhetoric and poetic as instruments of moral instruction and persuasion. In the debates of *Paradise Regained*, as in those of *Comus* and *Paradise Lost*, the false eloquence dissociated from truth is exposed and stripped of its pretensions through its encounter with true eloquence, the vehicle of true wisdom. In the Messiah's encounter with the devil, in the Lady's dialogue with the god of intemperate revelry, and in Abdiel's refutation of Satan's arguments for revolt, the eloquence of zeal is opposed to the seductions of persuasive oratory. In each case truth confronts cunningly disguised falsehood or the spurious and illusory wisdom of the world, the flesh, or the devil. The ordeal of temptation, as Milton portrays it, is a dialectical process in which truth and falsehood grapple at close quarters and "the scanning of error" leads "to the confirmation of truth" (*CP*, pp. 729, 746). To many of Milton's own contemporaries this confidence in dialectic and disputation would have seemed a major obstacle to the victory of truth, but it is consistent not only with his own belief in the value of contraries in eliciting a clear definition but also with Aristotle's insistence on the value of rhetorical debate in demonstrating the truth. "Rhetoric is useful," Aristotle declared, "because things that are true and things that are just have a natural tendency to prevail over their opposites." Even though dialectic and rhetoric draw opposite conclusions impartially, "the underlying facts do not lend themselves equally well to the contrary views. No; things that are true and things that are better are, by their nature, practically always easier to prove and easier to believe in."[4]

1

Before reexamining the idealistic view of rhetoric and its significance for Milton's dialectic of temptation, it is helpful to recall the context of seventeenth-century attacks on eloquence. These were launched in the

4. *Rhetoric*, in *Basic Works*, ed. McKeon, pp. 1327–1328.

name of scientific precision, theological decorum, or the stability and peace of church and state. However sweeping these denunciations may seem, they were not altogether blanket indictments.

Within prescribed limits the censors of language were usually willing to sanction the sport with words and figures as a kind of private recreation, or to concede that eloquence might not be out of place in addressing a popular audience. Nevertheless they profoundly distrusted the traditional alliance of rhetoric and philosophy. Techniques of persuasion were irrelevant to the methods of science; in a philosopher addressing philosophers, eloquence would be an unseemly and unnecessary ornament.

The same critics who condemned the excesses of rhetoric often condemned the defects of scholasticism, and it is only fair to recall that many of these men, exposed to humanistic methods at grammar school and to a kind of residual scholasticism at the universities, possessed firsthand experience of both. A chronic diet of figs and honey (as they perceived) could be just as unwholesome for sound learning as a diet of thistles, brambles, and vermiculate questions.

While sharing the humanists' disdain for the barbarous style, obscurity and pedantry, and alleged sophistries of the schoolmen, the reformers of science were by no means willing to allow the orator to replace the friar as spokesman for philosophy. As partisans of "new philosophy" they generally condemned humanism and scholasticism alike for ambiguous or meaningless diction. Both were offenders against truth of fact and truth of style. Both obstructed the advancement of learning and the investigation of nature by substituting false appearances, chimerical ideas or illusory words, for truth.

Like the humanists' own diatribes against scholastic philosophy, the scientists' assaults against eloquence on behalf of a philosophical language were directed against a conservative academic establishment, and their virulence reflects an awareness of the entrenched strength of the tradition they were challenging. During the great age of humanism, in the course of the fifteenth and sixteenth centuries, the idealistic conception of rhetoric as a vehicle of truth—the ideal championed by Cicero and Quintilian, St. Augustine and Petrarch— had virtually achieved the status of a critical and pedagogical orthodoxy. Antagonists to the ideal, committed to a laborious quest for certitude, distrustful of the authoritative names and systems of antiquity, dissatisfied with the methods and terminology of the schoolmen, yet equally skeptical of rhetorical attempts to embellish the truth while truth herself still awaited discovery and exantlation, felt the pursuit of eloquence, the cultivation of fine words, a poor and inadequate substitute for the pursuit of knowledge, the investigation of things. "Alas! what can they teach, and not mislead?" they might well have exclaimed, with Milton's Christ. To employ the techniques of persuasion on matters one did not yet know seemed foolhardy. The magisterial pretensions of eloquence must be countered by a frontal assault on the *ars rhetorica* itself.

In direct opposition to the Ciceronian ideal espoused by the majority of Renaissance humanists, Thomas Sprat explicitly demanded the dissociation of truth and eloquence. The Royal Society has "endeavored, to separate the Knowledge of Nature, from the Colours of Rhetoric, the Devices of Fancy, or the delightful Deceit of Fables" (*S*, p. 288). All "the art of rhetoric," asserted Locke, "besides order and clearness, all the artificial and figurative application of words eloquence hath invented, are for nothing else but to insinuate wrong *ideas*, move the passions, and thereby mislead the judgment, and so indeed are perfect cheat. . . . It is evident how much men love to deceive, and be deceived, since rhetoric, that powerful instrument of error and deceit, has its established professors, is publicly taught, and has always been in great reputation." Like the fair sex, eloquence "has too prevailing beauties in it, to suffer itself ever to be spoken against. And it is in vain to find fault with those arts of deceiving, wherein men find pleasure to be deceived" (*Essay*, pp. 202–203).

In sum, rhetoric was an art of persuasion rather than a method of dispassionate investigation, and therefore inappropriate for scientific inquiry. Since it usually selected its arguments from topics and commonplaces—from knowledge stored up in tins (so to speak), conveniently processed, packaged, and labeled for instant use—it did not yield fresh information or encourage the further discovery of truth.[5] Since it was concerned with probabilities or apparent probabilities rather than with certainties, it was a dangerous and unreliable guide

5. For the conservative associations of Renaissance Ciceronianism, and its relation to other dogmas of learning in the sixteenth century, see Croll, *Style*, pp. 119–122. Merely "because it was a *rhetorical* doctrine, Ciceronianism ideally represented the aims and interests of the conservative orthodoxies. . . . The method that characterized them all, Barthollist, Platonist, Aristotelian, was in a broader sense the method of rhetoric, in the sense . . . that they all tended toward the study of the *forms* of their various sciences rather than toward the direct observation of the facts; they all busied themselves, as their opponents constantly affirmed, with words rather than with things." Moreover, like other orthodoxies, Ciceronianism reflected "the love of authority and a single standard of reference which still flourished in . . . the sixteenth century."

through the labyrinth of errors and conjectures that confronted the seeker after certitudes. As it had no determinate subject matter but professed competency in virtually every field of specialization, it was apt to impose a false appearance of learning, exposing the laboriously acquired sciences to the pretensions of the charlatan or the superficiality of the amateur. Since it depended largely on common opinions and popular beliefs,[6] it did not befit the counsels of learned men. Appealing to the imagination and the passions no less than to reason, it obstructed sound judgment. Applied to natural philosophy, it rendered the obscurities of nature more obscure. Applied to morality and politics, it encouraged faction. Applied to theology, it darkened the divine word with human inventions.

Attempts to subordinate rhetoric to logic might lend it greater respectability, but they also tended to reduce it to an art of decoration and applied ornament. After Ramus had annexed invention and disposition to logic, little remained for the *ars rhetorica* except consider-

---

6. In Plato's *Phaedrus* professors of rhetoric are censured for maintaining that "the orator should run after probability" (i.e., "that which the many think") and thus "say good-bye to the truth." In a passage that could support a more idealistic view of eloquence, Socrates argues that an orator trained in philosophy would be the more plausible speaker: since probability is "engendered in the minds of the many by the likeness of the truth," the man who actually knows the truth will also know best how to "discover the resemblances of the truth" (*The Works of Plato*, trans. B. Jowett [New York, (1937)], 3: 439–440). Aristotle, in turn, defined rhetoric "as the faculty of observing in any given case the available means of persuasion." Like dialectic, it could be applied to virtually every kind of subject. Whereas every other art "can instruct or persuade about its own particular subject-matter," rhetoric considers "the means of persuasion on almost any subject presented to us," for it is "not concerned with any special or definite class of subjects." Moreover, it is directed to the limited capacities of a popular audience: rhetoric deals with "such matters as we deliberate upon without arts or systems to guide us, in the hearing of persons who cannot take in at a glance a complicated argument, or follow a long chain of reasoning." As some audiences are not easily convinced by even the most exact knowledge, the speaker must employ, as his "modes of persuasion and argument, notions possessed by everybody" (*Basic Works*, pp. 1327–331). Rhetoric is "an instrument invented to manipulate and agitate a crowd and a disorderly populace," declared Montaigne, "and an instrument that is employed only in sick states, like medicine." The stupidity and facility of the common people make them "subject to be led by the ears to the sweet sound of this harmony without weighing things and coming to know their truth by force of reason." Rhetoric has been justly defined as "the science of persuading the people" and as "the art of deceiving and flattering"; and those who "deny this in the general definition verify it everywhere in their precepts." The rhetoricians made a profession of "deceiving not our eyes but our judgment, and of adulterating and corrupting the essence of things"; accordingly, well-governed commonwealths have "made little account of orators" ("Of the Vanity of Words," in *The Complete Essays of Montaigne*, trans. Donald M. Frame [Stanford, 1965], pp. 221–222).

ations of delivery and style.[7] For an audience dependent on the written rather than the spoken word, style alone would be left. Rhetoric might indeed seem little more than the art of elocution. This, in turn, had been undercut by changing tastes in style.

Caught between changing attitudes toward truth and eloquence alike, rhetoric might easily seem a superfluous as well as a dangerous art. Its methods were too facile for philosophical discourse, yet too formal for private reflection and familiar dialogue. It could satisfy neither the demands of contemporary scientists for more rigorous methods of investigation and demonstration nor the demands of a new generation of literary critics for an easy, natural, plain style free from every trace of diligence and premeditated artifice, a style capable of suggesting the *natural* processes of thought and speech.

Attempts to define and differentiate styles sometimes end in disputes over words; ideas concerning characteristics of various styles are apt to become Baconian "idols." The plain style of the late seventeenth century occasioned such disputes. While the labels *Attic, anti-Ciceronian,* and *Senecan* debatably may be historically appropriate in the context of classical antiquity, their applicability to sixteenth- and seventeenth-century vernacular styles in England and on the Continent is more dubious. The categories themselves, as used by modern scholars or by Renaissance critics, are often too broad. The plain, science-inspired discourse advocated by Sprat would appear to be a reaction not only against a vestigial Ciceronianism but also against the excesses of earlier anti-Ciceronian modes. However, to associate Sprat's discourse specifically with "the stylistic views of science," dissociating it from Seneca and Aristotle and the anti-Ciceronian movements of the late Renaissance, would seem to be too narrow; later critics have considered too far-reaching Jones's views on the scope of the Royal Society's stylistic reform and its influence on the sermon, the prose essay, and other prose forms (*Studies*, pp. 91–160). In John Wilkins's insistence that the style of the sermon be plain and natural, unobscured by scholastic harshness or rhetorical flourishes, Jones perceived the spirit of experimental philosophy. In the same passage, however, Williamson detected the influence of Seneca, who had argued "that the philosophic or essay style should be plain and natural." The "stylistic programme of the Royal Society,"

7. See Paolo Rossi, *Francis Bacon: From Magic to Science*, trans. Sacha Rabinovitch (Chicago, 1968), pp. 178–185 and passim; and see Ong, *Ramus*.

Williamson maintained, reaffirms "Bacon's revolt against Ciceronian *copia,* and associates itself with Senecan requirements." The Society "reflected rather than initiated a stylistic reform." This "cannot be regarded as exclusive with the Royal Society, nor as divorced from the Anti-Ciceronian movement" (*S,* pp. 250–253, 275–276).

There were, of course, other classical models for the plain style, more natural and considerably easier than Seneca; there were medieval and Renaissance variants both in Latin and in the vernacular tongues; and there were other considerations, besides scientific precision and homiletic decorum, that prompted the demand for apparent simplicity and natural plainness. ("Apparent"—for these qualities are often the result of studied composition, the art of concealing art.) In poetry these qualities had been deliberately cultivated by Horace and consciously assimilated by Ben Jonson and Robert Herrick. The "diligent kind of negligence" (*S,* pp. 219, 226) sought by English prose stylists is reminiscent of a commonplace exploited by all three of these poets: "Simplex munditie"; "Such sweet neglect more taketh me, / Then all th'adulteries of art"; "A Sweet disorder in the dresse / Kindles in cloathes a wantonnesse"; "A carelesse shooestring, in whose tye / I see a wilde civility; / Doe more bewitch me, then when Art / Is too precise in every part." The "native easiness" desired by Sprat had long been cultivated in familiar epistles, in colloquies and dialogues, and in certain species of drama. Among classical orators Demosthenes, and among classical historians Thucydides, were regarded as models of Attic prose. And the simple style of Scripture had been frequently contrasted by English Protestants with the painted manner and "vayn perswasion" of worldly and fleshly eloquence.[8]

8. See Richard Foster Jones, *The Triumph of the English Language* (Stanford, 1966), pp. 59–61; cf. p. 112. For the greater part of the sixteenth century, Englishmen had commonly regarded their language as "plain, honest, substantial, but uneloquent," in comparison with the rich and "gorgeous" eloquence of the Latin tongue; but their attitudes toward their mother tongue varied, Jones observes, "according to the value placed upon eloquence, or rhetoric." The utilitarian and "antirhetorical spirit" of the Puritans appeared in their invectives against "the immorality of a deceitful and vain-glorious style" and in their insistence upon "plainness and simplicity as the natural vesture of truth, especially in religious matters" (pp. 18–23, 30–31; see also pp. 98–103, 281, 322).

For other discussions of the plain style, see Wesley Trimpi, *Ben Jonson's Poems;* Jonas A. Barish, *Ben Jonson and the Language of Prose Comedy;* and the forewords by John M. Wallace, J. Max Patrick, and Robert O. Evans in *Style.* As these and other studies indicate, such terms as *Attic style* or *plain style* actually comprehended a wide diversity of styles and stylistic levels. The plain style of an Anacreontic ode differs from that of an Horatian epistle; the plainness of epigram from that of elegy. Naked simplicity of expression might befit the sublime as well as the comic, familiar conversation as

2

"To distinguish rhetorical from intellectual process in the writings of professed naturalists," Croll observed, "is to divide between the bark and the tree; whatever the motions of their minds, they will betray themselves in their style" (*Style*, p. 198). Though Croll's botanical metaphor is appropriate to its subject, it is more applicable to the kind of bare and naked style that the new philosophers professed to be seeking than to the style they actually achieved. Their achieved style was less organic than the bark of a tree, less naked than bare skin, though less extrinsic than the figured brocades of the Ciceronians. It was, in short, a removable garment—albeit a plain one— and on occasion it might sport a rhetorical gewgaw or two, all the more conspicuous for their comparative rarity. The opponents of rhetoric never tired of the hackneyed imagery of cosmetics, haberdashery, and disease. In spite of their express disdain for figurative and oblique discourse, Hobbes and Locke were experienced masters at metaphor and simile and insinuative irony. In their concern for style, the "antitrhetorical" critics were rhetoricians in spite of themselves; and in their efforts to purify the language of learned discourse by banishing the art of eloquence they were, in fact, advancing yet another (and not altogether original) version of the idealistic view of style as the garment of truth.

Paradoxically, an easy, natural style rarely comes naturally or easily; it must be strenuously and deliberately sought for; it is, in fact, an effect of art. The plain style, the "native easiness" demanded by the "antirhetoricians," must be painstakingly cultivated; and (as their own writings reveal) it could be acquired only with difficulty and through the combined efforts of a duly constituted committee of experts.

The linguistic views of the Royal Society and other "new philosophers" were less radical than Jones and other literary historians have maintained. As Williamson observes, Sprat's reformation of style was to be "directed primarily towards the requirements of natural philosophy." He had no intention of banishing wit or eloquence from every kind of written discourse; and his own *History* of the society reveals

---

well as scientific discourse. The seventeenth-century critics who discussed the subject were not invariably precise in identifying which of numerous variants of the plain style they were recommending. The "native easiness" and the "mathematical plainness" commended by Sprat apparently derive from different and not altogether compatible traditions.

"two sharply contrasted attitudes toward eloquence," representing "two different ambitions of his time, literary and scientific, relative to different ends of writing" (*S*, pp. 275, 286, 294). In praising scientist, philosopher, and linguistic reformer alike, the poet Abraham Cowley commended their mastery of "eloquence and wit" (*SC*, pp. 384, 397, 406). Joseph Glanvill, who had formerly received plaudits for removing the inveterate antipathy between rhetoric and philosophy, subsequently defended the use of rhetoric and wit in sermons addressed to the people, whose "affections are raised by figures . . . and passionate representations." (*Studies*, p. 137).

Though Thomas Hobbes regarded judgment as more essential to wit than fancy, he allowed the latter a more ample scope in poetry and rhetoric and in familiar conversation than in other modes of discourse. In a good poem "fancy must be more eminent," but in a good history "judgment must be eminent," and fancy may serve only to adorn the style. In demonstrative oratory ("orations of praise . . . and invectives"), fancy is predominant, "because the design is not truth but to honor or dishonor." In other rhetorical modes such as "hortatives and pleadings," judgment or fancy predominates "as truth or disguise serves best to the design in hand." In demonstration, however, "in counsel, and all rigorous search of truth, judgment does all, except sometimes the understanding have need to be opened by some apt similitude, and then there is so much use of fancy." Finally, "in professed remissness of mind and familiar company, a man may play with the sounds and equivocal significations of words, and that many times with encounters of extraordinary fancy; but in a sermon, or in public, or before persons unknown or whom we ought to reverence, there is no jingling of words that will not be accounted folly. . . . Judgment therefore without fancy is wit, but fancy without judgment not" (*L*, pp. 66–67). Even Locke concedes that rhetorical figures may be "laudable or allowable . . . in harangues and popular addresses," though they must be totally avoided "in all discourses that pretend to inform or instruct" (*Essay*, pp. 202–203).

3

While advocating a naked, unadorned style for scientific discourse, the partisans of "new philosophy" were not unanimously hostile to the *ars rhetorica* as an instrument of popular persuasion. Moreover, many of them continued to regard eloquence and wit as desirable qualities of style, though they sometimes showed considerable fastidiousness in defining them. Like many of his contemporaries, Cowley drew a sharp distinction between true and false wit, and similar attempts to differentiate between true and false eloquence were not uncommon.[9]

Despite the contrary premises from which they started, the defenders and assailants of rhetoric were often less sharply divided than they believed themselves to be. On occasion they advanced the same arguments, employed similar imagery, and reached analogous conclusions. On the subordination of words to things and the priority of matter over manner, most of the contestants in both camps (with notable exceptions such as Ascham) held similar opinions. Many of them admired the same classical or modern authors and displayed analogous preferences in style. There remained a substantial community of taste in spite of divergent attitudes toward the *ars rhetorica*.

Though based on the conventional separation of truth and eloquence, the antirhetorical tradition tended on occasion to reconcile them by insisting on a style strictly accommodated to the discovery and demonstration of truth. This was essentially a rhetorical concern; and the native purity of language so assiduously pursued was in fact a species of eloquence, even though its advocates might refuse to acknowledge it as such. For some of them, however, such a style constituted true eloquence, as contrasted with the false eloquence of the traditional rhetoricians. Conversely, though apologists for rhetoric and poetic usually started from a viewpoint diametrically opposite— the conventional harmony of eloquence and truth—they sometimes drew so sharp a distinction between specious and solid eloquence and between the use and abuse of this art that they began to sound like their opponents. In denouncing false rhetoric using arguments that their adversaries were directing against rhetoric in general, and in insisting that true eloquence should be adapted to the truth of things (a thoroughly orthodox doctrine), they tended to approximate the stylistic views of their opponents. However, on the employment of schemes and tropes, the utility of fictions, and the role of the imagination and passions as aids to instruction and right action, they differed fundamentally from the antirhetorical school. Even on these points, though, some poets and prose writers tended to share the antirhetori-

9. Compare Croll (*Style*, p. 147) on the earlier definition of "true and solid eloquence" by Muret: "non tantum in verbis posita est, sed in rebus." See Cowley, "Ode of Wit."

cal school's distrust of ornamentation and to restrict imagery and fable to a minimum.

In condemning Ciceronian copiousness and Senecan brevity alike as diseases of learning, Bacon anticipated the arguments that antirhetorical critics would subsequently direct against both styles. Yet he also favored the idealistic view of rhetoric as an instrument of moral and political philosophy. Between these extremes he walked with the caution of a tightrope walker, balancing the utility of eloquence against its dangers and tempering qualified praise with warning. Like Aristotle, he contended that speech is "much more conversant in adorning that which is good than in colouring that which is evil" and that "Rhetoric can be no more charged with the colouring of the worse part, than Logic with Sophistry, or Morality with Vice." He endorsed Cicero's complaint that Socrates had "separated philosophy and rhetoric; whereupon rhetoric became an empty and verbal art." Like Cicero and numerous Renaissance apologists for rhetoric or poetics, he quoted Plato's statement "That virtue, if she could be seen, would move great love and affection" in order to justify the idealistic conception of eloquence: "so seeing that she cannot be shewed to the Sense by corporal shape, the next degree is to shew her to the Imagination in lively representation: for to shew her to Reason only in subtilty of argument, was a thing ever derided in Chrysippus and many of the Stoics; who thought to thrust virtue upon men by sharp disputations and conclusions, which have no sympathy with the will of man." The true duty and office of rhetoric is "*to apply Reason to Imagination* for the better moving of the will." Continually besieged by mutinous and seditious affections, reason itself "would become captive and servile, if Eloquence of Persuasions did not practise and win the Imagination from the Affection's part, and contract a confederacy between the Reason and Imagination against the Affections" (*SW*, pp. 268, 309–311).

In defense of rhetoric Bacon has in effect led us on a conducted tour through Spenser's Castle of Alma.[10] But he was not altogether satisfied with rhetoric; and the reader may be more forcibly reminded

10. In *The Faerie Queene* (bk. 2, canto 9) "sober Alma" (the soul) conducts her two house-guests, Prince Arthur and Sir Guyon, through her "house of Temperance" (the human body), leading them ultimately to "a stately Turret" (the head) and through the chambers of the brain associated with the faculties of reason, imagination, and memory. For the relation of Bacon's rhetorical theory to his conceptions of the human mind and its faculties, see Karl R. Wallace, *Francis Bacon and the Nature of Man* ... (Urbana, Chicago, London, 1967).

of Spenser's Duessa or Archimago. Eloquence paints and disguises the "true appearance of things," Bacon declared. The vanity of studying words instead of matter is like the frenzy of Pygmalion: "for words are but the images of matter; and except they have life of reason and invention, to fall in love with them is all one as to fall in love with a picture." To "clothe and adorn the obscurity even of philosophy itself with sensible and plausible elocution" is not hastily to be condemned; but "the excess of this is . . . justly contemptible." The "more severe and laborious sort of inquirers into truth . . . will despise those delicacies and affectations." (*SW*, pp. 182–183, 284).[11]

Lest philosophers should take comfort in the discomfiture of the rhetoricians, however, Bacon reminded them that false science is more hurtful than specious eloquence: "for as substance of matter is better than beauty of words, so contrariwise vain matter is worse than vain words." The "vermiculate questions" and "degenerate learning" of the schoolmen (*SW*, p. 183) were a disease of knowledge; and on this point the defenders and assailants of rhetoric usually concurred.

4

For Bacon, as for many of his contemporaries, poetry was essentially imaginative fiction, distinguished from other arts chiefly by its license to feign. In contrast to rhetoric, it tended to dissociate reason and imagination, submitting "the shews of things to the desires of the mind; whereas reason doth buckle and bow the mind unto the nature of things." Nevertheless it is precisely through this departure from the nature of things that poetry "serveth and conferreth to magnanimity, morality, and to delectation." The world itself is inferior to the human soul, and the "spirit of man" desires "a more ample greatness, a more exact goodness, and a more absolute variety, than can be found in the nature of things." Poetry portrays the merits of virtue and vice with greater justice than true history. It expresses "affections, passions, corruptions, and customs" more effectively than philosophy. For wit and eloquence it is little inferior to oratory. Allusive or "parabolical" poetry, in particular, may serve to illustrate or to conceal the teachings of philosophy, politics, and religion. Though Bacon was unwilling to assert categorically that the mythological fables of antiquity had been originally composed as philosophical allegories, he never-

11. See also Karl R. Wallace, *Francis Bacon on Communication and Rhetoric* (Chapel Hill, 1943).

theless insisted on the value of parables as "a method of teaching whereby inventions that are new and abstruse and remote from vulgar opinions may find an easier passage to the understanding." No man of ordinary learning should object to this use of fable, for it is "a thing grave and sober, and free from all vanity; of prime use to the sciences, and sometimes indispensable" (*SW*, pp. 243–247, 403–408).[12]

12. See also Don Cameron Allen, *Mysteriously Meant: The Rediscovery of Pagan Symbolism and Allegorical Interpretation* (Baltimore and London, 1970).

IV. The Dialectics of Temptation: Milton and the Idealistic View of Rhetoric

In asserting the moral and philosophical utility of poetry, Renaissance critics drew their arguments from a wide variety of sources: allegorical interpretations of pagan myth; the poetic theories of Horace and Aristotle and their numerous successors; commentaries on the figurative, visionary, and parabolic methods of Scripture; and traditional comparisons between the methods of rhetoric and poetics. Many of the arguments advanced on behalf of the *ars rhetorica* were urged, with equal or greater vigor, in support of the *ars poetica*. Like the apologists for rhetoric, the defenders of poetry tended to center their arguments on the use and abuse of their art, on the subordination of eloquence to truth, and on the need to engage the affections, the senses, and the imagination in teaching and persuading to wisdom and virtue. Affirming the poet's responsibility to moral and political philosophy, they usually insisted on his superiority to the philosopher as a public teacher and as an educator of youth. The best poet mixes instruction with delight, Horace had declared. Wisdom is essential for good writing, and the poet ought to study the philosophy of the Platonic Academy:

> The very root of writing well, and spring
> Is to be wise; thy matter first to know;
> Which the *Socratick* writings best can show:
> And, where the matter is provided still,
> There words will follow, not against their will.
> *(Ars Poetica)*

The poet Homer, Horace elsewhere asserted, "tells us what is fair, what is foul, what is helpful, what is not, more plainly and better than Chrysippus or Crantor" (*Epistles*, book 1, epistle 2).[1]

---

1. See Horace, *Ars Poetica* and *Epistles* in *Literary Criticism*, ed. Gilbert.

In Sir Philip Sidney's opinion, it was "that feigning notable images of virtues, vices, or what else, with that delightful teaching, which must be the right describing note to know a poet by." Though the philosopher "with his learned definitions" could replenish memory "with many infallible grounds of wisdom," these must "lie dark before the imaginative and judging power, if they be not illuminated or figured forth by the speaking picture of poesy." Whereas the philosopher teaches obscurely, "so as the learned only can understand him," the poet is "food for the tenderest stomachs," the true popular philosopher. Moreover, through his power to move his audience, the poet better fulfils the end of teaching, which is action rather than knowledge.[2]

Milton's scattered allusions to poetry and rhetoric in his prose works belong, on the whole, to the same idealistic tradition. In *Areopagitica* he extols Spenser as "a better teacher than Scotus or Aquinas," thus adapting to English poetry (possibly by way of the Italian poet Erasmo da Valvasone) Horace's eulogy of Homer as a moral teacher. Similarly, in *Reason of Church Government*, he reaffirmed the poet's responsibilities to church and state as moral and religious teacher: "Teaching over the whole book of sanctity and virtue through all the instances of example, with such delight to those especially of soft and delicious temper who will not so much as look upon Truth herself, unless they see her elegantly dressed, that whereas the paths of honesty and good life appear now rugged and difficult, though they be indeed easy and pleasant, they would then appear to all men both easy and pleasant, though they were rugged and difficult indeed" (*CP*, pp. 670, 728–729).

In the same treatise he combined two cardinal principles of Renaissance humanism—the civic responsibilities of eloquence and the pedagogical utility of pleasure as a stimulus to learning—to recommend "wise and artful recitations sweetened with eloquent and graceful enticements to the love and practice of justice, temperance, and fortitude" and to suggest that pulpit oratory be complemented "after another persuasive method" through "set and solemn panegyries, in theaters, porches, or what other place or way may win most upon the people to receive at once both recreation and instruction" (*CP*, p. 670). He also endorsed Plato's opinion that persuasion is "a more winning and more manlike way to keep men in obedience than fear" and his suggestion that important laws should be prefaced by

2. "Defense of Poesie," in *Literary Criticism*, ed. Gilbert, pp. 416–427.

some "well-tempered discourse, showing how good, how gainful, how happy it must needs be to live according to honesty and justice; which being uttered with those native colors and graces of speech, as true eloquence, the daughter of virtue, can best bestow upon her mother's praises, would so incite and in a manner charm the multitude into the love of that which is really good, as to embrace it ever after" (*CP*, p. 640).

Milton returns to these ideas decades later in *Paradise Regained*, where they play a significant role in the hero's moral education and the definition of his mission. Believing himself "born to promote all truth" and righteousness, he has considered and rejected the use of force as an instrument to this end; long before his encounter with Satan in the wilderness, he has already begun to conceive his role as one of teaching and persuasion:

> Yet held it more humane, more heavenly, first
> By winning words to conquer willing hearts,
> And make persuasion do the work of fear.
> (*CP*, p. 487)

And it is to this theme that both hero and Adversary continually recur in the course of the temptation:

> But to guide Nations in the way of truth
> By saving Doctrine, and from error lead
> To know, and knowing worship God aright,
> Is yet more Kingly; this attracts the Soul,
> Governs the inner man, the nobler part;
> That other o'er the body only reigns,
> And oft by force, which to a generous mind
> So reigning can be no sincere delight.
>
> The *Gentiles* also know, and write, and teach
> To admiration, led by Nature's light;
> And with the *Gentiles* much thou must converse,
> Ruling them by persuasion as thou mean'st,
> Without thir learning how wilt thou with them,
> Or they with thee hold conversation meet?
> (*CP*, pp. 504–505, 520)

Like Bacon, Milton regards false science as more pernicious than ignorance or false eloquence, and he bases his hero's rebuttal partly on the traditional subordination of eloquence to truth. Since the Gentiles have erred from the truth, their eloquence is also faulty. Their poets confuse virtue and vice; their orators are inferior to the prophets; their philosophers are retailers of idols, the counterfeit images of truth:

> Who therefore seeks in these
> True wisdom, finds her not, or by delusion
> Far worse, her false resemblance only meets,
> An empty cloud.
>
> (*CP*, pp. 522–523)

If strength divided from truth and justice merits nothing but dispraise and ignominy (*CP*, p. 333), the dissociation of reason and eloquence from justice and truth would seem to be a far worse abuse.

The same preference for persuasion over force appears in other late works. In the *Second Defense* Milton argues "that the truth, which had been defended by arms, should also be defended by reason; which is the best and only legitimate means of defending it" (*CP*, p. 819). In *Paradise Lost* Abdiel is praised for having fought

> The better fight, who single hast maintain'd
> Against revolted multitudes the Cause
> Of Truth, in word mightier than they in Arms;
> And for the testimony of Truth hast borne
> Universal reproach, far worse to bear
> Than violence.
>
> (*CP*, p. 324)

Subsequently, in challenging Satan to combat, Abdiel argues from the same *topos*:

> nor is it aught but just,
> That he who in debate of Truth hath won,
> Should win in Arms, in both disputes alike
> Victor; though brutish that contest and foul,
> When Reason hath to deal with force, yet so
> Most reason is that Reason overcome.
>
> (*CP*, p. 326)

Throughout his literary career Milton remains faithful to the patriotic ideal of the poet and orator as one who employs his eloquence to teach and exhort his countrymen and to celebrate their achievements in war or peace (*CP*, pp. 521, 523, 606, 668, 718, 819, 838). Yet with equal consistency he regards persuasion as a nobler instrument of polity than the martial force of the conqueror or the secular power of the magistrate. In his scale of heroic values the fortitude of the mar-

tyr, suffering reproach or violence for his solitary testimony to the
truth, ranks higher than the fortitude of the victorious soldier (*CP*,
pp. 323, 324, 379, 467, 507). Milton's supreme hero is, like Milton
himself, a teacher; and among teachers and orators the most eloquent is the impassioned speaker transported beyond the bounds of
art by moral or patriotic fervor or by religious zeal: Abdiel, the Lady
of *Comus*, the orators of a free Greece and a republican Rome, the
biblical prophets and evangelists. Though he parodies this ideal in
Satan, even its *eidolon* or counterfeit can be rhetorically effective (see
CP, pp. 108, 321, 323, 394, 614, 718).[3]

Like many other humanists, Milton maintained that true eloquence must be based on true wisdom and that accordingly the poet
and orator must be no less learned than eloquent.[4] As a student at

3. For examples on war and peace, see *CP*, pp. 521, 523, 606, 668, 718, 819, and
838. For views on heroic values, see *CP*, pp. 323, 324, 379, 467, 507. See also John M.
Major, "Milton's View of Rhetoric," *SP* 64 (1967): 685–711; and Joseph Anthony
Wittreich, Jr., "'The Crown of Eloquence': The Figure of the Orator in Milton's Prose
Works," in *Achievements of the Left Hand: Essays on the Prose of John Milton*, ed.
Michael Lieb and John T. Shawcross (Amherst, 1974), pp. 3–54.

4. On the relationship between truth and eloquence, see Ruth Wallerstein, *Studies
in Seventeenth Century Poetic* (Madison, 1950); Joseph Anthony Mazzeo, *Renaissance and Seventeenth-Century Studies* (New York and London, 1964); Josephine
Miles, *Style and Proportion: The Language of Prose and Poetry* (Boston, 1967); John
Hoskins, *Directions for Speech and Style*, ed. Hoyt H. Hudson (Princeton, 1935); Cic-
ero, *Orator*, trans. H. M. Hubbell (Cambridge, Mass., and London, 1939); Richard
McKeon, "Literary Criticism and the Concept of Imitation in Antiquity," "Aristotle's
Conception of Language and the Arts of Language," "Rhetoric in the Middle Ages,"
and "Poetry and Philosophy in the Twelfth Century: The Renaissance of Rhetoric," in
Critics and Criticism, Ancient and Modern, ed. R. S. Crane (Chicago, 1952).
   Ruth Wallerstein discusses the views of Sperone Speroni concerning the analogy
between painting and rhetoric. Just as the painter depicts the faces and bodies of
men, the orator paints "con lo stile delle parole" the truth, which is the proper object
of speculative doctrine (pp. 14–15). Josephine Miles reexamines the distinction between philosophy and rhetoric, the opposition between plain and elaborate styles,
and Renaissance adaptations of the metaphor of raiment in discussions of style (pp.
38–46 and passim).
   Analyzing St. Augustine's view of language as essentially and primarily "the immediate embodiment of thought," Wallerstein stresses this view's influence on his attitude
toward rhetoric. Investigating his "special Christian application" of the "conception
that style takes its form immediately from thought," she traces the Augustinian tradition in style through the Middle Ages and the Renaissance. Over time, this notion of
style—which first found clear expression in Socratic and Platonic criticism of the
Sophists—was "worked out in terms of an allegorical and schematic view of the Bible,
a symbolistic view of nature and of human reason." Yet Augustine also "helped to
kindle in the sixteenth and seventeenth centuries a view of the integral relation of
expression to the movement of the thinking mind which was quite independent of
symbolism and allegory and quite critical of it" (pp. 8–9, 28–29, 50–56).
   In "St. Augustine's Rhetoric of Silence: Truth vs. Eloquence and Things vs. Signs"

Cambridge he had insisted that "nothing mean or mediocre is tolerable in an orator any more than it is in a poet." It behooved "an aspirant to true, and not to merely specious eloquence, to be instructed and perfected in an all-around foundation in all the arts and in every science" (*CP*, p. 622). Though this argument served as an apology for speaking prematurely, he would subsequently develop it with greater seriousness in his treatise on education. Like Bacon he affirms the priority of *res* over *verba* and postpones the study of the "organic arts" (logic, rhetoric, poetics) until the students shall have mastered the substance of the other arts and sciences: "From hence, and not till now, will be the right season of forming them to be able writers and composers in every excellent matter, when they shall be thus fraught with an universal insight into things" (*CP*, pp. 636 –637).[5] Nevertheless even the ideal of a learned eloquence fell short of perfection. Like the idealized orator of Cicero and Quintilian, the ideal poet, as Milton describes him, must be a *vir bonus*, a good man: "a composition and pattern of the best and honorablest things—not presuming to sing high praises of heroic men or famous cities, unless he have in

---

(*Renaissance and Seventeenth-Century Studies*, pp. 1–28), Mazzeo explores Augustine's "attempt to assimilate classical rhetoric to Christian needs and . . . the profound transformations he made in the doctrine he received." From one point of view Augustine "brought rhetoric back to where Plato had left it in the *Phaedrus*, where eloquence and rhetoric are based on truth in contrast to mere show"; yet he also "established, or cast into authoritative form, often verbalistic conceptions of allegory, typology, symbolism, and metaphor" which (in Beryl Smalley's phrase) "made Scripture into a divine encyclopedia written in cipher."

In the *Orator* Cicero stresses the ideal relationship between philosophy and eloquence (pp. 313–315): "I confess that whatever ability I possess as an orator comes, not from the workshops of the rhetoricians, but from the spacious grounds of the Academy." Philosophy is "essential for the education of our ideal orator . . . for no one can discuss great and varied subjects in a copious and eloquent style without philosophy." John Hoskins followed Cicero in emphasizing the dependence of the orator on knowledge of truth: "The conceits of the mind are pictures of things and the tongue is the interpreter of those pictures. The order of God's creatures in themselves is not only admirable and glorious, but eloquent; then he that could apprehend the consequences of things, in their truth, and utter his apprehensions as truly were a right orator" (*Directions for Speech and Style*, pp. 2, 4–8). Cicero "said much when he said, *dicere recta nemo potest nisi qui prudenter intelligit.*"

5. Cf. *CP*, pp. 631–632. Francis Bacon similarly argued that "scholars in universities come too soon and too unripe to logic and rhetoric [which are] the rules and directions how to set forth and dispose matter." Therefore, "for minds empty and unfraught with matter, and which have not gathered that which Cicero called *sylva* and *supellex*, stuff and variety, to begin with those arts, . . . doth work but to this effect, that the wisdom of those arts, which is great and universal, is almost made contemptible" (*SW*, pp. 226–227).

himself the experience and the practice of all that which is praiseworthy" (*CP*, p. 694).

In subordinating eloquence to truth, and words to things, Milton
attached major importance to the writer's choice of theme and subject matter, and this emphasis is reflected in his remarks on the
themes of *Areopagitica* and the *Second Defense*, the subjects of his
epic plans, and even the topics of several of his academic exercises.[6]
To exalt the dignity of one's theme in this way was, of course, conventional oratorical strategy; but in Milton's major prose and poetry it is
usually more than rhetorical artifice. In the literary criticism of the
period, an epic or a panegyric might be judged according to the intrinsic merits of its subject as well as its artistic merit. Except in the
rhetoric of display or as a demonstration of the writer's technical
skill, comparatively little importance was attached to the principle of
art for art's sake. This emphasis on matter, however, did not diminish
the importance of style; in fact it presented an additional challenge to
the skills of the poet or orator. If he must choose a subject worthy of
praise, he must also demonstrate his ability to praise it worthily. In

6. Milton frequently employs modesty *topoi* and inexpressibility *topoi* to suggest
that his subject surpasses the power of his own eloquence. Alternatively he may claim
that the subject itself has inspired him and that passion and zeal for his theme have
transported him out of himself and beyond the conscious principles of his art. Though
Milton endeavors to "the best of my small ability to praise the Day," she herself "excels
the eloquence of all who praise her" (*CP*, p. 599). He concludes his oration on the
music of the spheres with the fear that "by my rough and inharmonious style I have all
along been clashing with this very harmony which I am proclaiming, and that I myself
have impeded your hearing of it" (*CP*, p. 604). The praise of learning exceeds the might
of eloquence, which is "best displayed on subjects which do not excite very great applause. Those which arouse the most applause can hardly . . . be kept within the limits
of a speech. The very richness of the subject encumbers it and straitens and hedges the
spreading parade of eloquence" (*CP*, pp. 622–623). The "very attempt of this address
thus made, and the thought of whom it hath recourse to, hath got the power within me
to a passion" (*CP*, p. 718). In "a cause so great and glorious . . . I can hardly refrain from
assuming a more lofty and swelling tone than the simplicity of an exordium may seem
to justify" (*CP*, p. 819). "I have delivered my testimony, I would almost say, have erected
a monument that will not readily be destroyed to the reality of those singular and
mighty achievements which were above all praise. [I] have heroically celebrated at least
one exploit of my cc ntrymen. I pass by the rest, for who could recite the achievements
of a whole people?" (*CP*, p. 838). The subject of *Paradise Lost* is more heroic than those
of classical epic, the poet declares; he further accentuates the magnitude of the events
he is describing by his apologies for comparing "great things with small" or for portraying spiritual realities in terms of their earthly counterparts. See Prolusions in *CP*:
"Whether Day or Night is the More Excellent" (pp. 595–602); "On the Music of the
Spheres" (pp. 602–604); "Learning Makes Men Happier than Does Ignorance" (pp.
621–629). See also *Areopagitica* (pp. 717–749); *The Second Defense of the People of
England* (pp. 817–838).

the interest of truth and decorum, a great subject required a comparable greatness in style. In *The Reason of Church Government* Milton protested that "if the Athenians, as some say, made their small deeds great and renowned by their eloquent writers, England hath had her noble achievements made small by the unskilful handling of monks and mechanics." In fixing "all the industry and art I could unite to the adorning of my native tongue," he had placed primary emphasis on matter rather than on words. To "make verbal curiosities the end" would be "a toilsome vanity"; and he had cultivated his native language chiefly in order "to be an interpreter and relater of the best and sagest things among mine own citizens" (*CP*, p. 668). In the *Second Defense* he found it agreeable to God's will, "that there should be others by whom those achievements should be recorded with dignity and with elegance. . . . And much as I may be surpassed in the powers of eloquence and copiousness of diction by the illustrious orators of antiquity, yet the subject of which I treat was never surpassed in any age in dignity or in interest" (*CP*, p. 819).

On other occasions both his praise and his condemnation of rhetoric were rhetorically motivated. In one academic exercise Milton suggested that he may "become eloquent and witty" by the "inspiration and secret impulse" of his learned audience (*CP*, pp. 614–615). In another prolusion he searched for "a rhetorical display" that might fascinate his audience, contrasting the charm and the persuasive power of the humanities—rhetoric, poetry, history—with the impotence of scholastic philosophy "to move the affections of the heart" (*CP*, pp. 604–605). Yet he was keenly aware that true praise might seem perilously close to flattery (*CP*, p. 718), and he frequently dismissed the arguments of his opponents as empty rhetoric. In *Tenure of Kings and Magistrates* he professed concern lest tender dispositions be "foolishly softened from their duty and perseverance with the unmasculine rhetoric of any puling priest or chaplain" (*CP*, pp. 752–753). In *Eikonoklastes* he opposed "the plain truth of a full and pertinent reply" to the "fair and plausible words," the "court-fucus," of that "politic contriver" King Charles (*CP*, pp. 783–786).

For Milton, as for Bacon, the efficacy of rhetoric for good or evil depended in large part on its power to engage the imagination and affections. But he was equally aware that the latter are frequently deceptive; and in *The Reason of Church Government* he portrayed their deceits in terms that had been traditionally applied to the sophist and the rhetorician. In the majority of men these "wily arbitresses" are solely responsible for ushering "truth and falsehood between the sense and the soul." Before truth can reach the understanding, she must "pass through many little wards and limits of the several affections and desires," where she must "put on such colors and attire as those pathetic handmaids of the soul please to lead her in to their queen." If she meets with their favor, "they let her pass in her own likeness; if not, they bring her into the presence habited and colored like a notorious falsehood. And contrary, when any falsehood comes that way, if they like the errand she brings, they are so artful to counterfeit the very shape and visage of truth that the understanding not being able to discern the fucus which these enchantresses with such cunning have laid upon the feature sometimes of truth, sometimes of falsehood interchangeably, sentences for the most part one for the other at the first blush" (*CP*, p. 675). The views expressed here are not irrelevant for the rhetoric of Milton's temptation scenes; the "subtle imposture of these sensual mistresses" is paralleled by the sophistries of sensual demons like Comus and Belial and the variety of lures, sensuous or intellectual, employed by the Father of Lies himself.

In the same treatise, however, the characteristics of true and false rhetoric are also transferred to true and false models of church discipline. Apologists for poetic or oratorical eloquence had extolled their ability to lend a visible shape to wisdom or virtue; Milton applies this *topos* to church government: "if any visible shape can be given to divine things," discipline is "the very visible shape and image of virtue, whereby she is not only seen in the regular gestures and motion of her heavenly paces as she walks; but also makes the harmony of her voice audible to mortal ears" (*CP*, p. 642; cf. p. 645). The conventional decorum between *res* and *verba*, truth and eloquence, is transferred to the relation between religion and "ministerial form": "If the religion be pure, spiritual, simple, and lowly, as the Gospel most truly is, such must the face of the ministry be. And in like manner if the form of the ministry be grounded in the worldly degrees of authority, honor, temporal jurisdiction, . . . it will turn the inward power and purity of the gospel into the outward carnality of the law, evaporating and exhaling the internal worship into empty conformity and gay shows" (*CP*, p. 649).

Against the ceremonies and vestments of prelaty Milton applies arguments that his near-contemporaries directed against pulpit eloquence:

Tell me, ye priests, wherefore this gold, wherefore these robes and sur-
plices over the gospel? Is our religion guilty of the first trespass and hath
need of clothing to cover her nakedness? . . . Believe it, wondrous doctors,
all corporeal resemblances of inward holiness and beauty are now past; he
that will clothe the gospel now, intimates plainly that the gospel is naked,
uncomely. . . . Do not, ye church maskers, . . . cover and hide [Christ's]
righteous verity with the polluted clothing of your ceremonies to make it
seem more decent in your own eyes. . . . What new decency . . . can be
added to this by your spinstry? Ye think by these gaudy glisterings to stir up
the devotion of the rude multitude. (*CP*, pp. 673–674).

As epic poet, Milton would subsequently denounce the idolatries of
the heathen in similar terms: "gay Religions full of Pomp and Gold"
(*CP*, p. 220). And in *Paradise Regained* he would return to the argument of his antiprelatical tract: the opposition between "the strength
of fleshly pride and wisdom" and "the pure simplicity of saving
truth" (*CP*, p. 673).[7]

Behind Milton's idealistic view of rhetoric there lay the classical
rhetorical tradition, as reinterpreted by Renaissance humanists, the
Ramist ideal of an eloquence ancillary to dialectic, and the Baconian
conception of style fitted to matter (*res et verba*) and a union of imagination and reason. Equally if not more significant, especially for
much of his controversial prose and for his later divine poetry, were
contemporary Puritan conceptions of the power of the Word of God
and of the austere and majestic eloquence of the Scriptures. (I do not
regard these, however, as peculiarly Puritan—and I should prefer to
stress the common ground shared with Anglican and, in many respects, with Roman Catholic views on poetic and prose style in religious matters.) Augustinian ideas of a redeemed eloquence dependent on and accommodated to the divine wisdom of the biblical
revelation, classical and Christian conceptions of the relationship between poetry and prophecy, and the Renaissance tradition of divine
poetry[8] (consecrated to sacred themes and, in varying degrees, condi-

7. Compare the similar emphasis on evangelical plainness in *Of Reformation in
England* and Milton's invective against "the new-vomited paganism of sensual idola-
try" as meretricious ornament: an attempt to "bring the inward acts of the spirit to the
outward and customary service of the body" (*The Prose Works of John Milton*, ed. J. A.
St. John [London, 1871], 2:364–366, 382, 387–388).
8. See Lewalski, *Protestant Poetics*; Joseph Anthony Wittreich, Jr., *Visionary Poetics: Milton's Tradition and His Legacy* (San Marino, Calif., 1979); Wittreich, ed.,
Milton and the Line of Vision (Madison, 1975); Michael Lieb, *Poetics of the Holy: A*

tioned by scriptural models), together with contemporary religious attitudes toward style helped to shape Milton's polemical prose[9] as well as the unique manner and method of his theological treatise. In a significant degree contemporary attitudes influenced the rhetoric of Heaven and Hell, and of fallen and unfallen mankind, in *Paradise Lost*—though critics are still debating the nature and extent of this influence.[10] Finally, they underlie the rejection of the philosophy and

---

Reading of Paradise Lost (Chapel Hill, 1981); William W. Kerrigan, *The Prophetic Milton* (Charlottesville, 1974); John Spencer Hill, *John Milton: Poet, Priest, and Prophet* . . . (Totowa, N. J., 1979); William G. Riggs, *The Christian Poet in Paradise Lost* (Berkeley, 1972); William G. Madsen, *From Shadowy Types to Truth: Studies in Milton's Symbolism* (New Haven, 1968); Lily Bess Campbell, *Divine Poetry and Drama in Sixteenth-Century England* (Cambridge, 1959); William Haller, *The Rise of Puritanism* . . . (New York, 1938), pp. 128–172, 386–389, on the Puritan "rhetoric of the spirit."

9. See Thomas Kranidas, "Milton and the Rhetoric of Zeal," *TSLL* 6 (1965): 423–432; Kranidas, "'Decorum' and the Style of Milton's Antiprelatical Tracts," *SP* 62 (1965): 176–187; Keith W. Stavely, *The Politics of Milton's Prose Style* (New Haven and London, 1975); Michael Lieb, "Milton's *Of Reformation* and the Dynamics of Controversy," in *Achievements of the Left Hand*, pp. 55–82; Mary Ann McGuire, "'A Most Just Vituperation': Milton's Christian Orator in *Pro Se Defensio*," *SLI* 10, no. 2 (1977): 105–114; James Egan, "The Satiric Wit of Milton's Prose Controversies," *SLI* 10, no. 2 (1977): 97–104; Peter Auksi, "Milton's 'Sanctifi'd Bitternesse': Polemical Technique in the Early Prose," *TSLL* 19 (1977): 363–381; Webber, *The Eloquent "I"*.

10. See J. B. Broadbent, "Milton's Rhetoric," *MP* 56 (1959): 224–242; George William Smith, Jr., "Iterative Rhetoric in *Paradise Lost*," *MP* 74 (1976): 1–19; Peter Berek, "'Plain' and 'Ornate' Styles and the Structure of *Paradise Lost*," *PMLA* 85 (1970): 237–246.

In *Surprised by Sin: The Reader in "Paradise Lost"* (London and New York, 1967), Stanley E. Fish emphasizes the deceptiveness of eloquence and argues that Milton "could rely on his readers to associate logic and the capacity for logical reasoning with the godly instinct in man, and the passions, to which rhetoric appeals, with his carnal instincts." It is not enough, Fish maintains, "to analyze . . . the speciousness of Satan's rhetoric." Logic is "a safeguard against a rhetorical effect only after the effect has been noted"; and the "deep distrust, even fear, of verbal manipulation in the seventeenth century is a recognition of the fact that there is no adequate defence against eloquence at the moment of impact. [The] appeal of rhetoric was traditionally associated with the weakness of the fallen intellect—the defect of our hearers." As Fish points out, the tradition begins with Plato's opposition to dialectic: "Socrates' interlocutors *discover* the truth for themselves, when, in response to his searching questions, they are led to examine their opinions. . . . The rhetorician, on the other hand, creates a situation in which his auditors have no choice but to accept the beliefs he urges on them."

Arguing that Milton endeavors "to educate the reader to an awareness of his position and responsibilities as a fallen man" by re-creating in the reader's mind "the drama of the Fall" and making him "fall again exactly as Adam did," Fish treats the distance between the reader's "initial response and the *obiter dictum* of the epic voice" as a means for simultaneously humiliating and educating the reader. The "reader is made aware that Milton is correcting not a mistake of composition, but the weakness all men evince in the

eloquence of Hellenic civilization in *Paradise Regained*, the protagonist's attack on the painted and verbose language of the Greek poets, and his preference for the "majestic unaffected stile" of the Hebrew prophets over "all the Oratory of *Greece* and *Rome*." These were "men divinely taught"; for Milton as for many of his Puritan and Anglican contemporaries, a wise eloquence or eloquent wisdom depended in some degree on divine revelation: on the written Word of God understood in the light of the Spirit.

---

face of eloquence" (pp. 1, 6–9). Cf. Fish, *Self-Consuming Artifacts* on "rhetorical" and "dialectical" presentation and their significance for the reader's experience in prose works by Milton, Bacon, Browne, and other seventeenth-century authors.

V. Persuasion or Inquiry: Methodology and the Revaluation of Rhetoric

Attacks on rhetoric and poetry during the seventeenth and eighteenth centuries comprehended a wide variety of charges and an equal variety of attitudes, neither of which were applied consistently to the two disciplines. Both rhetoric and poetry were censured on the grounds of utility, truth, and style. Poetry, it was said, presented fictions, while rhetoric argued mere probabilities, and the rhetorical topics of invention were useless for the discovery of truth. Both appealed to the imagination—the source of so many idols of the human mind—and both could be as easily exploited in the cause of error as of truth. Neither aided the advancement of science, the perfection of a sound methodology or the discovery of "real" knowledge and useful inventions. Unlike deductive logic, rhetoric could not yield certainty, and, unlike inductive methods, it could not contribute new facts. In seeking probable arguments it depended on commonly accepted opinions. These were often little more than superstitions and vulgar errors, "idols" of the human mind rather than clearly definable and verifiable ideas. Stylistically, both arts frequently obscured whatever useful facts or clear and distinct ideas they had borrowed from science and philosophy, overlaying them with verbal ornaments and difficult metaphors. The discourse of science and the language of the pulpit alike required a plain and unadorned style, stripped of the meretricious cosmetics of rhetoric.

1

Although criticism of rhetorical method—as contrasted with the methods of inductive and deductive logic—is generally directed against rhetoric per se, other, more specific protests against the devices of amplification and adornment are not, for the most part, indictments of the principles and methods of rhetoric as a whole, but attacks on variations from the plain style. The latter had long been a recognized *genus dicendi*, the *stilus tenuis* (or *gracilis, subtilis,* or *humilis*); as such it belonged to the *ars rhetorica*. In denouncing rhetoric for its ornaments, the advocates of the plain style were themselves engaging in rhetorical theory.

Anti-Ciceronians of the late sixteenth and early seventeenth centuries and Royal Society advocates of the plain style in the late seventeenth century were in fact debating issues that had previously confronted both classical Greek and Latin rhetoricians. Many of the charges they made and the formulas they employed to express them were an inheritance from classical controversies on style—the dispute over *res et verba*; the complaint of high-sounding words and little matter; the appeal to the senses and the passions; the imagery of tumors and winds, the cosmetic shop, and the bordello. The metaphors, conceits, and strong lines of the Senecan stylists were partly conditioned by Aristotelian rhetoric, and, like the emblems fashionable during the sixteenth and seventeenth centuries, they frequently involved the topics of invention. They are, in fact, logical arguments as well as rhetorical figures or tropes, and mid-Seicento treatises sometimes classified them as such, under topical headings.

Few of the assailants of rhetoric were willing to dispense with its topics or its ornaments themselves. In a century that prided itself on its wit—and not least in the age of the Royal Society—few desired to discard altogether the salt traditionally associated with the Attic style. Even in his philosophical treatises Hobbes displayed a restrained mastery of metaphor. In attacking eloquence or condemning dogmatism and superstition, in hailing the advancement of science and apotheosizing its heroes and its martyrs, the spokesmen for the experimental philosophy and a plain and perspicuous style exhibited their own command of the topics and images of demonstrative oratory—including the Ciceronian and Aristotelian commonplaces *honestas* and *utilitas*, nobility and utility. In censuring rhetoric, the proponents of plain diction rarely bothered to define it. Usually they were referring to the old humanist ideal, *copia verborum*, the orotundity associated with Ciceronianism, or to the obscurity and brevity and strong lines associated with the Senecan style. Less frequently they meant reliance on the topics of invention—the source for "finding" or discovering arguments in either logic or rhetoric. These had been attacked on the grounds that they were not a true art of discovery. Instead of providing new information, they merely enabled the speaker to organize information that he already possessed. Instead of providing "real" knowledge of concrete things, they encouraged the writer to juggle with words. In this respect, the attack on rhetoric may have been partly conditioned by the principle rhetoric shared with Aristotelian (and Ramist) dialectics and with scholastic disputations—the invention or "finding" of arguments under conventional headings or commonplaces. This system, like the disputes of the schoolmen, tended, in their opinion, to foster verbal controversies instead of advancing substantial and useful knowledge. If the conventional logic and its *topoi* could not provide an appropriate method for the discovery of nature and nature's laws, the topics and methods of rhetoric—admittedly less certain than logic—could hardly be expected to do so.

There were significant differences between the kind of plain style advocated by the Royal Society and the Senecan style fashionable earlier in the century, even though Croll and Jones disagree on the precise nature of these differences. While both schools borrow from Silver Age authors the emphasis on *res* as opposed to *verba* and both advocated the plain style as a more efficient instrument for philosophy and science, the partisans of the Senecan or Stoic style were, on the whole, content to take Latin authors as their models rather than to forge a new linguistic instrument specifically designed as a tool for scientific reasoning and communication. They were far more attached to the conventional goals of rhetoric, and they recognized the advantages of a style that could exploit paradox, arouse curiosity through its obscurity and ambiguity, persuade through its points and antitheses, and startle through its eccentricity, its clever metaphors, its "strong lines," and its enigmatic brevity. In short, the Senecan style exploited the resources of wit in the interests of rhetorical effect for the ends of persuasion as well as those of philosophy.

In its predilection for proverbs and aphorisms, the Senecan or Stoic style made exaggerated use of a familiar rhetorical convention. Aristotle had favored the use of adages since they usually reflected common opinion and therefore lent credibility and probability to the speaker's arguments. Medieval rhetoricians had recommended proverbs or exempla at the beginning of letters or other compositions, and medieval and Renaissance authors had made abundant use of them. In other contexts, however, the Senecan stylists were frequently contemptuous of common opinion. Besides attacking "vulgar errors," they consciously exploited the method of paradox. This could arouse marvel, display the author's ingenuity, and (in matters of faith) dramatize the limitations of human reason, but by definition a paradox posed a thesis contrary to common belief and ordinary opinion.

Moreover, in certain respects, the Senecan style was better suited for expressing an awareness of the epistemological crisis of the late Renaissance than for resolving it. The style could dramatize a state of indecision and the need for a suspension of judgment more easily than it could establish certainties. Still tied, in large part, to the old system of topics of invention, it could juxtapose contrary opinions, contradictory aphorisms and arguments, without resolving them. Its deliberate ellipses, its riddles and epigrams, its laconic brevity and clipped periods, its loose syntax and lax organization made it an effective vehicle for the "broken knowledge," the still unorganized and unsystematic wisdom that Bacon had admired in the aphorism. A problematic art, content with probabilities, it was able, through its usual looseness of structure, to present a variety of diverse opinions on a selected topic without decisively affirming or rejecting them. Conversely, when and if the author did attempt to sift authorities and opinions, he could still leave the final resolution tentative and problematical, as the record of his own personal opinion—an opinion he might change tomorrow. His conclusions are subjective and personal; he has argued probabilities rather than demonstrated certainties. His judgments remain within the realm of opinion—his own opinion—and they are not necessarily valid or binding or conclusive for all reasonable men. His reasonings are the meditation of an individual, aware of personal limitations as well as the general fallibility of human reason.

Not all writers who professed to be stoics or skeptics or who employed the Senecan style or its looser variant (the libertine style) exhibited such modesty or were content with probability. Some were far more sure of possessing a substantial measure of truth, and the aphoristic character of the Senecan style permitted them to string a rosary of exhortations and dogmas with little explanation or formal proof. In different contexts the same style could dramatize certitude or doubt, but it could rarely serve as an effective instrument of systematic logical demonstration. Writing on different subjects or for different effects, the same author could, if necessary, vary his persona. In one work, he could speak with the caution of a seeker or a skeptic. This was a style admirably adapted for presenting an achieved moral or political (or religious) philosophy as though it were *not* already achieved, as though it were still in process of formation—still being thought through and threshed out—or had just been achieved through a long and arduous process of inner debate and doubt and become essentially the solution to a personal crisis, the final summing up or choral exode (so to speak) of a drama of the soul.

Such a style was less suited, however, for rigorous logical demonstration, for evaluating evidence and testing a hypothesis, or for discovering new facts. It operated most effectively in expressing a personal ethos or a personal piety, a personal skepticism or a personal faith— the doubts and suspended judgment of the Pyrrhonist or the resolved mind and independent conscience of the Christian Stoic. In scientific matters, however, the style tended rather to adorn fact and dramatize speculation than to elucidate them. It was not (as Bacon ultimately realized and as Sprat subsequently perceived) the most effective vehicle for natural science, in spite of the notable precedent of Pliny. The stylistic qualities that late seventeenth-century British writers frequently regarded as requisite for scientific and philosophical discourse—simplicity, lucidity, and ease—were characteristic not so much of this Stoic style as of the style associated with Epicurus;[1] and it is not unfitting— and perhaps not accidental—that many of the British scientists who insisted on plainness and simplicity of style were, like Epicurus himself, empiricists, sensationalists, and atomists.

2

The rivalry between rhetorician and logician, poet and philosopher, was a quarrel of long standing, though marked by frequent truces and temporary reconciliations. It has appeared in Socrates' ridicule of the sophists, in Plato's strictures on rhetoric and poetry, in Aristotle's systematic effort to define the different methods of the or-

---

1. See Giambattista Vico, *On the Study Methods of Our Time*, trans. Elio Gianturco (Indianapolis, New York, Kansas City, 1965), p. 18, for a critique of ancient philosophical style: "The advocates of Stoicism (for whom . . . pure reason is the regulative standard of truth) were the thinnest and leanest of all philosophers. The Epicureans, according to whom the regulative standard of truth resides in sense perception, were simple in expression, and unfolded their doctrines in more detail. The ancient Academics instead, being disciples of Socrates who contended that he knew nothing but his own ignorance, were masters of an overflowing and lavishly embellished expression." Compare: "Epicurus, for whom sense perception was the only avenue of approach to knowledge, neither granted any proposition to his opponents, nor allowed them to grant any to him, but explained phenomena in the simplest and most unadorned language" (p. 77).

ganic arts and to demonstrate the utility of rhetoric and poetic in serving the ends of moral and political philosophy, and in the rivalry between philosophy and humane letters during the late Middle Ages and throughout the Renaissance. Seventeenth-century criticism of rhetoric by scientists and philosophers was essentially a continuation of traditional hostilities over diction and style appropriate for persuasion and for logical demonstration or instruction, and both its novelty and its importance may easily be exaggerated. What was new, and truly significant, was not so much the attack on rhetoric and poetry as the criticism of conventional logical methods and the search for new justifications and techniques for increasing the store of existing knowledge and enhancing its certitude and its utility. The new epistemological methods and resulting discoveries and problems resolved many long-standing controversies between rival schools by sweeping both away, impartially undermining Paracelsan as well as Galenic medicine, Hermetic as well as Aristotelian conceptions of the elements and principles of nature.

In place of the conventional logic of the schools, the seventeenth century contributed not the development of a new rhetoric or a radical reconception of the *ars rhetorica*, but the search for new and more certain epistemological methods. Though these methods owed much to classical and modern precedents such as Archimedes' conceptions of analysis and synthesis, the theories of the Paduan Aristotelians concerning induction and deduction, the axiomatic and demonstrative method of Euclidean geometry, and the views of classical as well as medieval authorities on the value of experiment, they led to a searching reassessment of traditional scientific or philosophical methodologies and to a radical revision of the conceptions of nature and the human mind that had persisted since classical antiquity. If the seventeenth century is, in a sense, the watershed between Renaissance civilization (still strongly influenced by medieval conceptions and values) and the modern world, the primary responsibility lies with new conceptions of scientific methodology rather than with new attitudes toward the nature and function of rhetoric and poetry.

The *ars rhetorica* and its allied arts, poetry and painting, still operated effectively as instruments of persuasion in areas of experience where the old public philosophies and the established dogmas of the church still possessed authority and conviction. The play of wit, the massive display of verbal or visual ornament, the lavish use of emblem and conceit and antithesis, the calculated appeal to the senses and emotions of the spectator—these features of baroque art and Seicento poetry and oratory could serve post-Tridentine piety as devotional aids, instruments for the confirmation of faith and for incitement to love and reverence of God. These features, these means of persuasion, performed the function and office of rhetoric; and, as the rhetorical element in contemporary artistic theory would suggest, they may have been influenced by rhetorical principles. The element of illusion in baroque art is, in a sense, the visual counterpart of the emphasis on verisimilitude and probability in rhetorical and poetic theory.

Baroque art, like the poetry of the period, sometimes strikes modern critics as an art of *vraisemblance*—problematical, subjective, deceptive, and indeed, at times, sophistic—rather than of positive truth; imitating fluid and changing phenomena rather than permanent forms; emphasizing the appearances of natural objects rather than their mathematical identity, and the shifting moods of nature rather than her geometrical and mechanical laws; and adapting modes of presentation to the senses and passions of the observer. The reason may lie partly in the recognized affinities between painting and poetry and rhetoric. Giacopo Mazzoni defined poetry as a branch of sophistic insofar as the poet is a maker of *eidola*;[2] and in the lighter erotic verse of the metaphysical and cavalier poets the play of wit and dialectic hinges on disguised fallacies that a trained reader (and the poet himself) could easily recognize as sophistical arguments. Such sophisms, idolisms, and paradoxes, frequently deployed as *suasoriae* for seduction or in defense of inconstancy, enhanced the sportive quality of these lyrics. Read ironically, as they were generally intended to be read, they could provide an additional source of marvel and delight. Like other sophistic genres such as the mock-encomium, they could demonstrate the poet's virtuosity, his skill in manipulating plausible or seemingly plausible arguments in support of an absurd thesis or an unjust end.

Most baroque painters and orators, however—and most poets in their more serious verses—would have vigorously rejected the sophist label. What distinguished the just rhetorician from the unjust was essentially his moral purpose or intent. To rely on verisimilitudes and probable or apparently probable images and arguments in the presentation of truths or in the cause of truth was to persuade to truth. The poet or painter might employ fables and myths to communicate

---

2. See the translation of Mazzoni's *On the Defense of the Comedy of the Divine Poet Dante*, in *Literary Criticism*, ed. Gilbert, pp. 359–403.

the principles of moral and natural philosophy or of natural and re-
vealed theology; in the same way he might introduce "probable circumstances" and *vraisemblances* into his imitation of scriptural his-
tories, the miracles of saints, or the dogmas of the faith, persuading to
belief and adoration through the techniques of illusion. One should
recall, however, that stricter critics in both Catholic and Protestant
countries frequently discountenanced the mixture of pagan and sacred traditions and that some of them insisted on historical accuracy
even in the details of sacred pictures or poems and literal adherence to
the biblical narrative as far as was possible. The nudity of mankind at
the resurrection was a notable exception.

3

In seventeenth-century England, Holland, and France the humanistic currents of the Renaissance still ran strong despite the challenge
of the new science and demands for a utilitarian education oriented
toward real information, or the knowledge of things rather than mastery of words. Latin was still an international language, the official
medium of diplomatic correspondence and the unofficial medium of
international controversy and scholarship.[3] Neo-Latin poetry still
flourished, and a major poet could still weigh the relative advantages
of his native tongue and the language of Virgil and Seneca. The command of the Latin language not only as the key to classical and modern learning but as a practical rhetorical instrument was still the os-
tensible aim of a grammar school education. The public and private
career of John Milton—as a student at St. Paul's, as schoolmaster and
secretary to the Council of State, as historian and lexicographer,
logician and poet, and as Latin controversialist and classical republican—would have seemed intelligible to many Quattrocento
or Cinquecento humanists. The topical classification of Milton's

3. Acutely conscious of the limited audience that he might expect for his English
works, Bacon was anxious about his posthumous reputation and desired to have his *Essays*, his *Advancement of Learning*, and other works translated into Latin. He composed
his *Meditationes Sacrae* (1597) in the Latin tongue, "believing, as he wrote to Tobie
Matthew, that 'these modern languages will at one time or another play the bankrowte
with books, and since I have lost much time with this age, I would be glad if God would
give me leave to recover it with posterity'" (A. Wigfall Green, *Sir Francis Bacon: His Life
and Works* [Denver, 1952], p. 89). See also Catherine Drinker Bowen, *Francis Bacon:
The Temper of a Man* (Boston and Toronto, 1963), p. 216. Matthew translated both the
Essays and *The Wisdom of the Ancients* into Italian (1618), dedicating his translation to
the Grand Duke of Tuscany.

commonplace book, his emendations to the text of Euripides, his predominantly philological approach to problems of scriptural interpretation, and his familiar letters also reflected his debt to the humanistic tradition.

Nevertheless, the position of Latin was already threatened by the
vernacular tongues. Within a few decades it would lose its importance as a language of state. Though scholars would continue to employ it in scientific or philosophical treatises well into the eighteenth
century (or indeed into the twentieth), many of the major treatises of
seventeenth-century thinkers were composed in the vernacular, or in
both the learned and the vulgar tongues. With Latin's decline as a
living language, and thus as an indispensable rhetorical medium and
an instrument for political and scholarly communication, two principal causes of the rise of humanistic pedagogy largely disappeared.
The grammar schools survived, and with them the classical curriculum, but the emphasis had shifted from the functional use of Latin as
a rhetorical instrument to the study of the classics for their own sake
and for a more polished command of the vernacular. University orators continued to deliver Latin addresses (as they still do) and school-
boys won prizes for Latin verse, but the age of Latin rhetoric was over.

Seventeenth-century scientists were at times almost as conscious of
living in a new age as the humanists of the fifteenth and sixteenth
centuries had been. At the beginning of the century they called for a
"restoration" of learning, much as earlier humanists and painters had
called for a rebirth of the arts. A few decades later they extolled the
advancement and progress of science and the "heroes" who had "ren-
ovated" natural philosophy. In the ancients-versus-moderns controversy they usually supported the latter, and they were as aware of
standing on the threshold of a new era as we ourselves are. They held
(or thought they held) the keys of a new learning based not on rhetorical inventions or logical topics but on a science of "real" discovery.

4

The alliance of philosophy and oratorical or poetic eloquence, suggested (perhaps grudgingly) by Plato in the *Phaedrus* and explicitly
affirmed by Cicero, Horace, and Aristotle, was strained to the breaking point by seventeenth-century philosophers; but the breach was
not irreparable. Bacon, the author of the *Novum Organum* (the "new
instrument")—an accomplished orator as well as the buccinator (or

trumpeter) of the great instauration—described the office of rhetoric as applying "Reason to Imagination for the better moving of the will." A century later, in an inaugural lecture as professor of rhetoric, Vico deplored the neglect of oratorical studies. Summarizing the deficiencies as well as the merits of Seicento critical philosophy, he called for a reconciliation of philosophy and eloquence: "What is eloquence, in effect, but wisdom, ornately and copiously delivered in words appropriate to the common opinion of mankind?" In placing "upon the same plane of falsity not only false thinking, but also those secondary verities and ideas which are based on probability alone," speculative criticism can be harmful in the education of the young. They must be educated in "common sense," and this arises from "perceptions based on verisimilitude." The disregarded art of "topics and invention of arguments," Vico explains, can enable those who know the *loci* to "grasp extemporaneously the elements of persuasion inherent in any question or case." Indeed, "criticism is the art of true speech; *ars topica*, of eloquence" (*On the Study Methods of Our Time*, pp. 13–19, 78).

Eloquence does not, Vico argues, appeal to "the rational part of our nature, but almost entirely to our passions, [which] can never be swayed and overcome unless this is done by more sensuous and materialistic means." The role of eloquence is to persuade, enticing the soul by "corporeal images" and impelling it to love. For "once it loves, it is easily taught to believe; once it believes and loves, the fire of passion must be infused into it so as to break its inertia and force it to *will*." Instead of wasting too much time on subjects "taught by abstract geometry," the youth who aspires to a political career rather than to physics or mechanics should "study topics," "defend both sides of a controversy," and "not spurn reasons that wear a semblance of probability and verisimilitude" (pp. 37–41).

The poet, like the philosopher, Vico continues, teaches moral duties, but he teaches "by delighting what the philosopher teaches austerely." Working with "invented" examples, he "induces persuasion by giving plastic portrayals of exalted actions and characters" and departing from "the daily semblances of truth, in order to be able to frame a loftier semblance of reality." He focuses his vision on "an ideal truth," on "truth as it ought to be by nature and reason" (pp. 42–43). Though the moderns are superior to the ancients in science, Vico judges the ancients superior in eloquence and wisdom and advocates that they be read first in the curriculum "since they are of proved reliability and authority" and may serve as "standards by which to gauge the quality and validity of the moderns" (pp. 41, 74).

As professor of rhetoric Vico was not, perhaps, a disinterested pleader, especially on the occasion of his inaugural lecture. His oration, delivered at the end of "the Cartesian century" and the beginning of the century of the Enlightenment, is valuable, however, not only for its strictures against Cartesian methodology but for its affinities with the Renaissance humanistic tradition. Like the neoclassical movements in other countries and in other fields (notably in the arts of design) it represents a partial but temperate reaction against the Seicento "moderns," while recognizing their scientific and philosophical achievements, and in favor of the ancients. It is a plea for the fusion of philosophy and eloquence as in antiquity and frequently in the Renaissance. It is a defense of rhetorical topics and probabilities, sensuous images and ornaments, against the insistence on strictly logical reasoning and unadorned speech. It is an affirmation of the value of persuasion as well as instruction and of appeals to the passions, the imagination, and the common sense as well as to the understanding. In these respects it is essentially a continuation of the Renaissance tradition in rhetorical and poetic theory. The Lamia and the philosopher are at last reconciled, even though the latter belongs to the school of Descartes, a master more rigorous than Apollonius.[4]

5

The actual effect on creative literature of seventeenth-century attacks on rhetoric and poetry must be assessed in historical context. The "Native easiness" that Sprat advocated is not identical with "Mathematical plainness,"[5] whether he realized it or not; the attempt of essayists and dramatic or lyric poets to achieve a familiar style, polished but unaffected and modeled on the conversation of gentlemen, does not necessarily coincide with the needs of the philosopher and scientist for an exact and unambiguous language. Though contemporary criticism of ornaments of style and figures of amplifica-

4. See Keats, "Lamia," *Complete Poems and Selected Letters*, ed. Clarence De Witt Thorpe (New York, 1935), pp. 356–375, for the tale of the young philosopher Lycius, who was enamored of a lamia and rescued by the sage Apollonius. Keats found the story in Robert Burton's *The Anatomy of Melancholy*. Burton himself had derived it from Philostratus's *De Vita Apollonii* (see Keats, *Complete Poems*, p. 375n).

5. Walter Jackson Bate, *From Classic to Romantic: Premises of Taste in Eighteenth-Century England* (New York, 1961), p. 31.

tion, the search for valid methods of invention and judgment, and the exaltation of reason over passion and imagination, truth over opinion, and certainties over probabilities may have bridled the Hippogriff, curbing flights of fancy and encouraging a more exact and succinct diction and a plainer and chaster style, there were precedents for these stylistic ideals in classical criticism, poetry, and oratory. Neoclassical poets in England and France alike operated within a critical frame of reference that presupposed, as had Horace and Aristotle, and indeed Cicero and Plato, a judicious alliance between philosophy and eloquence rather than their separation.

In western Europe the depreciation of rhetoric was conditioned partly by the traditional rivalry between oratory and science, which reflected the need for a reliable methodology and more exact vocabulary in the discovery and demonstration of truth. Though the techniques of rhetoric might persuade to certainties already discovered by other and sounder methods or to doctrines already affirmed by recognized authorities, its techniques were useless and indeed injurious for critical analysis and synthesis. The authorities and popular opinions to which the orator appealed were unreliable, and the passions he aroused were dangerous. His topics of invention were vague and uncertain. Words themselves, even on the tongue of a trained logician, were frequently unreliable instruments of thought and discourse, subject to ambiguity or, when applied to false or uncertain universals, meaningless.

In their quest for certitude and their attempt to purify their methodology from the uncertainties of rhetoric, the philosophers of the period were ultimately compelled, however, to recognize the limitations of their own methods. To avoid the extremes of dogmatism and skepticism, as well as the "probable" arguments of the rhetoricians, they were forced to search for a logic of probability and for degrees of verisimilitude. In attempting to narrow the denotation of words to things or ideas, they had first to demonstrate the possibility of certain knowledge of things and the validity of ideas and to ascertain what kinds of things or what categories of ideas could be known with certainty. Systematic and methodological demonstration of a proposition could not yield certain knowledge unless its terms were precisely defined and clearly known, and unless axioms and postulates as well as definitions had been solidly established. To purify language as the vehicle of ideas could aid the advancement of "real" knowledge very little unless the mind itself were purified, and the origin and reliability of its content—its store of ideas—had been fully investigated. The search for certitude led inevitably to inquiries into the nature and limitations of the human understanding and ultimately (as for some of the followers of Locke) away from certainty and back into the realm of probability and opinion.

For many seventeenth-century thinkers, the distrust of rhetoric was also conditioned by the political and religious controversies that had divided western Europe. Hobbes wrote against the background of the English civil war, the Thirty Years War on the Continent, and the religious conflicts that had destroyed the stability of French society in the previous century and led to the expulsion of the Huguenots in 1685. The excesses of religious zeal, the disruptive force of private conviction and enthusiasm, and rival appeals to conflicting political or religious principles heightened the prejudice against rhetoric and the desire to reestablish ethics and politics, law, and (with notable exceptions) religion on rational and verifiable grounds. The philosophers of the period were seeking a certain and infallible methodology not only for natural science but for moral and civil philosophy. Thus for Hobbes, the utility of ethical and political wisdom was to be estimated, not so much by the benefits one gains by knowing these sciences, as by the calamities one receives from not knowing them— notably the calamities of civil war.

The cause of civil war, Hobbes argues, was that few men had learned the rules of civil life, "these duties which unite and keep men in peace," for no one had hitherto taught them "in a clear and exact method." Whereas the few extant writings of geometricians were "sufficient for the taking away of all controversy in the matters they treat of," the "innumerable and huge volumes of *ethics*" had proved insufficient to resolve controversies for lack of certain demonstration. Whereas the former had increased science, the latter had "increased nothing but words." The former had been "written by men that knew, and the latter by such as knew not, the doctrine they taught only for ostentation of their wit and eloquence." Admittedly, "the reading of some such books is very delightful; for they are most eloquently written, and contain many clear, wholesome and choice sentences, which yet are not universally true, though by them universally pronounced." Lacking "a true and certain rule of our actions, by which we might know whether that we undertake be just or unjust," they are "no less frequently made use of to confirm wicked men in their purposes, than to make them understand the precepts of civil duties." From the "not knowing of civil duties, that is, from the want of moral science, proceed civil wars, and the greatest calamities of mankind"; and for the "production of the contrary commodities," there must be "a certain rule and measure of right established, which no man hitherto hath established."[6]

Declining to discuss the principles of religion, Hobbes confined his investigation to material bodies, demonstrating, as he believed, the moral and political principles and the legal rights and duties necessary for a stable and prosperous society and a secure and well-regulated state. Leibniz, in turn, believed that the essentials of religion as well as of law could be placed on a scientific foundation. Praising jurisprudence as a "science having very much to do with reasoning," he finds nothing in "the ancients . . . which approaches the style of the geometers as much as that of the pandects."[7]

Elsewhere Leibniz contrasts his own "universal characteristic" with rhetoric as an instrument of persuasion: "The stranger the representation or rather misrepresentation one party makes of this or that point according to his variable disposition, persuading others against his adversary by rhetorical effects of sharp relief and contrasting colors, the more dogmatically does he make up his own mind or indoctrinate others especially when he skillfully appeals to their prejudices." Yet, he continues,

> Whoever is firmly convinced of the truth of religion and its implications and at the same time in his love of mankind longs for its conversion, will surely have to understand, as soon as he grasps our method, that . . . there can be no more effective means conceived for the spread of the faith. . . . For once missionaries are able to introduce this universal language, then also will the true religion, which stands in intimate harmony with reason, be established, and there will be as little reason to fear any apostasy in the future as to fear a renunciation of arithmetic and geometry once they have been learnt. (*Selections*, pp. 24–25)

6

Despite the impact of the "new" scientific and philosophical movements on the content, and sometimes the style, of contemporary and later poetry, they could have only a limited influence on its form and

---

6. *Body, Man, and Citizen*, ed. Richard S. Peters (New York and London, 1962), pp. 28–29.
7. *Selections*, ed. Philip P. Wiener (New York, 1951), p. 580.

method. Even when he stooped to truth or attempted to discourse on moral or natural philosophy, the poet could not, as a rule, demonstrate his propositions with mathematical exactitude—establishing definitions and postulates and axioms, proving propositions and theorems, deducing corollaries and further propositions. Conversely, he could not amass and sift experimental data to derive general principles by induction and analysis. He must either depend on the authority of the scientists or philosophers who had followed the necessary steps of demonstration, or he must compress his arguments so drastically that they amounted to little more than the rhetorician's enthymemes and examples.

The emphasis that literary critics and poets of the period placed on method[8] should not be confused with scientific method—though perhaps the authors themselves would have been flattered by the comparison. It was not a new phenomenon, but a survival of classical, medieval, and Renaissance rhetorical and poetic theory and of Renaissance criticism of the arts of design. In their attitude toward the ancients, moreover, there was usually a fundamental divergence between the methodologists of science and philosophy and the neoclassical critics who stressed the importance of correct methods in art or literature. For the former, the methods of the ancients had lacked certitude. Natural and moral philosophy must be reestablished on a new and more reliable foundation. The authority of the ancients was a major obstacle to the further advancement of learning. For neoclassical poets and critics, in contrast, the correct methods in literary (and frequently in plastic) imitation had been discovered and systematized in antiquity. Their concepts of method were based largely on the poetics of Horace and Aristotle (with the additional influence of

8. Bate, *From Classic to Romantic*, pp. 26, 29, 34. Among studies of concepts of method in the sixteenth and seventeenth centuries, see Gilbert, *Renaissance Concepts of Method*; Ong, *Ramus*; John Herman Randall, Jr., "The Development of Scientific Method in the School of Padua," *Renaissance Essays*, ed. Paul O. Kristeller and Philip P. Wiener (New York and Evanston, 1968), pp. 217–251; Marie Boas, *The Scientific Renaissance, 1450–1630* (New York, 1962); A. Rupert Hall, *The Scientific Revolution, 1500–1800: The Formation of the Modern Scientific Attitude*, 2nd ed. (Boston, 1962).

Peter Schouls has argued that for both Descartes and Locke "the theory of method is intimately connected with the theory of knowledge." These men "took up a similar methodological stance when they approached any subject-matter of which they believed they could attain knowledge." For both, "the method of resolution and composition" imposed a "certain nature on the object to be known." Descartes's view of the efficacy of this method was based on his "view of reason as a faculty which gives man absolutely trustworthy information" (*The Imposition of Method: A Study of Descartes and Locke* [Oxford, 1980], pp. 26–28, 252, 257).

Longinus) and the example of the ancients themselves. "*Nature Methodiz'd*" was to be found in the "RULES of old *discover'd*," not in a new literary methodology, and the principles of nature were to be found in the idealized nature of Virgil and Homer. The neoclassical conception of method was essentially a continuation of the Renaissance emphasis on classical poetic theory and the idealized nature of classical poetry or art as the best and most certain guide to the imitation of nature and nature's laws.

Moreover, whereas the methodologies embraced by seventeenth-century philosophers aimed at certitude, the methods that neoclassical critics had derived from their classical authorities emphasized probability and verisimilitude. Whereas the former attempted to divest their arguments of emotional coloring, the latter inherited a poetic theory that laid down rules for imitating and arousing the passions in order to allay them. In both these respects, neoclassical poetics, like its classical predecessor, was more closely allied to rhetoric than to the new scientific methodology. Though writers of the period could hardly escape the influence of the new philosophy (or philosophies), though they might, as Vico himself suggested,[9] utilize it for new images or attempt to celebrate its achievements, they could not employ its methods; they could promulgate a truth already established, but they could not demonstrate it.

Even if they were content to present contemporary moral or natural science at second hand, writers would be compelled to rely rather on probabilities than on certainties, as the new philosophical schools often disagreed fundamentally with one another. Whether the principles of religious faith could be demonstrated by rational methods remained uncertain. Finally, near the end of the century, Locke's inquiry into the limitations of the human understanding left few valid ideas that a poet committed to the theory of ideal imitation—the representation of universals—could legitimately imitate. He had to be content, mostly to portray probabilities rather than ideal realities or to imitate particulars qua particulars rather than as images or exempla of universal truths.

Though poets are not usually expected to be epistemologists, they were often (as in the case of Virgil and Tasso, Spenser and Milton) expected to be teachers of moral philosophy; and those who aspired to the themes of divinity and natural science as well must have been aware of some of the basic divergences between their own methods of

9. *Study Methods*, pp. 43–44.

presentation or argument and those of contemporary philosophers. This raises the further question of the influence of the latter on poetic style and diction. The demand for perspicuity—a conventional stylistic virtue ever since Aristotle—was not a new ideal; criticisms of the obscurity, the extravagant conceits, and the scholastic imagery of metaphysical poetry were usually based on commonplaces of classical rhetoric and poetic, notably the principle of decorum. The ideal of a polished but familiar style was to be found in Horace's epistles and satires; his *Ars Poetica*, Virgil's *Georgics*, and numerous poems by later and minor authors could provide models for didactic treatises in verse; and Lucretius's summary of Epicurean doctrine (which Dryden translated)[10] could offer guidance to poets who desired to write on natural or moral philosophy.

Many of the qualities of neoclassical verse—characteristics that recent scholarship has attributed largely to the influence of the new science—could have been derived just as easily from classical models. Like their predecessors in antiquity, the neoclassical poets who treated scientific or philosophical subjects did not, as a rule, dispense with rhetorical ornament altogether. The "mathematical plainness" that Sprat demanded would no longer be truly functional when imposed on a mode of discourse and argument that, by its very nature, lacked mathematical certainty. The linguistic ideals of the French and English scientists of the seventeenth century were a necessary and integral part of their search for an exact, rigorous, and infallible methodology. They were less essential, and less relevant, to poetic methods, which could at most adorn philosophical or scientific doctrines with images or probable reasons, but could not demonstrate them with finality and apodeictic certainty.

7

Renaissance defenses of rhetoric and poetics usually presupposed a close cooperation between philosophy and eloquence, while attacks on rhetoric and poetics tended to appeal to the contrary but no less traditional argument: the separation of rhetoric and philosophy. (To the philosopher, such a separation might frequently be regarded as deplorable, though sometimes as necessary, inevitable, and desirable.) In arguing the power of the poet or orator to teach, delight, and

10. See Mary Gallagher, "Dryden's Translation of Lucretius," *Huntington Library Quarterly*, 28 (1964): 19–29.

move more effectively than the philosopher, and in asserting his ability to give concrete and sensuous form to abstract ideas, the defenders of these arts sometimes took for granted a comparatively stable system of recognized truths or bodies of doctrine whose validity was not generally subject to doubt and which could (without violence to their intrinsic certainty or probability) be restructured according to the methods of the poet or orator and invested with appropriate garments of style.

Moreover, defenders of rhetoric and poetics usually took for granted the conventional logical categories and rhetorical topics. Mythological and theological manuals, collections of adages and emblems or hieroglyphs, allegories and exampla, were often topically organized, or could easily be utilized as classified sources of invention. Metaphors and conceits were likewise discussed under logical or rhetorical headings. Seventeenth-century attacks on the topics of invention, on metaphor and allegory and other figures of speech or thought, on the argumentative force of proverbs and common opinions, and on the validity of universal ideas tended, accordingly, to weaken the traditional, but slender ties between the arts of demonstration and persuasion. When the principles of philosophy could be regarded as certain, its methods of discovery and demonstration valid, and its moral and natural doctrines established by incontrovertible proofs, poetry and oratory might safely and expediently serve as its handmaids or allies. But when philosophy itself was in doubt, its conventional principles and methods challenged and its traditional systems subjected to radical reappraisal, the conventional devices of eloquence might merely obscure the distinction between truth and falsehood and hinder its followers from the search for certitude. Not only were words (the images of ideas) deceptively ambiguous, but the ideas themselves were uncertain. Like Bacon's idols of the marketplace, ideas were often little more than chimaeras, and the responsibility for their uncertainty rested, in large part, on words, through the defects of common speech as well as through common opinion. Inevitably, therefore, the problem of correct method in the sciences entailed a critique of the nature and the use or abuse of language, a critique of words as well as of ideas and of methods of invention and demonstration.

Contemporary criticism of traditional logic and rhetoric was conditioned in large part by the need to reconstruct the arts and sciences on a new and more reliable foundation, applying to natural and moral philosophy methods of discovery and demonstration that might possess the certainty of mathematics. At the end of the seventeenth century major European thinkers were still concerned with many of the issues that had, in very different ways, engaged philosophers like Bacon, Descartes, and Hobbes. Leibniz was seeking an art of discovery; his search for mathematical precision in language and method ends in a "universal characteristic." Vico specifically takes up the issue of the relationship between rhetoric and the new science; beginning his oration *On the Study Methods of Our Time* with a tribute to Bacon, he vindicates the merits of eloquence against the rival claims of critical philosophy.

VI. "New Philosophy" and Seventeenth-Century Style

The influence of the scientific revolution on poetic technique and on prose style cannot be clearly defined, and in attempting to demonstrate such influence the critic is apt to oversimplify the literary and scientific methods of the age. The principle of decorum—still central in poetic and rhetorical theory—usually demanded variation in style and structure according to genre. Even within the same literary species, moreover, there were individual differences according to the subject, the personal tastes and affective intent of the author, the character of his persona (or personae), and the nature of his audience.

The philosophers, in turn, varied no less widely in their conceptions of the relationship between rhetoric and science, of the principles of correct method, and of the use and abuse of language. The grounds of certainty were not always the same for natural and moral philosophy, or for theology and politics; the principles that governed natural scientists in their search for an exact and unequivocal language were not identical with the motives that inspired contemporary attacks on pulpit eloquence. Against the background of contemporary political and ecclesiastical conflict, men of reason had ample grounds for distrusting modes of discourse that, by appealing to passion instead of reason and to uncertain opinions rather than demonstrable truths, could only perplex and embitter controversial issues instead of resolving them.

In natural science, and often in moral and political philosophy, the theory of language was inseparably linked with problems of methodology. In many instances, the distrust of rhetoric was conditioned not only by the charges that classical philosophers had leveled against oratory and sophistic but also (and more significantly) by distrust of the traditional logic. The Ramist reforms had attempted to reconcile logic and eloquence by compelling the rhetorician to base his arguments and their disposition or arrangement on logic. Dialectical topics of invention—and especially the topic and subtopics of causality—were now of central importance both for the rhetorician and the logician. The new philosophers required a more certain and more productive method of invention, however, and throughout the century, from Bacon to Leibniz, the search for a true and perfect "art of discovery" remained a central concern. Bacon contrasted the invention of the logicians and rhetoricians with the desired art of invention that could discover the true principles of nature, inventing new sciences and producing useful and "luciferous" (or "light-bearing") discoveries. He looked for such a method in observation and experiment, the collection and classification of data, and a gradual, cautious ascent to universals and axioms through induction—a Jacob's ladder of scientists climbing laboriously to general ideas and clambering down again to concrete and sensuous particulars.

Other Seicento thinkers found suggestions for an art of discovery and demonstration in the analytic and synthetic methods of the mathematicians. From language they demanded a precision comparable to that of the mathematician's signs. In their hands, the invention and judgment of the logician (or the rhetorician) were, in effect, reconstituted by a methodology modeled on that of mathematics. Invention was conceived primarily in terms of induction or analysis, combined in part, as Hobbes argued, with deductive or synthetic method. Demonstration consisted entirely in synthesis or deduction. Disposition, insofar as it followed the order and arrangement of geometrical demonstration—definitions, axioms, postulates, theorems, corollaries—was governed by mathematical principles.

Language or elocution, finally, was conceived not as extrinsic ornament (as in the traditional arts of rhetoric and also in the Ramus-Talaeus system) but as the instrument of thought, the medium of discovery and demonstration. Words must serve the philosopher in the same way that signs and symbols served the mathematician, and they must be equally naked and unequivocal. Without such "mathematical plainness" they would be unreliable and imperfect tools for either analysis or synthesis, induction or deduction. The "experimental" and "mechanical" philosophers of the period were, in part, looking for a mathematical or symbolic logic, though they did not usually press their demands for linguistic reform to this extreme. Most of them were content to attempt the virtually impossible task of fixing the precise significance of words and treating them as marks or signs.

A few, like Wilkins and Leibniz, did in fact attempt to dispense with words and to express ideas by visual rather than verbal signs.

The contrast between this mathematical approach to logic and language, and the older, more conventional views may be more easily apparent if one compares the mathematical approach with Milton's description in *Of Education* of the "organic arts": "Logic . . . is to be referred to this due place with all her well-couched heads and topics, until it be time to open her contracted palm into a graceful and ornate rhetoric" (*CP*, p. 636). Milton does not cite authorities on logic here, though he lists an abundance of authors for the rule of rhetoric; but the order of the arts in this passage recalls the Ramist subordination of rhetoric to logic. The topics of invention, challenged by the new philosophers as fostering little more than verbal controversy instead of producing new and certain knowledge, remain central to his conception of logic and rhetoric, as they had been in Ramus's system.

1

With their criticism of the old logic and their disdain or indifference to its topics of invention, the methodologists of the new philosophy widened the gulf between scientific method and the methods of the poet, the orator, and, to a certain extent, the painter and sculptor. These had been taught to base their inventions on commonplaces, deriving arguments and images from standard topical headings. In spite of the limited sanction that some of the philosophers—Bacon, Leibniz, and even Hobbes—granted to rhetoric and poetry, and the emphasis they sometimes placed on reconciling both these arts with reason, they had nevertheless increased the difficulty of combining philosophy and eloquence. Poets might celebrate the new science or utilize its discoveries for images and examples; but they could not, as a rule, imitate its methods. Imagination—the chief source of poetic imagery and wit—was suspect, for it often fostered false images of things, idols or phantasms instead of true ideas. The passions were suspect—despite their traditional role in both poetry and rhetoric—for they prejudiced judgment and obscured reason. Truth could best be observed in a dry light, not through the haze of passion, the cloudy mists of the humors. Verbal ornament was suspect, for it was deceitful and superfluous, disguising truth and falsehood, portraying great as small or evil as good, and substituting words for solid substance.

Similarly, the traditional philosophical systems were suspect, for they were based on inadequate induction or on latent, though unintentional, fallacies. The poet or orator who drew his arguments from these systematic philosophies could only increase the estrangement between reason and imagination; instead of reuniting philosophy and eloquence, he would be confirming their divorce. If he attempted (as his office theoretically demanded) to represent abstract concepts, he must recognize the unpleasant fact that many general ideas—including some of the conventional topics of invention—had been dismissed by his scientific contemporaries as mere idols and chimaeras. The transcendental realm of ideas no longer existed; the rhetorician's store of universals consisted largely of phantasms or "insignificant noise," vain imaginations or empty words.

Though Bacon had found the principles of natural and moral philosophy in pagan myth, and had adorned his own treatises with such allegorical fables, many of his descendants, such as Hobbes and Sprat, condemned metaphors and allegories alike as equivocal and deceitful. These devices were also vulnerable to the charge of obscurity, like the enigmas that Bacon and Browne had favored, but which a later generation frequently disregarded as incompatible with clarity of discourse. Examples and similitudes, in contrast, fared better. They were recognized tools of inductive reasoning. The investigator discovered principles and formed universals by comparing particular examples and similitudes and abstracting general ideas from them. The empirical strain in the new philosophy, by emphasizing sensation as the source of knowledge and concrete particulars as the objects whose existence is most easily known, tended, indeed, to undermine one of the traditional objections against poetry: the sensuous and concrete character of its medium. By the criteria of the empiricists themselves, poetry stood closer to the primary sources of knowledge than its Platonic censors had believed.

Though most poets, and perhaps a majority of prose writers, could not follow the strict analytic and synthetic methods advocated by seventeenth-century philosophers, these methods may nonetheless have influenced contemporary efforts to portray the process of thought, the act of invention or discovery. Bacon argued that in the probative method knowledge should be communicated in the order in which it had been discovered. Descartes described his *Meditations* as all analysis. Although Descartes himself presents the act of invention in narrative form, it could also be portrayed with greater immediacy and vividness. A writer could endeavor to imitate the action of the mind directly, investing the process of invention, the search for truth, with dramatic tension. In the older and traditional kind of logical or rhetorical invention, the writer first chooses his arguments and then arranges them systematically; the process of invention lies outside the work itself, and the structure of the work is determined by the requirements of logical (or quasi-logical) demonstration. In the new analytic mode, which depicts the actual process of discovery, the act of invention is inherent in the work itself. It is the object of the writer's imitation and determines the structure or disposition of the entire work. Presenting his principles in the order in which he discovered them, the writer imitates the process of analysis, the act of invention.[1] As Hobbes observed, "the causes of the motions of the mind are known, not only by ratiocination, but also by the experience of every man that takes the pains to observe those motions within himself." Men who have not "learned the first part of philosophy, namely, *geometry* and *physics*, may, notwithstanding, attain the principles of civil philosophy, by the *analytical method*." They may be known "by any man's experience, that will but examine his own mind."[2]

2

Like other currents in late Renaissance thought—the traditions of Catholic and Protestant meditation, the spiritual warfare of the *miles Christianus*, the moral combat of the Stoic, the contemplations of the neo-Platonist and the self-analysis of the skeptic, the self-dramatization of the "original genius"—the new philosophy tended to encourage introspection as well as scientific experiment, study of the microcosm of human nature as well as the nature of the universe, discovery of the principles of the world within as well as the external world. Investigation of the nature of man fostered a kind of intellectual autobiography, a "romance" or "fable" (as Descartes termed his own works) of the quests and adventures of reason, much as investigation of the operations of grace stimulated spiritual autobiography, a record of the ordeals of faith and conscience. Descartes had originally planned to entitle his *Discourse on Method* "A History of my Mind,"

1. See Webber, *The Eloquent "I"*; Leonard Nathanson, *The Strategy of Truth: A Study of Sir Thomas Browne* (Chicago, 1967).
2. *Body, Man, and Citizen*, ed. Richard S. Peters (New York and London, 1962), p. 78.

and it remains, as Arthur Wollaston observes, "a sort of memoir."[3] The analytical method of Descartes's *Meditations* leads to self-knowledge[4] and a clearer recognition of his relationship to God and the world. His *Discourse* is the autobiography of a personal and individual quest for certainty, intended merely "to try and reform my own thoughts and to build on a foundation of my own."[5] It attempts to establish, through the introspection of a particular individual, universal principles, certain and infallible knowledge of the existence of God and the nature of mind and matter.

This species of meditative literature (for it is not the only kind), inquiring rather than demonstrating truths already discovered, properly belongs to the art of invention, but it might serve as demonstration. Bacon and other seventeenth-century thinkers considered truly instructive that knowledge "delivered and intimated . . . *in the same method wherein it was invented*" (*SW*, p. 304). Since it lent itself more readily to dramatic presentation, the writer could, if he chose, depict his reflections as an imitation of thought, the mimesis of a mind, perhaps speaking through a persona. The meditative genre— to which Bacon's *Thoughts and Conclusions*, and Pascal's *Pensées*, no less than Descartes's analytical *Meditations*, belonged—permitted the writer to present his speculations as though they were an interior monologue, a philosophical impromptu. He could also, at will, lighten his discourse, by temporarily giving rein to fantasy, enlivening judgment with wit, without violating verisimilitude or probability— for he was, after all, painting an image of the human mind in action.

The dialogue form or a one-sided conversation could be conducted without sacrificing the dramatic character of the mimesis of invention. Like the soliloquy, the dialogue was well adapted to the representation of invention, the process of inquiring after uncertain and unknown truths. As Hume observes in *Dialogues Concerning Natural Religion*, there are "some subjects . . . to which dialogue-writing is peculiarly adapted, and where it is still preferable to the direct and simple method of composition," the "methodical and didactic manner," "accurate and regular argument" and deductive proofs, common in contemporary philosophical treatises. Any question of philos-

3. Wollaston, trans., Introduction to *Discourse on Method and Other Writings*, by René Descartes (Baltimore, 1960), p. 12.
4. *The Meditations . . . of René Descartes*, trans. John Veitch (La Salle, Ill., 1968), p. 90.
5. Descartes, *Discourse on Method, Optics, Geometry, and Meteorology*, ed. Paul J. Olscamp (Indianapolis, New York, Kansas City, 1965), p. 14.

ophy "which is so *obscure* and *uncertain*, that human reason can reach no fixed determination with regard to it; if it should be treated at all; seems to lead us naturally into the style of dialogue and conversation. Reasonable men may be allowed to differ, where no one can reasonably be positive."[6]

In choosing the dialogue form, Hume was returning to a well-established though somewhat old-fashioned genre that had been a favorite vehicle for philosophical and critical speculation for Plato and Cicero, many Renaissance humanists, and seventeenth-century critics like Dryden. Since it pretended to imitate actual conversation, it required a natural and familiar style. Comparable simplicity in the soliloquy and in the author-to-reader dialogue was sometimes sought, but writers in these forms were often more notable for their rhetorical variety than for their systematic use of familiar style. Contemporary manuals for meditation sometimes included detailed directions for the exploitation of rhetorical figures as well as logical arguments. The literature of private devotion could not always escape the techniques of public oratory. The writer frequently addressed his deity as though he were flattering a prince, and exhorted or rebuked his own soul as though he were haranguing an audience or prosecuting a felon at the bar.

3

The cultivation of a personal style, or what appeared to be a personal style, was not dissociated from rhetorical ends. As the natural and spontaneous expression of an individual personality, it could serve as ethical proof. By avoiding the appearance of dogmatizing, by presenting his arguments as valid in his own eyes but not necessarily binding on others, and by appearing to speak only his own opinion, the writer might paradoxically persuade his reader more effectively than through open persuasion, by describing a personal search for truth rather than arguing from first principles.

Such personal styles were not always familiar or plain. Some abounded in tropes and schemes and periods; others sought Senecan brevity. Some were fanciful, idiosyncratic, and deliberately whimsical, mixing levels of style and subject matter, exploiting macaronic and burlesque techniques, converting *copia* into inarticulated abun-

6. In *The English Philosophers from Bacon to Mill*, ed. Edwin A. Burtt (New York, 1939), pp. 690–691.

dance, and consciously producing the effect of incoherence. Some were collections of aphorisms; others pursued a continuous and carefully reasoned argument, point by point, and stage by stage. Some were deliberately obscure; others painstakingly lucid and precise. Some endeavored to strike the imagination and stir the emotions; others were directed to reason alone. The clear and plain style of some of the philosophical meditations, such as those of Descartes, was conditioned primarily by the linguistic demands of their epistemological methods rather than by considerations of verisimilitude in presentation, though the latter may have influenced other meditative writers of the century.

Discussions of seventeenth-century prose have sometimes blurred the distinction between the Senecan style and the kind of plain style that the spokesmen for the new science required as a medium for discovery and demonstration. Adherents of the Senecan style insisted on a closer correlation between words and things, including a more concise delivery of the matter of discourse and less concern for adorning and amplifying it. They were consciously renewing the old battle between philosophy and eloquence; and they were, in many cases, partisans of the Stoic philosophy associated with the curt or pointed style. The Stoics had been noted, or notorious, in antiquity for their contempt of eloquence, and the style of Chrysippus in particular (whom Horace compares unfavorably with Homer as a teacher of moral philosophy) had been an obvious target for the rhetoricians. In the reaction against an exaggerated Ciceronianism, seventeenth-century philosophers could appeal to the authority and example of Seneca, just as historiographers could turn for support to Tacitus and Sallust. In contrast, many of the new scientists were demanding a mathematically precise language that could effect a radical and certain reconstruction of philosophy. Though some were influenced by Stoicism, as others were by Epicureanism and Platonism, they refused to accept any of the classical systems on authority or *in toto*. Where adherents of the Senecan style admired wit, the scientists often professed to distrust fancy. Where the former sought striking and ingenious metaphors, the latter rejected such devices as equivoques. Where the former delighted in strong lines and riddling epigrams, the latter sought lucidity. Though both regarded words as the images of things, the latter carried the *res et verba* formula to its logical conclusion: the word becomes a mathematical sign for an idea.

As R. F. Jones recognized, there is a significant difference between the kind of plain style advocated by late Cinquecento and early Seicento anti-Ciceronians and that demanded by the Cartesians in France and the Royal Society in England. Nevertheless the distinction may not have been obvious to all writers of the period. The ideal of mathematical plainness, as closely linked with mathematical conceptions of discovery and demonstration, had to be fought for. Many of the English Senecans may have believed themselves to be writing scientific and philosophical prose, when by the standards of Descartes or Sprat they were merely affecting a mannered brevity and an equivocal obscurity, reporting experiments of light in the idiom of Egyptian darkness.

4

In the *querelle des arts*, from antiquity through the Renaissance, the attack on poetry and rhetoric is directed not only at their methods of persuasion and their vulnerability to abuse but also at their claims to teach as well as delight. Unlike the sciences, poetry and oratory were not confined to a particular subject matter. According to Petrarch, the poet might treat any subject belonging to history, ethics, or natural philosophy; his office was to veil such material in pleasing fictions. In theory, within the inevitable limitations imposed by the several poetic genres the poet possessed virtually unlimited license in his choice of subject, and his rights to so comprehensive an empire of the mind seemed confirmed by the variety of doctrines that exegetes had discovered under the integument of Gentile myths. These myths had traditionally been interpreted as historical, moral, or physical allegories. Similar claims to license in choice of subject had been made on behalf of the orator. They underlay Plato's attack on rhetoricians ignorant of the realm of ideas and Cicero's demand for a union of eloquence and philosophy, and they reinforced the ideal of the poet or orator as *vir bonus* and *doctus*, endowed with learning and character as well as verbal skill.

Such professions of universal competence would be meaningless without universal learning, without special competence in each of the sciences that the writer proposed to treat. In an age when formal education still centered on the trivium and quadrivium, such universality was theoretically possible; the Renaissance ideal of the *uomo universale*—whether prince, courtier or gentleman, artist or poet— was partly conditioned by Cicero's ideal of the orator. In practice, eloquence might disguise superficiality as easily as it adorned solid learning. In natural and moral philosophy the poet or orator often remained little more than an amateur; it is hardly surprising that professional philosophers sometimes dismissed him as a dilettante.

The influence of the new science on poetry, especially during the early part of the seventeenth century, has perhaps been exaggerated by modern scholars. The early metaphysical poets wrote before Descartes and Hobbes. Even though some of them felt the influence of Bacon's thought and encountered Continental conceptions of "resolutive" and "compositive" methods, the logical and scientific arguments that they frequently employ belong, as a rule, rather to the old-fashioned scholastic modes of demonstration than to those of the new science, though they allude to new philosophy and recent scientific discoveries. These poets may demonstrate, like scientists and logicians, from definitions, from Aristotelian categories and Ramist dialectical topics, or from the principles of geometry, physics, or metaphysics; but they are arguing according to methods and principles already condemned as obsolete, anachronistic, and fallacious.

Moreover, they often employ traditional methods ironically, aware that their arguments contain egregious fallacies and that their demonstrations do not actually demonstrate. Theirs is a rhetoric of seduction, prosecuted with sophistic and affective proofs, parodying mysticism as well as logic and combining jejune erudition and intellectual subtlety with passion. Its mimetic range extends from religious ecstasy to debauchery, from devotion to guile. Imitating passion or the pretense of passion, it portrays the lover's arguments (*dianoia* or "thought") as seemingly genuine and sincere expressions of his affections (*pathos* or "passion") and character (*ethos* or "moral purpose"),[7] or alternatively as conscious lies and amorous deceits, the kind of vows at which Jove proverbially smiled.

The delight of such poetry proceeds partly from its challenge to literary conventions and expectations, and to the usual decorum of the lover. The *ars amatoria* has become, in effect, a scholastic discipline prosecuted by the techniques of academic disputation, utilizing logical demonstration as well as rhetorical topics, and exploiting arguments derived from the whole encyclopedia of the arts and sci-

7. See Aristotle's *Poetics* for discussion of *dianoia, ethos,* and *pathos* in dramatic poetry. For the use of *ethos, pathos,* and *logos* as rhetorical terms in Aristotle's *Rhetoric* and elsewhere, see Sister Miriam Joseph, *Shakespeare's Use of the Arts of Language* (New York, 1947), pp. 34–40, 386–399.

ences—physics and metaphysics, mathematics and theology. Its wit derives in part from its ability to flout the conventions of rhetorical persuasion at the same time that it parodies the methods of logical demonstration, and from its fusion of two different (though not altogether incompatible) stances: the decorum of the scholar and that of the lover. In much of this verse—written by university men trained in scholastic methodology and conscious of satiric treatments of the scholar-lover in jest-books and on the stage—there is a strong element of self-parody. The writer is conscious of the requirements of the double decorum—conscious (to invert John Livingston Lowes's remarks on Chaucer's Prioress) of the imperfect submergence of the scholar in the lover.

5

Whatever its innovations in scientific and philosophical methodology, the Century of Genius was, on the whole, more conservative in its literary methods and its critical standards. The cult of wit was strongly influenced by classical precedents[8]: the epigrams of Martial and the example of Seneca, Tacitus, and other writers of the Silver Age; Aristotle's analysis of metaphor and the role of wit in discovering the "middle term" in demonstrative and dialectical arguments; classical discussions of *ingenium* (talent, natural genius) and Tacitus's discourse on style. The attempts by Hobbes, Sprat, and others to exclude metaphors and other equivoques from scientific discussion were not a new development; Aristotle had banned them from definitions and from dialectical disputations. Indeed the pattern of reaction and counterreaction that recent critics have detected in the art or literature of the period—the interplay between classical and anticlassical movements; the quarrel between ancients and moderns; the tension between originality and imitation, natural talent and the rules of art, innovation and tradition; the conflicting demands of eloquence and reason, words and matter—roughly recapitulates the struggle between writers of Golden and Silver Age Latinity. Neoclassical critics protested the excesses of metaphysical and Senecan style—and

8. For discussion of sixteenth- and seventeenth-century attitudes toward the metaphorical ingenuity exhibited in the Scriptures, the wit of the Holy Spirit, see Lewalski, *Protestant Poetics*; Webber, *The Eloquent "I"*; Saint Augustine, *On Christian Doctrine*; Louis L. Martz, *The Wit of Love: Donne, Carew, Crashaw, Marvell* (Notre Dame, Ind., 1969).

neoclassical artists the irregularities of the styles we would label mannerist or baroque—on grounds similar to Quintilian's condemnation of the "corrupt" eloquence of Silver Age writers and Vitruvius's censure of bizarre and fantastic trends in mural decoration.

Despite the attacks of scientists on the topics of invention, and on the use of metaphors and allegories, writers continued to exploit them. Allegories underlie much of the emblem literature of the period, and emblems themselves continued to flourish well into the eighteenth century.[9]

9. For further discussion of emblems, see the Appendix.

VII. Conclusion: A Rhetoric of Inquiry?

For some modern critics, the history of styles is a topic in the history of ideas. The weatherwise, trained to observe the signs of the times, perceive a period style as a kind of psychic barometer, faithfully registering changes in intellectual climate. In the frequency and violence of metaphors, the discontinuities or distortions of syntax, and the unresolved tensions within the medium of discourse itself, the skillful analyst traces the intellectual vicissitudes of the seventeenth century as easily as a meteorologist follows the progress of a storm. Philosophical and religious orthodoxies, it has been argued, found correlative expression in the controlled orotundities of the Ciceronian period; the Stoic revival, a correlative in the Spartan brusqueness of the curt Senecan style; and skepticism and libertine speculation a model in looser and freer variants of the Senecan mode. These styles were succeeded by the naked plain style of Restoration savants in response to the demands of the new science for greater clarity and precision.

Despite qualifications by a few recent scholars, this view remains substantially intact. Though it sounds suspiciously pat—a trifle too good to be true—it is still the standard scheme for the *general* characteristics of English seventeenth-century prose styles. Croll himself applied it to poetry,[1] and in the analysis of individual authors recent

---

1. As Croll observed (*Style*, pp. 96, 176), the revived interest in writers of the Latin Silver Age tended to foster similar tastes in a variety of poetry and prose genres. In the seventeenth century "Lucan had a more effective influence on the ideas and style of poetry than Virgil did; . . . Seneca was more loved and much more effectively imitated in prose style than Cicero had been in the previous generations; . . . Tacitus almost completely displaced Livy as the model of historical and political writing; . . . Martial was preferred to Catullus, and Juvenal and Persius were more useful to the satirists than Horace; . . . Tertullian, the Christian representative of the Stoic style of the Empire, . . . exercised a stronger power of attraction . . . than St. Augustine, who is the Cicero and Ciceronian of patristic Latin." The English translator of Lipsius helped to disseminate the neo-Stoic style but also influenced the taste for Martial and the epigram. Noting the "new distaste . . . for the copious and flowing style of Ariosto and

criticism has emphasized the epistemological implications of style. (For Ciceronianism in prose style, read Petrarchism as a poetic fashion. For Seneca in philosophical prose, read Martial in poetic epigram; and for Senecanism in prose style, read metaphysical poetry.)

Some modern critics consider a period style to be interdisciplinary as well as international. As an expression of the changing sensibility of an age, it appears, more or less concurrently, in the arts of discourse and design, reflecting attitudes and assumptions, patterns of thought and feeling, of which contemporary writers and artists are often less than fully aware. Croll describes the shift in the seventeenth century from Ciceronian to anti-Ciceronian forms and ideas as "exactly parallel" with changes that occurred in the nonliterary arts, and he posits the former to be "perhaps more useful to the student of the baroque impulse than any of the others, because it was more self-conscious, more definitely theorized by its leaders, and more clearly described by its friends and foes" (*Style*, p. 208). Ernst Robert Curtius described as "mannerist" features of style that others have preferred to characterize as Senecan, baroque, or metaphysical; Heinrich Wölfflin's criteria for distinguishing Renaissance and baroque styles in painting, sculpture, and architecture have been extended to literature; and Wylie Sypher has distinguished four successive stages in Renaissance style: "a provisional formulation, a disintegration, a reintegration, and a final academic codification—a cycle roughly equivalent to a succession of art styles or forms technically known as 'renaissance,' ... mannerism, baroque, and late-baroque (having close affinities with academism and neoclassicism)." "Every style," Sypher suggests, "is a symptom"; perhaps the "most sensitive and explicit vocabulary of any society," it also functions as "a syntax of consciousness [that

---

Spenser, and the 'tedious uniformity' of Petrarchanism," Croll contrasted the rhythms of Spenser and the Petrarchans with those of Donne (*Style*, pp. 64, 208). As a parallel to the anti-Ciceronian movement other critics point to the reaction against the aureate and mellifluous qualities of Elizabethan lyric and narrative style: its copiousness and lavish ornamentation, its smoothness and preoccupation with verbal harmony, its leisurely and carefully rounded stanzas, its profusion of mythological detail. In brevity and point the verse epigram resembles the *stile coupé*; in its deliberate harshness, its mixture of colloquial plainness and learned obscurity, its "strong lines" and conceited wit, and its avowed concern for portraying the natural process of thought through a natural manner of speech, the Senecan mode possesses significant affinities with metaphysical poetry. Finally, similar tastes underlie the "Attic" poetry and prose of the period. In its concern for clarity and precision, simplicity and restraint, the tradition of Jonson, Denham, and Waller, and the "proto-Augustans" parallels the concerns of Restoration prose style.

expresses] the way in which a society feels, responds, thinks, communicates, dreams, escapes. . . . Syntax is conditioned by the structure of the world in which we believe we live; and the whole organization of the artist's sensibility is a screen through which appears the world he represents."[2]

1

For many of our contemporaries the pursuit of the baroque has been as compelling as the chase of the White Whale.[3] Cultural historians, art historians, literary critics, and musicologists have entered the pursuit, as motley a crew as that of the *Pequod*, while the quarry has seemed as monumental and as elusive as Moby Dick. But the definition of the baroque ("that Sea-beast," which man "of all his works / Created hugest") must be left to more intrepid critics with sharper harpoons. Questions arise that demand answers I cannot give. Are art-historical categories genuinely applicable to literary criticism? Or do they undergo such radical changes of meaning when transferred to specifically literary contexts that they obscure the essential characteristics of art and literature alike? Are analogies between literature and painting[4] to be interpreted—like baroque con-

2. *Four Stages of Renaissance Style: Transformations in Art and Literature, 1400–1700* (Garden City, N.Y., 1955), pp. 6, 16–17; cf. pp. 33–34.

3. For Wölfflin, the essential characteristic of Renaissance classical style is harmony of proportions; Alberti had defined beauty as "a harmony of all the parts, . . . fitted together with such proportion and connection, that nothing could be added, diminished or altered, but for the worse." In contrast, the aim of the baroque style was "not to represent a perfected state, but to suggest an incomplete process and a movement towards its completion." The baroque is "bold enough to turn the harmony into a dissonance by using imperfect proportions" (*Renaissance and Baroque*, trans. Kathrin Simon [Ithaca, 1966], pp. 66–67). For Arnold Hauser, the principal feature of mannerism is the disturbance of classical harmony and the disintegration of the Renaissance unity of space. In the two "post-classical styles," mannerism and baroque, he found diverse responses to "the intellectual crisis of the opening decades" of the sixteenth century: "mannerism as the expression of the antagonism between the spiritualistic and the sensualistic trends of the age, and the baroque as the temporary settlement of the conflict on the basis of spontaneous feeling." Mannerism, he suggests, was "the first movement to raise the epistemological question: for the first time the agreement of art with nature is felt to constitute a problem." The baroque, in turn, reflected the "new scientific world-view" that resulted from Copernicus's discovery: "[The] art of the baroque is . . . full of the echo of the infinite spaces and the interrelatedness of all being. The work of art in its totality becomes the symbol of the universe as a uniform organism alive in all its parts" (*The Social History of Art*, trans. Stanley Godman, vol. 2, *Renaissance, Mannerism, Baroque* [New York, n.d.], pp. 102–104, 128, 180–182).

4. Hauser perceives mannerist qualities in Cervantes and Shakespeare. Roy Daniells associates Milton's *Comus* and *Lycidas* with mannerism and *Paradise Lost* with

ceits—metaphorically rather than literally? At what point do these parallels exceed the limits of good sense and become tendentious or misleading? To what extent are our notions of the relationships between the thought and style of an age based on circular reasoning? Do they not, in fact, represent a kind of critical *contaminatio* in which stereotypes of style and stereotypes of an age endlessly mirror each other? Do we not, as a rule, tend to define the period in terms of the style, and the style in terms of the period? To what extent is our understanding of the thought and sensibility of an age predetermined by our reactions to its stylistic techniques? Conversely, to what extent is our analysis of style prejudiced by preconceived notions concerning the spirit of the age? The ghost of an era—the *Zeitgeist*—has thus far resisted most critical attempts at exorcism, and those of us who regard it as a mere superstition are still haunted by it.

Satisfactory answers to rhetorical questions are like the dentures of a gift horse; one assumes they can be found, but one prefers not to look for them. Of more immediate relevance is the assumption that a period style is the conscious or unconscious expression of a contemporary world view. Arnold Hauser stresses the epistemological implications of mannerism and the cosmological significance of the baroque. Sypher explains the disintegrative tendencies of mannerism in terms of "a crisis in fact and conscience." As the "formal dissolution of a style," mannerism is a reflection of "personal unrest" and "holds everything in a state of dissonance, dissociation, and doubt." The "baroque canon of style," in contrast, "does not depend upon mannerist contingencies, but upon assurances and certainties," confidently affirmed and "exhilarating to the eye" even if not "wholly convincing to the mind." For Odette de Mourgues, baroque art is a response to the spiritual crisis of the late Renaissance; it reflects uncertainty and disquiet, a loss of self-confidence, a conflict between the

---

the baroque; see his "Milton and Renaissance Art," in *John Milton: Introductions,* ed. John Broadbent (Cambridge, 1973), pp. 186–207. For Harold Segel, the epics of Ariosto and Spenser were essentially mannerist, in contrast to the baroque epics of Tasso and Milton (*The Baroque Poem: A Comparative Survey* [New York, 1974]). Sypher describes Spenser and Botticelli as masters of "the renaissance style of decorative isolation"; Milton's *Nativity Ode* and *Lycidas* are mannerist works; *Paradise Lost* is an exemplar of the high baroque; *Paradise Regained* belongs with Racine's *Berenice* as a "late-baroque encounter of opposing spiritual forces" (*Four Stages,* pp. 87, 106, 205, 289). For critiques of the baroque as a literary category, see René Wellek, "Concept of the Baroque in Literary Scholarship," *JAAC* 5 (1946): 77–100; and Rosemond Tuve, "Baroque and Mannerist Milton?" *Milton Studies in Honor of Harris Francis Fletcher* (Urbana, Ill. 1961), pp. 209–225.

spirit and the senses, a "confusion of reality and illusion," and the fragmentation of reality, consciousness, and time. Roy Daniells emphasizes the opposition between mannerist uncertainty and the "somewhat forced alliance of faith and reason that characterizes Baroque." Harold B. Segel contrasts the mannerist "sense of dissolution" and fragmentation, and its emphasis on the irreconcilable dualism of man's nature, with the unified vision of baroque and its reintegration of flesh and spirit.[5]

Though recent criticism still tends to interpret the characteristics of a period style in terms of a contemporary world view, this approach has not passed unchallenged, and several of its defenders have found it necessary to introduce qualifications. Segel endeavors to "delineate the contours of both a Baroque Weltanschauung and a Baroque aesthetic," but advances his views with caution. In contrast to earlier critics, who associated the metaphysical or mannerist style with the disintegration of the older, more harmonious world order, Frank J. Warnke maintains that the metaphysical poetry of English and continental writers alike was "based implicitly on a world-view which assumes the validity of universal correspondences or analogies which relate everything to everything else, a view which assumes also a solidly hierarchical arrangement of entities in a rationally comprehensible universe." Even though "the old world-view had become untenable in a straightforward form" by the middle of the seventeenth century, the "unitive impulses" underlying metaphysical poetry had not become extinct; and in England "a number of expedients manifest themselves in what amounts to an unconscious re-formulation of the bases of metaphysical style." In a study of baroque style Lowry Nelson, Jr., argues that the reconstruction of the world view underlying a period style ought to be based primarily on stylistic analysis rather than on cultural history: "The process of isolating characteristic features, relating them to poetic structure, and defining the style of a period cannot but entail the gradual discovery of a world-view." Though one may glean "hints and guesses" from "social and cultural history," these are apt to "become *idées fixes* or molds into which poems are forced to fit."[6]

5. Sypher, *Four Stages*, pp. 33–34, 102, 116–117, 185. De Mourgues, "The European Background to Baroque Sensibility," in *From Donne to Marvell*, ed. Boris Ford, *The Pelican Guide to English Literature*, vol. 3 (Harmondsworth, Middlesex, and Baltimore, 1970), pp. 89–97. Daniells, "Milton and Renaissance Art," pp. 188, 190, 196. Segel, *Baroque Poem*, pp. 62–65.
6. Segel, *Baroque Poem*, Warnke, "Metaphysical Poetry and the European Con-

2

Having conjured up the apparitions of mannerist and baroque sensibility, the *Zeitgeist* has brought us full circle: we must end where we began—with the perilous attractions of an interdisciplinary theme. At first glance, few subjects would seem more specialized than seventeenth-century rhetoric. Yet, for many of our contemporaries, its roots are almost as extensive as those of an ombù tree: to uncover them the literary historian must defy property laws and excavation rights. We have already watched him hard at work in the fields of his neighbors, digging up the root-system with hand-spade or bulldozer, tracing the the phenomenology of style through art history, the history of science, the history of ideas. Unfortunately we cannot follow him further afield as he pursues his subject through anthropology and epistemology to the foggy water-meadows of *Geistesgeschichte*. In effect he has extended the context of seventeenth-century criticism well toward the outer limits of universal history—an appropriate tribute to the baroque vision of time and space.

However strained these interpretations may seem, they usually contain a substantial core of truth. But it is too late to begin a hunt for the occasional pearl in the pile of oyster shells, and we must conclude instead by noting some of the methodological difficulties implicit in this approach.

To describe the characteristics of a period style is far easier than to analyze its meaning or to trace its origins. To seek its causes in the sensibility or world view of a period seems plausible to many of our contemporaries. Nevertheless this is merely one of several alternative possibilities, and it has been partly compromised by ambiguous terminology. *Weltanschauung* and *sensibility* are as hard to pin down as *wit* and *taste*. Too, the various meanings of *style*[7] in Renaissance and modern criticism are seemingly inexhaustible. In the sixteenth and

text," in *Metaphysical Poetry*, ed. Malcolm Bradbury and David Palmer (Bloomington and London, 1971), pp. 270–271. Nelson, "The Baroque Style" in *Key Essays on Metaphysical Poetry and the Major Metaphysical Poets*, ed. Frank Kermode (Greenwich, Conn., 1969), pp. 95–96. On Warnke's discussion of world view, cf. Marjorie Nicolson, *op. cit.*, and Joseph Anthony Mazzeo, "A Critique of Some Modern Theories of Metaphysical Poetry," *MP* 50 (1952): 88–96.

7. See David A. Hansen, "Redefinitions of *Style*, 1600–1800," in *New Aspects of Lexicography: Literary Criticism, Intellectual History, and Social Change*, ed. Howard D. Weinbrot (Carbondale and Edwardsville, Ill.; London and Amsterdam, 1972), pp. 95–116, 186–189; and Meyer Schapiro, "Style," in *Anthropology Today*, ed. A. L. Kroeber (Chicago, 1953), pp. 387–412.

seventeenth centuries it could refer not only to elocution (its normal and proper sense) but also to the design and composition of a work. The rhetorical distinction between invention and disposition (the choice of arguments and the order of their arrangement) also became blurred: the structure of a lyric or satire, the plot of a dramatic or narrative fiction, or the formal organization of an essay might be conceived primarily as a kind of presentational (or representational) schema for a process of inquiry or gradual discovery; in such cases invention and disposition would tend to coincide. Perhaps more frequently in the criticism of art than of literature, the design or idea of a work might be described either as invention or as composition. The term *invention* also designated certain traditional elements of style. Virtually any kind of correspondence or similitude—allegories and emblems, metaphors and conceits—might be described as inventions. Though tropes conventionally pertained to elocution, they could also serve as arguments from analogy. The practice of transferring the terminology of rhetoric to other arts and sciences enhanced its ambiguity; it acquired new shades of meaning in these altered contexts.[8] Finally, the traditional schemas for analyzing levels of style— based as they are on social levels and on a hierarchy of themes and genres—are often too general to be of much practical value for modern criticism; the student of the *genus grande* or *genus humile* must perforce distinguish between several modes of each. The ambiguities of other stylistic labels—Ciceronian and anti-Ciceronian, Petrarchan and anti-Petrarchan, Attic and Asiatic, Senecan, metaphysical, Renaissance, mannerist, baroque—are already familiar to us.

3

Although the notion that a period style originates in the world view of the period may seem plausible in the context of Romantic aesthetics, it provides a dubious frame of reference for literary criticism. The principal hazards are methodological. Instead of basing its arguments on established facts, this approach takes for granted the very thesis it ought to demonstrate. Moreover, its fundamental assumptions are often derived from other fields; whether applied to literature or other arts, they are dogmas of cultural history. On the whole,

8. Cf. Alberti's application of rhetorical terminology to the arts of design (in *Della pittura*) and Bacon's adaptation of rhetorical terms to scientific method (in *The Advancement of Learning*).

it has tended to obscure rather than illuminate the interrelationships between seventeenth-century thought and style.

The correlation between syntax and *Weltanschauung* in particular has been greatly exaggerated. To associate the structure of a Ciceronian period with belief in the Ptolemaic cosmos and in a hierarchical model of society seems convincing only as metaphor; the image of the world as a complex sentence is a novel variation on the commonplace of the world as a book. Such metaphors are not necessarily reversible: one cannot assume that every book is a cosmic symbol, every ladder an emblem of the scale of creatures, or every well-rounded sentence an epitome of the universe.

For those who assume a causal relationship between the structure of a world view and that of a sentence, it is tempting to associate the fragmentation of syntax with the disintegration of society and the dissolution of the orthodox cosmology. The inferences drawn from mannerist and baroque style are apt to be no less cosmic in extension and scarcely more probable. Chiaroscuro becomes a symbol of doubt and uncertainty—the universal solvents of systems—or a correlative of mystical theology, dissolving the flesh in ecstasies. One must look hard, however, to find *formal* incoherence in Donne's classic statement of the theme of universal incoherence.

> And new Philosophy calls all in doubt,
> The Element of fire is quite put out;
> The Sun is lost, and th' earth, and no mans wit
> Can well direct him where to looke for it.
> And freely men confesse that this world's spent,
> When in the Planets, and the Firmament
> They seeke so many new; they see that this
> Is crumbled out againe to his Atomies.
> 'Tis all in peeces, all cohaerence gone;
> All just supply and all Relation:
> Prince, Subject, Father, Sonne, are things forgot,
> For every man alone thinkes he hath got
> To be a Phoenix, and that then can bee
> None of that kinde, of which he is, but hee.
> This is the worlds condition now, and now
> She that should all parts to reunion bow,
> She that had all Magnetique force alone,
> To draw, and fasten sundred parts in one;
> . . . .
> Shee, shee is dead; shee's dead: when thou knowst this,
> Thou knowst how lame a cripple this world is.

> And learn'st thus much by our Anatomy,
> That this worlds generall sickenesse doth not lie
> In any humour, or one certaine part;
> But as thou sawest it rotten at the heart.[9]

For many critics this passage sounds the death knell of the Renaissance world order. The bell tolls for a dying cosmology as well as for Elizabeth Drury. Despite the ingenuity with which Donne reverses the roles of microcosm and macrocosm, making the lesser cosmos seem the greater and the great world seem the small—extolling Elizabeth as the *anima mundi* and reducing the world to "the Microcosme of her"—he is actually lamenting the dissolution of the traditional world view. His principal topics—"The sicknesses of the World," the "Decay of nature," "Disformity of parts," "Disorder in the world," and "the want of correspondence of heaven and earth"—diametrically counter the commonplaces usually exploited in praise of nature: the beauty and order of the world and its resemblance to its maker.[10]

It would be a mistake, however, to isolate these motifs from their context or to exaggerate the importance of the passage on "new Philosophy." Donne is writing as poet and rhetorician rather than as an epistemologist; like Pauline allusions to vain philosophy, his reference to universal doubt and the conflict of rival philosophies reinforces the claims of faith. Because he draws so extensively on the thought of his own times, because he manages so cleverly to make ancient commonplaces look like new and startling discoveries, it is easy to forget that his poem is a meditation on the most traditional of themes and that his cosmological allusions are subordinated to an exhortation familiar to virtually every medieval or Renaissance poet:

> Repeyreth hom fro worldly vanyte.
>
> Her is non hoom, her nis but wildernesse;
> Forth, pilgrim, forth! Forth, beste, out of thy stal![11]

9. "An Anatomy of the World: The First Anniversary," *Poetical Works*, pp. 213–214.

10. There is a paradoxical mixture of sophistry and dogma in Donne's rhetorical technique. Like the sophistic orator, he can make small appear great, and vice versa, but this deliberate illusionism serves not only as a basis for contrasting Elizabeth's virtues with the vices of the world but also as a device for emphasizing the superior nobility of the soul to the world itself. Bacon appeals to the same *topos* in his discussion of poetry: "the world being in proportion inferior to the soul" (*SW*), p. 244.

11. Chaucer, *Troilus and Criseyde* and "Truth: Balade de Bon Conseyl," *The Complete Works of Geoffrey Chaucer*, ed. F. N. Robinson (Boston, New York, 1933), pp. 564, 631.

Though many of Donne's allusions are contemporary, the arguments they support are conventional and the attitudes they reflect, orthodox. By a series of hyperboles the poet adapts each of these arguments to the praise of Elizabeth Drury; but collectively they serve the ends of consolation and moral persuasion. As a sequence of variations on the theme of *contemptus mundi* they function as *suasoriae* ("hortatory arguments") to despise the world for the sake of heaven—and, on the same grounds, they are intended as arguments of comfort:

> nothing
> Is worth our travaile, griefe, or perishing,
> But those rich joyes, which did possesse her heart,
> Of which she's now partaker, and a part.

Pathological imagery seems inevitable in a postmortem, and in "An Anatomie of the World" one would expect to encounter images of disease and decay, developed with characteristic ingenuity. ("How witty's ruine!"—as Donne himself remarked.) Consumption, ague, lethargy, hectic fever, cardiac degeneration—any one of these maladies could be fatal in the world's old age; to these one must add cerebral concussion and other injuries suffered in infancy:

> Then, as mankinde, so is the worlds whole frame
> Quite out of joynt, almost created lame.
> . . . .
> The world did in her cradle take a fall,
> And turn'd her braines, and tooke a generall maime,
> Wronging each joynt of th'universall frame.

From these and from similar tropes in satire and tragedy, critics have constructed a stereotype of the late-Renaissance world view and imposed it categorically on cultural history and on the interpretation of period styles. Because the world is out of joint, syntax must be likewise disjointed, space and time dislocated, the human figure wrenched into postures that would have daunted a martyr. With the breakdown of the old cosmology, literary structures must also disintegrate: prose style into aphorism and epigram, poetry into a sequence of conceits. Literary taste tends to prefer variety to uniformity, multiplicity to unity, informality to formal design, and briefer or relatively unstructured modes of presentation—journals and diaries, essays and epistles, *sylvae* or miscellanies, meditations and "pious ejaculations," loosely organized collections of lyrics or epigrams, anthologies—to longer and more integrated poetic genres. The incoherence of the cosmos is mirrored in the confusion of style. The sickness of the age may be expressed in terms of dislocated vision as well as disjointed syntax. The "unreal" space and uncanonical proportions of mannerist art express an awareness of epistemological crisis, or unresolved tensions between sense and reason or between flesh and spirit. This approach achieved its *reductio ad absurdum* in the suggestion that the greatest of mannerist painters suffered from astigmatism.

4

Criticism of the baroque style also demonstrates a tendency to project stereotypes of seventeenth-century society upon its literature and art. *Contrapposti* become symbols of historical or cultural dialectic, expressions of political or theological conflict. The tension (or *Spannung*) in a baroque poem or painting mirrors the spiritual tensions of the age. "The baroque age was torn between extremes," writes Carl J. Friedrich. "The worldliness and *Sinnenfreude* of the Renaissance turned to coarse materialism and carnal debauch, while the philosophical and scholarly inquiries of humanism led to skepticism and scientific discovery. On the other hand the religious protest against renaissance and humanism, which Reformation and Counter-Reformation share, intensified otherworldly beliefs." In these "conflicting attitudes" he finds a primary source of the "ideas and feelings which animated the baroque artist." In contrast to the "debonair worldliness of the Renaissance, reflected in the luminous harmony of the paintings of Raphael, baroque was tormented by doubts, shot through with conflicts and tension." Friedrich's views are shared by many literary critics, though the latter are more likely to emphasize the integrative power of the baroque style and its ability to contain and resolve the siege of contraries.[12]

Attempts to associate metaphysical wit with belief in universal analogy seem more plausible. Nevertheless these also tend to be excessive in their claims, and they are subject to some of the same objections that can be raised against efforts to explain other aspects of seventeenth-century style in terms of a contemporary world view. In literature at least (not to speak for art history) the characteristics of a period style can for the most part be satisfactorily explained by literary principles.

12. Friedrich, "Baroque in Life and Letters," in *Metaphysical Poets*, ed. Kermode, pp. 80–81. Cf. Sypher, *Four Stages*, pp. 34, 184–185.

There is no need to invoke the "spirit of the age" as a *deus ex machina* to solve the problems of the literary historian. To appeal to a hypothetical *Weltanschauung* as remote or proximate cause seems perilously close to begging the question. Writers naturally used contemporary styles to express their views on society, religion, or cosmology; but neither world view nor politics determined the characteristics of style. One does not have to believe literally (if that is the right word) in a *mundus symbolicus* to use symbols effectively, or regard the world itself as an emblem and nature as a hieroglyph to compose an emblem book. Some writers did believe in an emblematic universe, but the majority of Renaissance emblems are based on analogies that readers must have regarded as ingenious fancies.

Similarly, it is most likely putting things backward to seek the origins of metaphysical wit in the concept of the world as metaphor or in the theory of universal analogy. (The roots of *concettismo* are to be found in the role of *ingenium*—natural ability or talent—in the invention of arguments and discovery of analogies; the major treatise on this subject—Emanuele Tesauro's *Il Cannocchiale aristotelico*—was strongly influenced by Aristotle's *Rhetoric*.) Some of the writers of metaphysical poetry and prose did believe in cosmic correspondences and sometimes based their conceits on traditional Hermetic analogies, yet they also employed analogies that they must have regarded as little more than fantastic inventions. In much the same way the use of antitheses or *contrapposti* could heighten and intensify the representation of virtually any kind of conflict—moral or intellectual, political or spiritual; but essentially these were a means for representing conflict, not the effects of conflict. In each of these cases some modern critics seem to have mistaken rhetorical expression, the deliberate adaptation of style to subject, for historical causation. In their view, it would seem, the choice of style and the power of expression belonged less to the individual poet than to the spirit to the times.

To allow for the historical conditioning of style while avoiding the excesses of the cultural-historical approach is difficult; it is not surprising that the literary historian occasionally loses his balance. He must in fact make his way along the sharpest of blades—the edge of Occam's razor—keeping strictly to those causes or principles that seem necessary. For the analysis of literary styles the concept of a world view has been both unnecessary and misleading. The notion of a period sensibility is attractive but too ambiguous to be reliable. Attempts to correlate changing tastes in style with philosophical or scientific movements have clarified the relationship between language and method—and the need for a scientific discourse independent of the technical vocabulary of school philosophy but also free from the rhetorical excesses of the Ciceronian and Senecan styles—but these are more relevant to the history of science and philosophy than to the literature of the imagination. Finally, analogies between the styles of the verbal and visual arts seem attractive in theory but often disappointing in execution; the literary critic is usually an amateur in the field of art history, and it is disturbing to find the same poet's style characterized alternatively as Renaissance, mannerist, and baroque.

It would be fanatical, however, to insist on the autonomy of style: to dismiss the *geistesgeschichtliche* approach as erudite charlatanism or *docta ignorantia* would be too radical. Nevertheless, if the literary historian is to apply this method judiciously, he must be aware of its defects as well as its merits. First, it tends to divert attention from the qualities of a particular writer to those of a period style, from the concrete work of art to a hypothetical construct as paradigm. (An increasing number of critics have preferred, therefore, to concentrate on the technique of a particular author or, more narrowly, on stylistic analysis of a single poem or essay.) Second, many of the images and concepts commonly regarded as characteristic of the late Renaissance were inherited from earlier periods. The image of the world upside-down is older than Chaucer. The decay of nature and the old age of the world are commonplaces familiar to St. Cyprian and the author of *Second Esdras*.[13] The progressive decadence of human society, and of mankind in general, was implicit in the myth of the four world ages. The doctrine of cosmic correspondences and the concept of the world as metaphor are no less venerable—and critics who regard them as determinants of seventeenth-century style must explain why they should flower so late. Perhaps this approach has taken too literally the analogies so frequently drawn between the artistry of the cosmos and the composition of a poem or painting, which heighten the dignity and nobility of art.

5

The degree to which the "epistemological crisis" of the late Renaissance influenced the style (as distinct from the content) of literature is more controversial than the influence of world view on mannerist and

13. Richard Foster Jones, *Ancients and Moderns: A Study of the Rise of the Scientific Movement in Seventeenth Century England*, 2nd ed. (Berkeley and Los Angeles, 1965), pp. 23, 279n.

baroque styles. Under the influence of Ramism, a speaker might turn
to logic for the choice and arrangement of his arguments and to rhetoric for the principles of style and delivery, but unless he was addressing an exceptionally learned and unusually patient audience, he
would have to resort to a crypsis ("concealment" or "dissimulation")
of method, suppressing or abbreviating certain stages in his argument.[14] On controversial issues he might aspire to probability, but
rarely to certainty. The rigorous inductive methods of the Baconian
tradition and the quasi-mathematical demonstrations of the Cartesians would be almost as unsuitable for oratory as for poetic fiction.
As Milton himself observed, the methods of the poet must differ from
those of the logician. A poet might imitate the process of discovery, or
the tension between doubt and faith, or dialectical conflict. But if he
aspired to certainty, he must seek it from another discipline—from
established scientific doctrines and philosophical systems or the dogmas of the orthodox faith—though all these were being challenged by
his contemporaries. Like the methods of the rhetorician, the techniques of the poet could produce a plausible likeness of truth, but
they could not, of themselves, establish truth. Verisimilitude and
probability were concerns of method and style; the truth (if the poet
sought to convey it) must reside primarily in the content rather than
in the method of his poem. Moreover, in conveying doctrines that he
believed to be true, the poet might deliberately sacrifice probability
and verisimilitude for the sake of the marvellous, as in allegory and
some of the more extravagant baroque conceits. Conversely, he could
invest falsehood with the appearance of truth and make fiction seem
like fact.

In considering the influence of the "epistemological crisis" of the
late Renaissance on poetic method and prose style, one should guard

14. Cf. Ong, *Ramus*, pp. 252–254. Ramus treats the "procedure" or "use" observed by poets, orators, and historians "as 'dissimulation in method' (*de crypticis
methodi*), styling it also simply dissimulation (*crypsis*), imperfect method, and word-
reversal (*hysterologia*)." When the poet "sets out to sway the people, the many-headed
monster," he "deceives ... in all sorts of ways," such as beginning *in medias res* and
"getting on to the end by some equivocal and unexpected dodge." As Ong points out,
the "uncomplimentary view which Ramus takes of the 'people' . . . is also extended to
the poets, orators, and historians, for these all have as their chief objective not teaching, but delighting and moving. This qualifies them as deceivers ... not because they
do not teach, . . . but because they do so in such a roundabout and underhand way.
They 'ambush' their audience into drawing conclusions which the audience has no
inclination to draw."
According to the *New English Dictionary* (s.v. "cryptic"), a *cryptic syllogism* is "a
syllogism of which the premises are not fully or explicitly stated."

against oversimplifying either the philosophical or the literary aspects of the problem and its solutions. The epistemologists themselves differed in their appraisal of the crisis and in their response to it. Some drew a sharp distinction between the methods of proof, discovery, or expression appropriate to the natural sciences, to moral or political philosophy, to matters of faith and religion, or to the requirements of learned or common citizens. Their assessments of the imagination diverged, as did their views on mathematical method, experimental method, inductive and deductive logic, the possibility of certainty, the utility of the syllogism, the value of probability, the origin of ideas, methods of invention and demonstration, the value of the rhetorical commonplaces (or topics of invention), and the use of figurative language and mythological fable.

The epistemologists' views on language were conditioned by their conceptions of methodology and cannot be considered in isolation from these conceptions. The demand for mathematically exact language was the inevitable concomitant of the demand for a mathematically exact method of demonstration—a method that belonged to the scientist and the philosopher rather than to the poet or the orator. Though some epistemologists endeavored (with limited success) to impose their linguistic reforms on the latter, they were, in fact, demanding the impossible. Though the poet and orator might clip their periods, prune their epithets and anaphoras, and expunge their metaphors, equivoques, and mythological allusions, they could never hope to achieve the rigorous certainty of a geometrical demonstration or a scientific experiment. The poet or orator could no more aspire to the rigorous logic of mathematical method than he could hope to adhere strictly to the methods of scholastic or Ramist logic. If he attempted as some did to follow the Ramist method, he must nevertheless, as Milton recognized, employ a "crypsis" of method—just as under the Aristotelian system he must normally use the enthymeme rather than the perfect syllogism or make a highly restricted use of the example instead of a thorough induction. As Milton observed at the end of his chapter on method, poets and orators could most profitably follow the principles of method peculiar to their own disciplines.

Insofar as method concerns the arrangement of material proceeding from what is more clearly to what is less clearly known, the method of an oration would appear to concern its disposition; the method of a dramatic or narrative poem, the construction of the plot and arrangement of incidents; the method of a lyric, the logical and affective development of its arguments and images. In a didactic verse-essay or philosophical poem, the poet might attempt to approximate the methods of the philosopher, but he would usually be compelled to amplify or ornament certain points and to diminish or omit other stages in the development of his argument. He must remove or disguise much of the scaffolding, the underpinning, the joinings, and contignations that were a necessary though unsightly part of the philosopher's demonstrative proofs.

Even though the impact of the epistemological crisis on poetic and rhetorical method was real, its nature, significance, and degree may easily be exaggerated. In the hands of many of the principal writers of the late-sixteenth and seventeenth centuries, skepticism frequently functions as a traditional rhetorical *topos*, reinforcing Stoic or Christian commonplaces concerning the limitations of the human condition and in particular the restricted scope of human knowledge. In Donne's "Anniversaries," the doubts fostered by the new philosophy serve as an argument for the misery of the human condition and for contempt of the world. In *Paradise Lost* the uncertainties of astronomical knowledge reinforce the argument for intellectual humility—the exhortation to be "lowly wise" and the injunction against the pursuit of forbidden knowledge. In *Samson Agonistes*, initial doubt, despair, and impatience serve as the ethical and emotional precondition for the dramatic progression toward their contraries—ultimate faith, hope, and patience. Browne and Burton convert the scientific treatise into a vehicle of moral and religious persuasion—a meditation on death and the vanity of worldly renown, and a satire on human folly.

6

With certain notable exceptions, such as the literature of "private" reflection, the intellectual and spiritual crises of the late Renaissance appear to have made less impression on the style of poetry than on its content.

Like its counterparts in prose, the poetry of reflection often varied widely in organization and style. On the one hand, the method and structure of a meditation, in prose or poetry alike, could appear so loose and informal as to seem a deliberate denial of method.[15] On the

15. For criticism of the meditative tradition in the sixteenth and seventeenth centuries, see Louis L. Martz, *The Poetry of Meditation*, rev. ed. (New Haven and London,

other hand, they might be as systematically and methodically conceived as those of an oration. Like the latter, even the most informal of meditations might be designed to teach, delight, and move—in short, to persuade—and on occasion even an informal meditation might make copious use of rhetorical tropes and schemes. Even though presented as no more than an aid to private reflection or a record of personal opinion, it was often intended for a public audience; like an actor on the contemporary stage, the author expected his soliloquy to be overheard. Occasionally it was composed for oral presentation—just as (conversely) a formal oration would be written not for actual recitation but for an audience of readers. Thus Croll's useful distinction between the essay style and the oratorical style apparently needs qualification.

The meditation and the essay often overlap, in content as in manner and style, as both Bacon and Montaigne recognized. Though critics are justified in emphasizing the interdependence of the essay style and the intellectual crises of the late Renaissance, one cannot limit its associations to a single philosophical approach, or even to philosophy in general; many of its principal features can be explained largely on specifically literary grounds. The frequent disavowal of dogmatism and the pretense of expressing no more than the temporary opinions of a private individual who makes no claims to certitude or even consistency seem to reflect contemporary intellectual attitudes: the stance is skeptical and relativistic, distrustful of authority, aware of the deceits of reason as well as imagination, and unwilling to rely either on traditional philosophical systems or on general opinion. While in some cases traditional systems and general opinion are avoided, in other cases, the essayist, like the rhetor and the dialectician, may appeal to them. Like the dialogue, the essay could reflect a variety of viewpoints, serving the empiricist or the rationalist as well as the skeptic; and like the dialogue it sometimes approached the frontiers of drama. Portraying the "wily subleties and refluxes of man's thoughts from within" (*CP*, p. 670), it could on occasion acquire the characteristics of monody, or literary discourse by a single speaker as in dramatic monologues.

As Croll recognized, the essay style is admirably adapted not only to the representation of doubt but also to the quest for certitude; the

---

1962); Lewalski, *Protestant Poetics*, and *Donne's "Anniversaries" and the Poetry of Praise: The Creation of a Symbolic Mode* (Princeton, 1973).

deceptively loose method of Montaigne's *Essays* differs as radically from the rigorous analytical method of Descartes's *Meditations* as Bacon's essays differ from those of Addison and Steele. Some essays are deliberately digressive, even capricious in method, sedulously avoiding the appearance of premeditated or systematic order, introducing topics seemingly at random or by association. By suppressing the traces of formal disposition, the author produces the illusion of spontaneity; the sequence of arguments and images appears to follow his natural train of thought or the idiosyncratic sport of private fantasy. Instead of first inventing his arguments and afterwards arranging them methodically in accordance with the principles of art, he creates the impression of inventing them on the spur of the moment during the actual process of composition. Another essayist may be more rigorous in argument and organization. Though his method may be introspective and subjective insofar as it purports to be an analysis and critique of the ideas in the author's own mind, it makes little or no pretense of representing the natural flow of thought, the energy of the imagination, or the personal idiosyncracies of the author. On the contrary, it is an intense and highly concentrated examination of the nature of knowledge and the grounds of certitude.

Other essays bear a closer resemblance to the topics and commonplace books of the rhetorician and dialectician. They tend to present an abundance of matter with comparatively little effort to sift and reorganize it. The author may mass quotations and topical headings, citing authorities and aphorisms or summarizing arguments that could be advanced on either side of a question, but without developing or elaborating them—and sometimes without taking a definite stand himself. To a considerable degree he is still thinking in terms of the traditional *copia rerum* of rhetorical theory while avoiding *copia verborum*, copiousness of words.

However embarrassing the new science and new philosophy might be for the school-divine, the poet had ample license to ignore them altogether, attack them, or adapt them to his own ends. Milton introduced the Copernican hypothesis into his Ptolemaic universe in order to bring philosophy down from heaven to earth, pointing a moral not irrelevant to the curiosity-prone hero of *Paradise Lost*: "Solicit not thy thoughts with matters hid." Donne adapted the new systems to the theme of *contemptus mundi*, but he generally treated them just as he treated the more traditional learning, as a source for arguments and images. In much of his secular poetry he parodies the scholastic disputation, but to regard this sportive sophistic as "philosophical method" is to make earnest of game. The ingenuity he displays in demonstrating paradoxes is a kind of dialectical exhibitionism. Like his extravagant analogies, his arguments merely appear to prove the thesis they are demonstrating; they are, for the most part "idolisms," and he does not, of course, expect them to be taken seriously. Their primary function is to display his own *ingenium* and his versatility in inventing.

7

Though critics have rightly emphasized the seventeenth-century preoccupation with the mind and conscience of the private individual and with his personal quest for certainty, they have been less successful in analyzing its causes and its implications for literary style. The causes for this preoccupation have been plausibly sought in Reformation and Counter-Reformation spirituality, but also in a variety of philosophical or scientific influences: nominalism and idealism; empiricism and rationalism; Stoicism, Neo-Platonism, or skepticism; relativism and psychological theory; the resoluto-compositive method; and the theory of humors. Among predominantly literary influences, scholars have emphasized the tradition of self-revelation in the familiar epistle and the dramatic soliloquy; self-examination in autobiography and the literature of meditation; the tendency toward individuation in poetic and rhetorical theories concerning the variety of emotions and types of character; and the analysis of moral categories in the extensive literature on virtues and vices.

Contemporary efforts to dramatize the movements of the mind and to portray the natural processes of thought in a natural manner are believed to have been partly influenced by contemporary literary doctrines. Some critics have stressed classical or patristic influences, the literature of the Latin Silver Age or the example of St. Augustine's *Soliloquies*. Others have detected the influence of humanist pedagogical theories concerning the natural variety of temperaments (or "personality differences") discernable among students, and the distinctive styles and characters of various authors. Still others have associated the literature of introspection with a reaction against humanist rhetorical doctrine.

Perhaps each of these explanations represents a partial approximation of the truth, providing only a tenuous foundation for large-scale generalization. The element of self-portraiture, the dramatic presentation of the movements of the mind, and the emphasis on the personal tastes and idiosyncrasies of the author are comparatively rare in stricter philosophical or scientific inquiries, although they sometimes occur, in varying degrees of frequency and intensity, in devotional literature. The mind-searching of the secular essayist or reflective poet frequently parallels the soul-searching traditional in Catholic and Protestant meditative techniques; indeed it may have been partly influenced by the latter.

In purely dramatic terms, the choice of monologue rather than dialogue as the vehicle for the process of inquiry or for dialectical conflict is not irrelevant to the characterization of the authorial persona. In the dialogue or debate different viewpoints are assigned to various characters, but in the monologue all points of view must be represented by a single dramatic persona: the narrator himself must present them. Dialectical process appears, accordingly, as inner conflict, and the process of inquiry as a personal quest. The treatise itself often resembles a private meditation or a spiritual autobiography. In such a work the ideal narrator would be a man of open mind and flexible opinions, tolerant of a wide variety of viewpoints, undogmatic to the point of inconsistency, capable of arguing for or against the same thesis or hypothesis. There is a characteristic persona for the essayist as for the satirist; and this persona displays on occasion several of the features conventionally associated with mannerism, though some of these result at least in part from generic demands rather than from the author's predisposition. For example, the impression of inner conflict and unresolved personal tensions, the multiple and uncoordinated perspectives, the shifting point of view all follow necessarily from an author's choice of a monologue form rather than a dialogue structure.

The most significant features of this "drama of inquiry" appear in its development of the oldest of philosophical and poetic themes: the interrelated motifs of self-knowledge and the quest for truth. The quest for truth is a traditional theme in allegory; whether seafarer, pilgrim, or knight-errant, the quester was commonly interpreted as a fictional symbol of mankind. (Dante, Odysseus, and Aeneas were all regarded as contemplative heroes.) The quest for self-knowledge was usually conceived in terms of the nature and end of man, the greatness and misery of the human condition—though interpretations range from Epicurean to Stoic, and from Calvinist to theosophical. In both motifs the individual is overshadowed by the concept of man in general, that "ingens hominis archetypus gigas" (*CP*, p. 57) whom

Milton locates among the stars or beside the waters of Lethe. In the "drama of the mind" represented in much of the prose and poetry of the earlier seventeenth century, the quester has not infrequently become a single individual, the author himself, writing or affecting to write in *propria persona*. It is a personal quest; and among its discoveries (or rediscoveries) not the least is privacy.

8

The representation of inquiry and discovery is itself essentially mimetic in mode, and the authorial persona is himself in a significant degree a dramatic fiction.[16] To some extent such representation is more characteristic of writers belonging to the late sixteenth century or the first half of the seventeenth (Montaigne, Browne, Burton, Donne) than of the Restoration period. Moreover, it is only one of several modes of delineating the search for truth or emphasizing the difficulties or even the impossibility of achieving certainty. The same poet or prose writer might assume a private and introspective mode on one occasion and a public mode on another, and both stances are in contrast to the collective, cooperative pursuit of truth advocated by Bacon and partly implemented by the Royal Society. In exploring himself as an individual, the author may be reasoning inductively from particular to universal, from the individual self to the nature and condition of mankind in general. Though the emphasis varies with different authors, there is on the whole continuous interplay between subjective and objective viewpoints and between universal and particular.[17]

16. Jackson I. Cope comments that "the distinction among levels of authorial awareness of his audience and of himself in Savile's work forces upon one ... an awareness that rhetoric was succumbing to drama, that the orator was become actor." Cf. Savile's remarks on Montaigne: "'He let his *Mind* have its full *Flight*, and sheweth by a generous kind of *Negligence* that he did not Write for Praise, but to give the World a true Picture of himself and of Mankind'" ("Modes of Modernity in Seventeenth-Century Prose," *MLQ* 31 [1970]: 92–111). Robert Adolph contrasts the kinds of *mimesis* associated with the classical plain style and with libertine prose. The former "demanded an artificial copy of an Ideal Soul, the Self or an ideal Attic or Roman or London gentleman or, in Jonson's comedies, the Typical Gull or Mistress. ... The libertine writer, on the other hand, reflects a different ideal of *mimesis*," the roots of which (as Erich Auerbach has demonstrated in *Mimesis*) "lie in the Judeo-Christian experience" (*The Rise of Modern Prose Style*, pp. 157–158).

17. See William H. Youngren, "Generality, Science and Poetic Language in the Restoration," *ELH* 35 (1968): 158–187; "Generality in Augustan Satire," in *In Defense of Reading*, ed. Reuben A. Brower and Richard Poirier (New York, 1962), pp. 206–234; and "Conceptualism and Neoclassic Generality," *ELH* 47 (1980): 705–740.

At the end of the seventeenth century, Bacon's distinction between a method of teaching and a method of inquiry was still vital for Locke; and in the following century the rival claims of eloquence and philosophy were no less significant for Hume. "I pretend not," Locke declares, "to teach, but to inquire," following "nature in its ordinary method" in order to trace and discover simple ideas in "their rise, progress, and gradual improvements" (*Essay*, pp. 73–74; cf. pp. 3, 10). His work consists rather in invention than in demonstration. Hume, in turn, compares two sorts of moral philosophers, whom he calls the scientists of human nature. The first considers man as "born for action" and attempts to paint virtue "in the most amiable colors; borrowing all helps from poetry and eloquence, and treating their subject in an easy and obvious manner, and such as is best fitted to please the imagination, and engage the affections." These philosophers "place opposite characters in a proper context; and alluring us into the paths of virtue by the views of glory and happiness, direct our steps in these paths by the soundest precepts and most illustrious examples. They make us *feel* the difference between vice and virtue; they excite and regulate our sentiments; and so they can . . . bend our hearts to the love of probity and true honor, they think, that they have fully attained the end of all their labors." The second "species of philosophers," in contrast, consider man "in the light of a reasonable rather than an active being, and endeavor to form his understanding more than cultivate his manners. They regard human nature as a subject of speculation; and with a narrow scrutiny examine it, in order to find those principles, which regulate our understanding, excite our sentiments." Such philosophers "think it a reproach to all literature, that philosophy should not yet have fixed, beyond controversy, the foundation of morals, reasoning, and criticism; and should for ever talk of truth and falsehood, vice and virtue, beauty and deformity, without being able to determine the source of these distinctions." Popular opinion, Hume protests, favors the "easy philosophy": "[the] fame of Cicero flourishes at present; but that of Aristotle is utterly decayed. . . . And Addison, perhaps, will be read with pleasure, when Locke shall be entirely forgotten."[18]

Against these views we should set those of Vico. Attacking the geometrical method in philosophy, he objects that, though "geometrical procedure" may be excellent for "demonstrating mathematical truths,"

---

18. *An Enquiry Concerning Human Understanding*, in *The English Philosophers from Bacon to Mill*, ed. Edwin A. Burtt (New York, 1939), pp. 585–586.

it may easily become a "faulty and captious way of reasoning" in subjects "unsuited to deductive treatment." Those principles of physics that are "put forward as truths on the strength of the geometrical method are not really truths," but merely "wear a semblance of probability." Moreover, this method is a hindrance to "eloquent exposition" of the subject. It enables us "to set forth matters in a purely geometrical apodeictic form" and to teach them "in a plain, unadorned way, devoid of any aesthetic charm."[19] These strictures on the geometrical method in philosophy are a counterattack against Seicento attacks on rhetoric, a reaction against the reaction against eloquence. Although Vico's target is the influence of Cartesian methodology and French scientific style (which he regards as essentially alien to the genius of the Italian language), his plea for a reunion of philosophy and eloquence stands in striking opposition to Sprat's demand for a divorce of "the knowledge of *Nature* from the Colours of Rhetorick" and a return to primitive purity and brevity and a naked, natural manner of speaking "as near the Mathematical plainness" as possible.

9

To conclude with an apology for the title of one's work may seem a breach of method, if not of manners—though in seventeenth-century eyes the world itself was upside-down. The appropriate title for this discussion has been preempted by Lévi-Strauss: "The Raw and the Cooked." Many writers of the period expressed a decided taste for the former. Echoing Plato's remarks on cookery, they professed disgust for the confections of the rhetoricians and "hatefullest disrelish" for the predigested pabulum of commonplace books. They preferred the ingredients of discourse raw, served up *au naturel* with a minimum of preparation, seasoning, and ceremony.[20] Yet they might, on occasion, devour a piece of marzipan or a methodical heading on the sly; and the ideal of style as a kind of chopped salad or *satura* was only one of several contemporary alternatives—most of them considerably more palatable. But I must leave the analogies between rhetoric

19. *Study Methods*, pp. 21–25. See Walter Jackson Bate, *From Classic to Romantic*, pp. 38–39.
20. Sir William Cornwallis, the Younger, regarded the essay as a "maner of writing" well befitting "undigested" motions (Ted-Larry Pebworth, "Not Being, But Passing: Defining the Early English Essay," *SLI* 10, no. 2 [1977]: 17–27). But Ben Jonson criticized the essayists, including "even their Master *Mountaigne*" for presenting matter, "raw, and undigested" (Trimpi, *Ben Jonson's Poems*, p. 38).

and gastronomy to others, though there is ample material in Milton alone. Instead, I have chosen a title less reminiscent of the anthropologist's field-table and more faithful to the seventeenth-century spirit of intellectual pilgrimage.

Seventeenth-century poets did not write without reflection, and though one is skeptical of recent attempts to explain their literary tastes as formed by the new science and the new philosophy, few of them could have remained indifferent to the intellectual conflicts of their age. (These were probably less keenly and less personally felt than were contemporary religious tensions, which might imperil life, limb, and livelihood, as well as the fate of the soul.) Even though they could not employ the methods of contemporary philosophy, they could adapt its doctrines or its terminology to their own ends, either facetiously or in high seriousness. More significantly, they sometimes shared its attitudes; and these, reflected in style, helped to develop a kind of rhetoric of inquiry. Although poetry—like rhetoric—could not establish the grounds of certitude, it could heighten the dramatic suspense of the search for certainty, portraying its hazards with fear or hope and investing the success or failure of the quest with passion or admiration. This interior epic—or, rather, dramatic monody— sometimes left its mark on syntax and diction or (more notably) on imagery. Alternatively smooth or rugged, easy or difficult, clear or obscure, the qualities of style could convey the serenity of achieved vision as well as the strenuous labor of attaining it: the uninterrupted prospect from the steep hill of Truth, or the circuitous and labyrinthine path to the summit.

1. Verité. *Iconologie ou Nouvelle Explication . . . Tirée des recherches & des figures de Cesar Ripa, Moralisées par J. Baudoin* (1681).

2. Verité. *Iconologie ou Nouvelle Explication . . . Tirée des recherches & des figures de Cesar Ripa, Moralisées par J. Baudoin* (1681).

3. Proteus as a symbol of truth. Achille Bocchi, *Symbolicarum Quaestionum* . . . (Bologna, 1555).

4. Eloquence. *Iconologie ou Nouvelle Explication . . . Tirée des recherches & des figures de Cesar Ripa, Moralisées par J. Baudoin* (1681).

5. Cannon and lightning-bolt as a symbol of eloquence. Achille Bocchi, *Symbolicarum Quaestionum . . .* (Bologna, 1555).

ΠΕΡΙΚΛΗΣ

6. Wisdom and eloquence. Achille Bocchi, *Symbolicarum Quaestionum*... (Bologna, 1555).

7. Chimaera as an emblem of rhetoric. Achille Bocchi,
Symbolicarum Quaestionum ... (Bologna, 1555).

8. Hercules Gallicus as a symbol of eloquence.
   Alciati . . . Emblematum liber (1531).

9. Hercules Gallicus as a symbol of eloquence.
   Alciati . . . Emblemata (1608).

10. Hercules Gallicus as a symbol of eloquence. Achille Bocchi, *Symbolicarum Quaestionum*... (Bologna, 1555).

11. Hercules Gallicus as a symbol of eloquence. Laurens van Haecht,
Mikrokosmos (Amsterdam, 1610).

Appendix:
Renaissance Emblems of Truth
and Eloquence

Among the topics discussed in the numerous mythographical and iconographical manuals of the Renaissance are commonplaces concerning rhetoric and dialectic, eloquence and truth. Of particular interest for the study of style is the relationship between naked Truth and sumptuously clad Eloquence. The two are sometimes depicted as antithetical, other times as interdependent, as the following summary of several of the more influential descriptions of Veritas and Eloquentia reveals. (In quotations, Greek words have been transliterated, and *u* and *v* have been adapted to standard modern usage.)

1

Renaissance images of truth often center on the motifs of concealment and revelation. The motif of truth hidden in a pit or a well recurs in a number of Renaissance emblem books, sometimes in association with the motto *Veritas in puteum demersa* (traditionally derived from Democritus) or with the mottoes *Veritas filia temporis* or *Veritas tempore revelatur, dissidio obruitur*.[1] In other emblems frogs are silenced by a bright light, signifying the victory of truth over sophistry or falsehood (*Emblemata*, cols. 602–604). An emblem depicting fire struck from stone signifies that truth does not appear without a great effort being made (col. 80): "sans faire grand effort, La Verité ne sort en evidence." The operation of combing flax is compared to separating truth from falsehood (col. 1098), an interpretation that Milton, in *Areopagitica*, associates with the miscellaneous seeds of the Psyche myth. In an emblem representing the differences between grammar, history, rhetoric, and philosophy, History is portrayed as nude in consonance with her simplicity and her association with truth. Rhetoric is clad in a

---

1. Arthur Henkel and Albrecht Schöne, eds., *Emblemata: Handbuch zur Sinnbildkunst des XVI. und XVII. Jahrhunderts* (Stuttgart, 1967), cols. 1816–1817.

long and ornate gown, in consonance with her resort to "venustis . . . coloribus." Dialectic (Logic) is roughly dressed and draws forth the hidden Truth from a well: "Aspera, non habitu sequitur Dialectica culto, Sagaciter verum eruens puteo abditum." Each of the three is associated with an animal: History with a winged dog, Rhetoric with a chimaera, and Dialectic with a sphynx (cols. 1537–1538).

In his description of Truth, Lilio Gyraldi cites Philostratus's account of Aletheia as a virgin appareled in white, along with Hippocrates' description of her as a beautiful woman, simply adorned:

> Veritas dea existimata a gentibus *alētheia* [Greek transliterated] à graecis vocata. Fingebatur, ut Philostratus in Amphiarao scribit, virgo niveis induta vestibus: quin et eodem authore in Heroicis, Virtutis mater effingebatur. Hippocrates verò in quadam ad Philopoemenen epistola hoc modo describit: Mulierem pulchram, magnam, simpliciter ornatam, illustrem ac splendidam, cuius oculorum orbes puro lumine nitebant, ut astrorum ac stellarum fulgorem imitari viderentur. . . . Veritas Temporis filia, & virtutis mater dicta. . . . Hanc in putei fundo delitere scripsit Democritus & ab eo Lactantius.[2]

Alciati's emblem of faith (emblem no. 9, "Fidei symbolum") portrays Honor joining hands with Truth, while Love stands between them. Although the verses refer to "nuda Veritas," the picture in the 1577 edition portrays Veritas as lightly dressed. Claude Mignault's commentary on this emblem explains that Truth is the mother of Faith, cites the descriptions of Aletheia by Philostratus and Hippocrates, and quotes Horace's verses on "naked Truth":

> Veritatem matrem habet, illam quidem nudam & simplicem, non comptam fuco aliquo, non velo tectam. Et quidem fides definitur, dictorum conventorumque constantia & veritas, quae ideò parentem habere Veritatem dicitur, & eam nudam, quòd in pactis, conventionibusque nihil fucatum esse, aut à vero alienum debeat. . . . Nuda hîc dicitur, quòd qui eam colunt, aperti sunt ac simplices, nullo modo fraudulenti, aut insidiosi, aut quòd veritatis oratio simplex esse debeat, aut quòd in luce & oculis omnium agnosci velit. Hinc Horat. I. Carm.

> *& Iustititiae soror*
> *Incorrupta Fides, nudaque Veritas.*[3]

    2. *De Deis gentium varia & multiplex historia . . . Lilio Gregorio Gyraldo Ferrariensi Auctore* (Basel, 1548), p. 37; facsimile edition in *The Renaissance and the Gods*, ed. Stephen Orgel (New York and London, 1976).
    3. *Omnia Andreae Alciati V. C. Emblemata: Cum commentariis . . . Per Claudium Minoem Divisionem* (Antwerp, 1577), pp. 82–83. Cf. Mignault's discussion of the

In his *Hieroglyphica* Pierius Valerianus interprets the sun as a hieroglyph of Truth. The myth of Proteus, in turn, symbolizes the difficulty that we experience in discovering the truth of things, confronted as we are by so many deceptive appearances, and by the tricks and subterfuges of sophists and dialecticians, which bear the outward appearance of truth.[4]

In the opinion of Vincenzo Cartari, the tripod serves as a sign of Truth, since the ancients believed that the Oracle always spoke truly. Citing the descriptions of Truth by Hippocrates and Philostratus, and Democritus's reference to Truth's concealment in a deep well until Time should draw her forth, Cartari also alludes to Alciati's emblem. Like Mignault, he maintains that Truth is painted naked in order to demonstrate that her followers are open and of good faith, or else that "toute parole de verité doit estre simple, sans fard, & faut que soit cogneuë & veuë de tout le monde."[5]

In a sculpture by Bernini, as described by Emil Mâle, Truth holds "a sunlike disk darting forth rays of light, and rests her foot on a globe."[6] Mâle notes that Cesare Ripa in his *Iconologia* (1603) similarly describes Truth as naked with "a sun in her hand and a globe beneath her feet," explaining that she must "be represented quite naked because her nature is simplicity itself" (Fig. 1). The sun signifies "that she loves the light and is herself the light," while the globe beneath her feet indicates "that she is more precious than all the riches of the world" (p. 193). This icon and its interpretation enjoyed considerable popularity. The 1758–60 Hertel edition of Ripa's *Iconologia* quotes from the 1603 edition: "Truth's nudity indicates that truth is a natural state and, like a nude person, exists without need for any artificial embellishment."[7] Similarly the English translation of Ripa's

power of Truth ("Veritatis magna vis") in his commentary on emblem no. 28 ("Tandem tandem iustitia obtinet"), pp. 149–150.

4. See *Les Hieroglyphiques de Ian-Pierre Valerian . . .*, trans. I. de Montlyart (Lyons, 1615), pp. 543, 586–587; fac. ed., Orgel, *Renaissance*.

5. See Cartari, *Les Images des Dieux*, trans. Antoine du Verdier (Lyons, 1624), pp. 191–192, 455, 470–471. Plutarch discussed the symbolism of the tripod of truth in "The E at Delphi," *Moralia*, trans. F.C. Babbitt (London, and Cambridge, Mass., 1936), 5: 211, 213.

6. *Religious Art from the Twelfth to the Eighteenth Century* (New York, 1949), p. 192.

7. See *Baroque and Rococo Pictorial Imagery: The 1758–60 Hertel Edition of Ripa's "Iconologia"*, ed. and trans. Edward A. Maser (New York, 1971), pp. 499–502.

work, published by Pierre Tempest in 1709, explains that Truth is depicted naked, "because *downright* Simplicity is natural to her." The sun in her right hand shows "her great Delight in *Clearness*." The open book in her left hand indicates "that the Truth of Things may be found in good *Authors*," while the palm symbolizes "her *Rising* the more she is depress'd." The globe beneath her foot signifies "that being *immortal*, she is the strongest of all Things in the World, and therefore tramples upon it."[8]

The 1630 edition of Ripa's *Iconologia* describes Verità in the following terms: "Una bellissima donna ignuda, tiene nella destra mano alta il Sole, il quale rimira, & con l'altra un libro aperto, e un ramo di Palma, e sotto al destro piede il globo del Mondo." Her nakedness is interpreted as a sign of her natural simplicity, on the authority of such classical authors as Aeschylus, Euripides, and Seneca: "Ignuda si rappresenta, per dinotare, che la simplicità le è naturale: onde Euripide in *Phoenissis*, dice esser semplice il parlare della Verità, nè gli fà bisogno di vane interpretationi; perciò che ella per se sola è opportuna. Il medesimo dice Eschillo, & Seneca nell' Epistola quinta, che la Verità è semplice oratione, però si fà nuda, come habbiamo detto, & non deve havere adornamento alcuno."[9]

Of the five images of Verità described in the 1630 edition, this alone is accompanied by an illustration. Truth is alternatively described as a golden-haired woman dressed in white, who holds a mirror and a pair of golden scales (Fig. 2). In a third image she is portrayed as naked but adorned with a few white veils. These indicate that verbal ornament should not obscure the essential beauty of her form, for her own intrinsic beauty is her principal adornment: "Fanciulla ignuda, con alcuni veli bianchi d'intorno, per dimostrare, che essa deve esser ricoperta, & adornata in modo con le parole, che non si levi l'apparenza del corpo suo bello, & delicato, e di se stesso più, che d'ogni altra s'adorna, & s'arrichisce." A fourth icon depicts Truth as "ignuda," holding a sun in her right hand and a timepiece ("un tempo d' horologio") in her left; as the commentary explains, this detail identifies her as the daughter of Time. Similarly, in the fifth image the naked Truth ("Giovinetta ignuda") holds an hourglass ("horologio da polvere") in her left hand, and a peach ("Persica")

8. See Ripa, *Iconologia: Or, Moral Emblems* (London, 1709), p. 78; fac. ed., Orgel, *Renaissance*.
9. *La più che Novissima Iconologia* (Padua, 1630), pt. 1, pp. 168–169.

with its foliage in her right hand, near her heart (*Iconologia* [1630], pt. 1, p. 170). According to the commentary, the peach had been an ancient hieroglyph for the heart, while its linguiform foliage served as a hieroglyph for the tongue. In signifying the conjunction of heart and tongue, it provides an appropriate symbol for Truth: "La Persica è antico Geroglifico del cuore, come la sua foglia della lingua, & si è usato sempre in molti simili proposti la similitudine, che hanno con l'una, & con l'altra, & insegna, che deve esser congiunto il cuore, & la lingua, come la Persica, & la foglia, acciòche quello, che si dice habbia forma, & apparenza di Verità."

This detail in Ripa's emblem reveals a confusion between the peach tree (*persicus* in Latin) and the *persea*. The latter, according to Plutarch, was sacred to Isis, because its fruit resembled a heart, and its leaf a tongue (*Moralia* 5:159). Hadrianus Junius introduced it in his *Emblemata* (Antwerp, 1565), specifically mentioning its consecration to Isis, and Alciati had already portrayed it in the 1531 edition of his *Emblematum liber* (*Emblemata*, cols. 236–237).

Like Ripa, Pierius Valerianus confuses the *persea* and its symbolism with the peach. Thus in book 54 of his *Hieroglyphica* (chapters 19 and 20) he represents the peach as a hieroglyph for the heart and for Truth. For Plutarch, according to Valerianus, had declared "que le Pescher estoit consacré à Isis, dautant que son fruict ressemble à un coeur humain, & la feuille à la langue." The hieroglyph of a peach with a leaf ("une pesche avec une feuille") served as the sign of Truth, inasmuch as this figure demonstrated that the tongue was conjoined with the heart (*Hieroglyphiques*, pp. 724–725).

In Achille Bocchi's emblem collection, the shape-shifting god Proteus is allegorized as an image of Truth. Depicting the attempt to seize the god during his sleep (Fig. 3), the emblem bears the title UNAM VIDENDAM VERITATEM IN OMNIB[US]. The accompanying verses illustrate the theme OPINIONIBUS SOPITIS FIRMITER / TENENDA CAPTA VERITAS:

> Quidnàm aliud Proteus, quàm Veri ipsius imago est
> Omnia vertentis sese in miracula rerum?
> Ille eadem divina hominis forma interioris,
> Quam variae illudunt facies, & Opinio fallax.[10]

10. Bocchi, *Symbolicarum Quaestionum* ... (Bologna, 1555), symb. LX, pp. cxxiiii–cxxv.

2

The power of eloquence is a recurrent motif in the emblematic literature of the Renaissance; writers and artists depicted it through a variety of symbols. The 1630 edition of Cesare Ripa's *Iconologia* includes six different representations of Eloquence, and one of Rhetoric—though without graphic illustrations. Rhetoric is portrayed as a beautiful woman, richly dressed, with a pleasant and cheerful demeanor. On the border of her garment are written the words *Ornatus persuasio*; there is a chimaera at her feet: "Donna bella, vestita riccamente, con nobile acconciatura di testa, mostrandosi allegra, & piacevole, terrà la destra mano alta & aperta, & nella sinistra uno scettro, & un libro portando nel lembo della veste scritte queste parole, *Ornatus persuasio*: & il color del viso sarà rubicondo, & alli piedi vi sarà una chimera" (*Iconologia* [1630], pt. 3, p. 19). *Ornatus persuasio* denotes the office of Rhetoric, which is to teach the art of persuasion: "di instruire altrui à parlare conveniente per persuadere." The chimaera, according to St. Gregory Nazianzen and a Greek exposition of Hesiod's *Theogony*, signifies the three traditional parts of rhetoric—judicial, demonstrative, and deliberative—symbolized respectively by the lion, the goat, and the dragon.

Rhetoric is depicted as "Fair and complaisant, because there is none so ill bred that is not sensible of the *Charms* of Eloquence. Her open Hand shews Rhetoric discourses in a more *open* Way than Logic. The Scepter, her *Sway* over Mens Minds. The Book, *Study* requisite" (*Iconologia* [1709], p. 78). The symbolism of Rhetoric's open right hand ("la destra mane alta, & aperta") derives from Zeno's contrast between the clenched fist of logic and the open palm of rhetoric: "perciòche la Rettorica discorre per le vie larghe, & dimostratrationi aperte, onde Zenone per le dita quà, & là sparse, & per le mani allargate per tal gesto la Rettorica interpretava" (*Iconologia* [1630], p. 19). Milton alludes to this commonplace in his tractate *Of Education*: "Logic . . . is to be referred to this due place with all her well-couched heads and topics, until it be time to open her contracted palm into a graceful and ornate rhetoric, taught out of the rule of Plato, Aristotle, Phalereus, Cicero, Hermogenes, Longinus" (*CP*, p. 636).

Ripa describes Eloquence as a beautiful young woman ("Giovane bella"), wearing a helmet encircled by a crown of gold. She holds a rod in her right hand, and a lightning-bolt in her left. She is dressed in purple and wears a breast-plate, but her arms are bare. Since Eloquence has no other end or intent than persuasion—and since she must persuade by alluring and moving—the beauty and ornament of her words are figured by the beauty of her countenance: "vaghissima d'aspetto, essendo l'ornamento, & la vaghezza delle parole, delle quali deve esser fecondo chi vuole persuadere altrui." Hence the Ancients had portrayed Mercury as a youth, "piacevole" and beardless; for the manners of that age conform to the style of Eloquence, which is "piacevole, audace, altera, lasciva, & confidente." Eloquence's bare arms and armored breast indicate that verbal delicacy would be powerless without doctrine and reason: "La delicatura delle parole s'insegna ancora nelle braccia ignude, le quali escono fuora dal busto armato, perche senza i fondamenti di salda Dottrina, & di ragione efficace l'Eloquenza sarebbe inerme, & impotente à conseguire il suo fine. Però si dice che la Dottrina è madre dell' Eloquenza, & della persuasione" (*Iconologia* [1630], pt. 1, p. 213). Because of their difficulty the arguments and reasonings of Doctrine are heard unwillingly and with little comprehension. When adorned with gracious words, however, they can be understood and often have the power to persuade. Eloquence is effective, therefore, in setting forth difficult arguments and in spurring the mind to passion or restraining it. It can move and incite the proud or high minded ("l'altiero"), or awake the dormant spirit of the low and lazy ("huomo basso, & pigro") with the rod of the lower and more common style of discourse, or with the sword of the middle and more ornamental style, or with the lightning of the high style ("col folgore della sublime").

In a French adaptation of Ripa's book, Eloquence is depicted in a copperplate engraving by Jacques de Bie as an armed female figure holding a lightning bolt and an open book, but the sword and the hourglass described in the text are not illustrated (Fig. 4). Jean Baudoin's moral commentary explains that Eloquence is portrayed as

> jeune, belle, & armée, à cause qu'elle ne se propose point d'autre fin que la persuasion; dequoy ne pouvant venir à bout que par le moyen de ses attraits & de ses charmes, on luy en met quantité sur le visage, pour montrer par là que les ornemens & les graces des paroles sont absolument necessaire à quiconque veut persuader autruy. Aussi n'estoit-ce que pour cela qu' anciennement on peignoit jeune & agréable le Dieu Mercure, pour figurer que l'Eloquence, qui peut agréer difficilement, si elle n'est belle, vigoureuse, fleurie, & pleine de majesté.[11]

---

11. *Iconologie ou Nouvelle Explication . . . Tirée des recherches & des figures de Cesar Ripa, Moralisées par J. Baudoin*, nouvelle edition (Paris, 1681), pt. 1, p. 73. See also pt. 1, pp. 189–190, for an emblem of Persuasion.

Stressing the union of Doctrine or Science with Eloquence, the commentator explaines that

> La delicatesse des paroles nous est encore denotée par ses bras nuds: car sans les fondemens d'une solide doctrine & d'un fort raisonnment l'Eloquence seroit desarmée, & ne pourroit jamais donner dans le but où elle vise; d'où vient qu'elle & la Persuasion sont à bon droit appellées les creatures de la Doctrine. Mais parce que les raisons que produit la Science, ont des difficultez qui empeschent qu'on ne les entende si aisément, l'on y adjoute pour cet effet les ornemens & les graces des paroles, qui les éclaircissent, & qui engendrent souvent des effets, par le moyen desquels l'on develope les embarras d'un esprit defectueux & grossier. Pour cette mesme fin encore, soit qu'il s'agisse ou d'expliquer par raisons les matières difficiles, ou d'émouvoir les passions de l'ame, ou d'arrester ses mouvemens déreglez, il est necessaire que l'Orateur soit ingenieux à couvrir son art d'un agréable mélange de paroles choisies & bien rangées: car quelque endormy que soit un esprit, elle l'éveillera sans doute par la subtilité de ses argumens, ou l'attirera par la douceur de son langage; jusques là mesme que son action & les paroles comme des foudres redoutables étonneront les plus audacieux, & leur feront tomber les armes des mains. (*Iconologie* [1681], pp. 75–76)

The golden crown that Eloquence wears is a mark of her great authority, whereby she reigns in the hearts of men. The open book and the hourglass teach us first that "les paroles tissuës avec art, & animées par la vivacité de l'action, ou mises par écrit pour le bien de la posterité, sont les instrumens de l'Eloquence," and second "qu'il faut apporter l'ordre requis, & la juste mesure du temps, qui donne au periodes le nombre, au stile la grace, & à tout le corps du discours l'ame de la persuasion."

Finally, the lightning-bolt, which Valerianus had ascribed to Eloquence (*Hieroglyphica*, bk. 33), signifies "qu' avec la mesme facilité qu'elle met par terre les plus hautes tours, l'Eloquence abbat l'obstination des ignorans, & ruine les opinions qu'ils ont basties sur de mauvais fondemens."

In addition to this highly influential icon of Eloquence, the 1630 edition of Ripa's *Iconologia* included five other descriptions of personifications of this concept. In this second emblem, Eloquence is represented as a woman clad in a garment of variegated colors with a garland of iris on her head. She holds a lightning bolt in her right hand and an open book in her left. "Il vestimento sopradetto dimostra che si come sono varij i colori, cosi l'Oratione deve essere vestita, & di piu concett[i] ornata." The iris is likewise notable for the variety

and ornamental beauty of its colors, which resemble those of the rain-
bow. The classical deity Iris, messenger of Hera, had been regarded as
goddess of Eloquence and, according to Homer, the Trojan orators
had eaten of this flower: "come quelli che erano eloquentissimi, ha-
veano mangiato l'Iride fiorita." By this detail Homer intended us to
understand that they had learned the principles of ornate discourse
by diligence and study:

> cioè che eglino haveano con ogni diligenza, & studio imparato i precetti
> dell' ornato parlare, & di cio questa è la cagione che il fiore di questa
> herba per la sua varietà & ornamento de colori, habbia con l'Iri de celeste
> similitudine grandissima, che pure era ancor lei tenuta per Dea dell' Elo-
> quenza. (*Iconologia* [1630], pt. 1, p. 213)

Ripa attributed this interpretation to Valerianus (*Hieroglyphica*, bk.
60); but it depends in part on a misinterpretation of Homer's *Iliad*, a
point to which we will later return.

The third image of Eloquence is a woman dressed in red, holding a
book in her right hand, and pointing with the index finger of her
raised left hand. At her feet are a book and an hourglass ("horologgio
da polvere") and a parrot on top of an open cage. As Ripa explained,
the parrot ("papagallo") symbolizes the eloquent man because it imitates human speech:

> perche si rende maraviglioso con la lingua, & con le parole imitando
> l'huomo, nella cui lingua solamente consiste l'essercitio dell' Eloquenza.

The parrot is depicted outside the cage, moreover, because eloquence
is not confined to a particular subject matter, but may discourse with
probability on any kind of matter:

> perche l'Eloquenza non è ristretta à termine alcuno, essendo l'offitio suo
> di saper dire probabilmente di qual si voglia materia proposta, come dice
> Cicerone nella Rettorica. (*Iconologia* [1630], pt. 1, p. 214)

The fourth image of Eloquence is a matron modestly dressed ("vestita d'habito honesto"), with a parrot on the top of her head. She
holds her right hand open and outwards ("aperta in fuora"), and
attempts to hide her clenched left hand under her garments. For,
according to Zeno the Stoic, Ripa observes, "la Dialettica era so-
migliante â una mano chiusa, perche proceda astutamente, & l'Eloquenza à una mano aperta, che si allarga, & diffonda assai più
(*Iconologia* [1630], pt. 1, p. 214).

The fifth and sixth images portray Eloquence in terms of the myths of Orpheus and Amphion respectively. Orpheus wears a Persian tiara and the garments of a philosopher. As he plays the lyre, wild animals crowd around him; forests and mountains move to hear him, streams stand still. Following the interpretation of Ovid's *Metamorphoses* by Giovanni Andrea dell' Anguillara, Ripa regards Orpheus as a symbol of Eloquence, and Eloquence itself as the offspring of Wisdom: "dicendo che Orfeo ci monstra quanta forza, & vigore habbia l'Eloquenza, come quella, che è figliuola di Apollo, che non è altro che la Sapienza." The lyre symbolizes the art of discourse ("l'arte del favellare propriamente"); and the miraculous effect of Orpheus's playing on beasts and hills and streams represents the effects of eloquence on various kinds of men: "Le selve, & i monti, che si muovono, altro non sono, che quegl' huomini fissi, & ostinati nelle loro opinioni, & che con grandissima difficoltà si lasciano vincere dalla suavità delle voci, & dalla forza del parlare." The streams which pause to listen to his music signify wicked men ("i dishonesti, & lascivi huomini"), restrained from evil by his eloquence. The beasts tamed and rendered mild by his playing signify bloody and cruel men converted to a more humane and praiseworthy life by his speech (*Iconologia* [1630], pt.1, p. 214).

In the sixth image Amphion draws to himself many widely scattered stones with the sound of his cithara and his song. This symbolizes the power of persuasive eloquence, which brings rough and ignorant men together into one society and teaches them to live together in a civilized fashion: "che la dolce armonia del parlare dell' Eloquenza persuade, & tira à sè gl' ignoranti, rozzi, & duri huomini, che quà, & là sparse dimorano, & insieme convenghino, & civilmente vivino" (*Iconologia* [1630], pt. 1, pp. 214–215).

In Renaissance emblem books, eloquence is often associated with the god Mercury or with the Celtic god Ogmios (or Hercules Gallicus) as well as with Orpheus and Amphion. In *Petri Costalii Pegma* (Lyons, 1555), Orpheus's power over beasts and stones and trees symbolizes the power of eloquence, "vis eloquentiae" (*Emblemata*, col. 1609). In the *Emblemata* of Nicolas Reusner (*Frankfurt*, 1581), the myth of Orpheus and the wild beasts represents the power of music and poetry: "Musicae, et poeticae vis" (*Emblemata*, col. 1610). In the *Emblemas* of Hernando de Soto (Madrid, 1599), the example of Ulysses on the island of Alcinous demonstrates the utility of eloquence to exiles and strangers (*Emblemata*, col. 1701). According to Alciati's *Emblemata* (Lyons, 1550), the herb moly, which Mercury offered to Ulysses as an antidote to Circe's drink, symbolized eloquence. The emblem bears the motto FACUNDIA DIFFICILIS; and the accompanying verses assert that "Eloquii candor facundiaque allicit omnes: / sed multires est tanta laboris opus" (*Emblemata*, cols. 315–316). In the *Picta Poesis* of Barptolemaeus Anulus (*Lugduni*, 1552), Mercury's flight to the temple of Pallas Athene at Athens illustrates the maxim SAPIENTIAM SEQUITUR ELOQUENTIA. The accompanying verses pose the rhetorical question concerning the reasons for his flight: "An quia ubi regnat Sapientia mox volat illuc / Facundi ille lepos Atticus eloquij?" (*Emblemata*, col. 1770).

In an emblem dedicated to the "most sapient orator," Bishop Claudio Ptolomaeo, Bocchi illustrates the force of eloquence by depicting Pericles seated aloft in the clouds wielding lightning-bolts and by portraying the bombardment of a town by cannon fire (Fig. 5). The accompanying verses elucidate the motto VIS ELOQUENTIAE POTEST UNA OMNIA:

> Fulgurat ecce, tonatque, & miscet cuncta Pericles
> Ut rutilans perterricrepum, & penetrabile fulmen:
> Utque imitata ipsum fulmen bombarda trisulcum
> Munitas arces, immensa repagula, turres,
> Oppida, & horribili evertit concussa fragore.
> . . . .
> Sic oratoris summi admiranda facultas,
> Quum se se ipse refert totum à caelestibus illis
> Rebus ad humanas, excelsius omnia certè, &
> Magnificentius eloquitur, sentitque movetque
> Fortius, ut valent prorsum nil sistere contra
> Ignivomo fatuos propulsans ore sophistas.
> (*Symbolicarum Quaestionum*, symb. XCII,
> pp. cxciiii–cxcv)

Bocchi specifically associates Wisdom and Eloquence in an emblem of Athene as goddess of wisdom and Hermes as god of eloquence (Hermathena), with the title: SAPIENTIAM MODESTIA, / PROGRESSIO ELOQUENTIAM, / FELICITATEM HAEC PERFICIT (*Symbolicarum Quaestionum*, symb. CII, p. ccx) (Fig. 6). Another emblem in Bocchi's book portrays the art of rhetoric through the traditional symbol of the chimaera; the tripartite monster overcome by Bellerophon mounted on the winged horse Pegasus (Fig. 7). The title (or motto) emphasizes the tripartite function of rhetoric—to teach, to delight, to move—and the divine power of Truth: ARS RHETOR[ICA] TRIPLEX MOVET, IUVAT, DOCET,

/ SED PRAEPOTENS EST VERITAS DIVINITUS. / SIC MONSTRA VITIOR[UM] DOMAT
PRUDENTIA. The accompanying verses explain the mythical monster as
an allegory of the three parts of rhetoric.[12]

> Forense enim horridus Leo notat genus:
> Nam exterret, ac elinguat adversarios.
> Sed capra: idest, Chimera ipsa, obtinet typum
> Plausibilis laudationis: laetius
> Lascivit etenim orator ore, ut auribus
> Auditor. At quod consulit, draconis est
> Persimile varij, ac flexuosi anfractibus.
> (symb. CXXXV, p. ccciiii)

Valerianus associated eloquence with a variety of "hieroglyphs": the
parakeet, the torrent, the open hand (extended forefingers and hand),
the bee, "Eloquence agreable" was symbolized by "la Mousche à
miel." In particular, the god Mercury serves as an emblem of speech
and eloquence: "la force de la parole & la vertu de l'interpretation, &
l'eloquence, comme messager & truchement des Dieux." The tongue
is consecrated to this god, for the Egyptians believed that Mercury
was the first to arrange words in order and give names to various
objects. He invented letters and instituted the adoration and service
of the gods, accomplishing these civilizing tasks through the force of
eloquence: "ce qui n'a peu, sans une merveilleuse force d'eloquence
entrer en la fantasie des hommes." Mercury's caduceus likewise symbolizes eloquence; and the serpents wound about it indicate that prudence and finesse were essential for true eloquence (*Hieroglyphiques*,
pp. 195, 288, 324, 424–425, 457, 783).

3

Derived ultimately from Lucian's *Heracles*, the image of the Gallic
Hercules as a symbol of eloquence appears frequently in Renaissance
mythographies and emblem literature. According to Lucian, "The
Celts call Heracles Ogmios in their native tongue," and portray him
"in a very peculiar way. To their notion, he is extremely old, bald-
headed, except for a few lingering hairs which are quite gray, his skin
is wrinkled, and he is burned as black as can be." Nevertheless, "in
spite of his looks, he has the equipment of Heracles: he is dressed in

12. See the discussion of Ripa above. For the currency of this interpretation in Renaissance emblem literature, see John M. Steadman, *Nature into Myth: Medieval and
Renaissance Moral Symbols* (Pittsburgh, 1979), pp. 160–162, 280.

the lion's skin, has the club in his right hand, carries the quiver at his side, displays the bent bow in his left." Yet, singularly enough, "that old Heracles of theirs drags after him a great crowd of men who are all tethered by the ears! His leashes are delicate chains fashioned of gold and amber [*chrysou kai ēlektrou*], resembling the prettiest of necklaces. Yet, though led by bonds so weak, the men do not think of escaping, as they easily could, and they do not pull back at all. . . . In fact, they follow cheerfully and joyously, applauding their leader and all pressing him close and keeping the leashes slack in their desire to overtake him." Since "the painter had no place to which he could attach the ends of the chains, . . . he pierced the tip of his [Heracles'] tongue, and represented him drawing the men by that means! Moreover, he has his face turned toward his captives, and is smiling."[13]

As a Celtic bystander explains to Lucian's narrator, his own people "do not agree with you Greeks in thinking that Hermes is Eloquence: we identify Heracles with it, because he is far more powerful than Hermes." He is "represented as an old man, for eloquence and eloquence alone is wont to show its full vigour in old age." According to Euripides (*Phoenissae*, line 530), "Old age has wiser words to say than youth." In the *Iliad* "Nestor's tongue distils honey" (1:249) and "the Trojan counsellors" on the walls of the city have a voice like lily-flowers (3:152; "*leirioessan*"). "That being so," the bystander continues, "if old Heracles here drags men after him who are tethered by the ears to his tongue, don't be surprised at that, either: you know the kinship between ears and tongue. Nor is it a slight upon him that his tongue is pierced. Indeed . . . I call to mind a line or two of a comedy which I learned in your country: 'the talkative / Have, one and all, their tongues pierced at the tip.'" The Celts consider, in fact, "that the real Heracles was a wise man who achieved everything by eloquence and applied persuasion as his principal force. His arrows represent words, . . . keen, sure and swift, which make their wounds in souls."

Valerianus also includes Hercules as a "hieroglyph" of eloquence, citing Lucian's account of the god Ogmios, or Hercules Gallicus (*Hieroglyphiques*, pp. 780–781). Cartari raises the question whether, in fact, Hercules was not the same as Mercury, citing the same story in Lucian concerning the gold and silver chains of eloquence, attached to the tongue of the Gallic Hercules and to the ears of his audience. Natale Conti transferred this detail specifically to Mercury: "Hunc [Mercurium] finxerunt antiqui aurea cathena auribus hominum annexa, mor-

13. See *Lucian*, trans. A. M. Harmon (London and New York, 1921), 1:61–71.

tales quocunque collibuisset trahere solitum, sicuti de Hercule dicitur."[14] Alexander Ross similarly declares that "He is called *Mercurius,* quasi *Medius currens*; for speech, whereof he is said to be god is that which runs between man and man. . . . And to shew the force of eloquence, they painted him drawing of people by the ears with a small chain reaching out of his mouth."[15]

Alciati included a picture of the Gallic Hercules in his *Emblematum liber* (1531), with the motto ELOQUENTIA FORTITUDINE PRAESTANTIOR (unnumbered folio [E6]) (Fig. 8). The accompanying verses emphasized the singularity of this representation of the hero as an old man drawing a multitude by the chains attached to his tongue, explaining that he ruled the people by language rather than by force:

> Quid quod lingua illi levibus traiecta cathenis,
>   Quis fissa facili allicit aure viros.
> An ne quod Alcyden lingua non robore Galli,
>   Praestantem populis iura dedisse ferunt.
> Cedunt arma togae, et quamvis durissima corda,
>   Eloquio pollens ad sua vota trahit.

Jeremias Held retained this emblem in his German version of Alciati's emblems (Frankfurt, 1567); and both Bocchi and Laurens van Haecht also use this motif.

Later editions of Alciati's *Emblemata* retain the same motto and verses, while substituting a different illustration of Hercules Gallicus (Fig. 9). In his commentary on this emblem, Claude Mignault cites Lucian's description of the Celtic god Ogmios, "eloquentiae prudentiaeque Deum." The icon that Lucian had described indicated "nihil aliud, . . . quam Herculem eloquentia & fortitudine praestantem, dissipatos olim Gallos & efferatos, ad iustitiam & mitiorem vitam vivae viribus eloquentiae reduxisse" (emblem no. 180, pp. 580–581). According to the Celts, Hercules was a man of wisdom and eloquence who had accomplished all things by his oratory: "Herculem oratione omnia perficisse, virum quidem sapientem, qui facundia quamplurima subegerit." Servius stressed the hero's strength of mind rather than of body: "Herculem â prudentioribus mentem magis quàm corpore fortem habitum"; and Cicero asserted the priority of the arts of speech over those of the battlefield ("Cedant arma togae,

---

14. *Natalis Comitis Mythologiae* (Venice, 1567), fol. 134v; fac. ed., Orgel, *Renaissance.*

15. *Mystagogus Poeticus, or The Muses Interpreter* . . . (London, 1658), p. 262; fac. ed., Orgel, *Renaissance.*

concedat laurea linguae") in his *Oratio in Pisonem.* Mignault favors
the ideal of a Hercules who is also a distinguished orator and tri-
umphs through eloquence rather than physical strength: "non quidem viribus corporis, sed facundiae vi auditores trahet quò velit."
Such a Hercules is comparable to Orpheus, who had similarly excelled in eloquence: "Nam & Orpheum aiunt, citharae dulcisonae
modulo feras & saxa movisse: quod est referendum ad vim eloquentiae, quam Euripides reginam, & Ennius flexanimam appellavit" (pp.
583–585). Mignault refers to the same legend in his commentary on
Alciati's emblem no. 137 on the twelve labors of Hercules (p. 465):
"Herculem virum fuisse Gallum, qui tum sollerti quadam prudentia,
tum admirabili eloquentia, qua maxime valebat, praeclara facinora
insigni fortitudine sit exantlatus, & ingenii dexteritate summas quas-
que difficultates superarit [*sic*]: quae tamen omnia Graecia, ut quam-
plurimum mendax, ad armorum gloriam convertere maluit." Apuleius regarded Hercules as a philosopher who had subdued the
monsters of the mind, such as ire and envy, avarice and lust; Plutarch
associated him with the knowledge of literature and wisdom ("li-
terarum & sapientiae cognitione").

In his *Symbolicarum Quaestionum* Bocchi portrayed Hercules
seated upon an oxcart, surrounded by a throng of people with chains
attached to their ears (Fig. 10). Above the picture appeared the cap-
tion: HIC HERCULES EST GALLICUS: / INTELLEGAT QUI AURES HABET; and on the
opposite page, the motto CURA ET LABORE PERFICI ELOQUENTIAM. The accompanying verses emphasize the need for ardor and labor, study
and care, in learning to speak eloquently. The man who once "draws"
the Gallic Hercules with his ears will be not only eloquent but wise:

> Discere quisquis avet bene dicere, discat oportet
> Ille prius. studium id, cura, laborque facit.
> Si studium affuerit summum, & quidam ardor amoris,
> Tum nihil obfuerint cura, laborque tibi.
> Qui Gallum Alcidem semel aurib[us] hauserit ultrò,
> Ille disertus erit non modò, sed sapiens.
>
> (symb. XLIII, p.lxxxix)

Bocchi's emblem is a deliberate variant of the traditional image of
Hercules Gallicus, for here the god is drawn forward by others, and
the oxen are urged forward by youths whose ears are chained to the
god's tongue. This variation serves to emphasize the essential point of
the motto; the verses, in turn, exploit the double sense of the verb
hauserit ("to draw out" and "to drink in").

The Celtic god also appears in an emblem book compiled by Laurens van Haecht and entitled *Mikrokosmos* (Greek transliterated), published in Amsterdam in 1610 (Fig. 11). The emblem bears the title GALLORUM HERCULES, and quotes the Latin text of 1 Corinthians 13:1: "Si linguis hominum loquar & angelorum, charitatem autem non habeam: sum velut aes sonans: aut cymbalum timiens [*Sic* for tinniens]." The accompanying picture portrays several dispersed individuals (or small groups of men) united by the chains of Hercules' eloquence, while the verses on the opposite page emphasize the power of eloquence to ravish, and to bind men together in concord, so that they freely desire to listen to the precepts of God:

> Ogmion Herculeo referunt hunc nomine dictum,
> Cuius lingua fuit chordis religata solutis.
> Et simul aurata, laxè pedente [*sic*], cathena.
> Ingens qua populus connexus restibus, ibat.
> Non secus eloquium Galli latiale figurant,
> Cum rapit huc homines, concordi fune ligatos,
> Ut praecepta Dei cupiant audire libenter.
> Quae dum mundus erit, nunquam peritura manebunt.
>
> (*Mikrokosmos*, no. 43)

According to Gyraldus, "Ogmion Hercules à Celtis dictus, ut Lucianus. . . . ostendit. eum enim eloquentiae ac prudentiae deum existimabant, itaque effingebant: . . . catenulis verò ex auro & electro admodum tenuibus, linguae suae extremitate perforata insertis, maximam hominum multitudinem, non invitam, sed sponte sequentem auribus alligatis trahentem" (*De Deis gentium*, p. 453). Cartari likewise bases his description and interpretation of the god on Lucian's account, though the chains are of gold and silver rather than of gold and amber:

> haveva poi allo estremo della lingua attaccate molte catene di oro, e di argento sottilissime, con le quali ei si traheva dietro per le orecchie una moltitudine grande di gente che lo seguitava però volontieri. Facile cosa è da vedere che questa imagine significa la forza della eloquenza, la quale davano quelle genti ad Hercole, perche, come dice il medesimo Luciano, fu Hercole creduto più forte assai, e più gagliardo di Mercurio, e lo faceano vecchio, perche ne i vecchi la eloquenza è più perfetta assai che ne i giovani.[16]

16. *Le Imagini de i dei de gli antichi* (Venice, 1571), p. 340; fac. ed., Orgel, *Renaissance*.

Lucian's reference to chains *chrysou kai ēlektrou* (cf. Harmon, *Lucian*, "of gold and amber") is rendered as "*auro & electro*" by Mignault and Gyraldus, but interpreted as gold and silver chains by Valerianus, Cartari, and others. The ambiguity of the word *electron* or *electrum* in the classical tongues and in Renaissance vernacular languages made it possible to interpret Ogmios's chains of *electron* either as amber or as an alloy of gold and silver resembling amber in color.

A further variation on Lucian's description of the Gallic Hercules occurs in Ripa's association of the iris with eloquence on the authority of Homer's *Iliad* (13:152) (*Iconologia* [1610] , part. I, pp. 213–214). According to Homer, Ripa declares, the Trojan orators had eaten flowering iris; in his discussion of the iris as a symbol of eloquence he cites the *Hieroglyphica* of Valerianus. In book 60, chapter 30 of this work, Valerianus represents the iris as a symbol of eloquence, adducing the example of the Trojan ambassadors in the *Iliad*. In asserting that they had eaten of the flowering iris ("l'Iris florisante"), Homer had shown that they were experienced in the art of eloquence; "pource que ceste herbe par sa bigarrure & diversité de couleurs resemble à la celeste Iris, laquelle mesme on reputoit la Deesse d'eloquence" (*Hieroglyphiques*, p. 805).

In fact, however, in Homer's *Iliad* the old men on the walls of Troy are compared (as good speakers) to cicadas which "pour forth their lily-like voice" (*opa leirioessan*). In citing this passage in *Herakles*, Lucian declares that these "Trojan counsellors" (*agorētai*) "have a voice like flowers" (*opa . . . euanthē*), adding that "the flowers mentioned are lilies, if my memory serves." In commenting on the cicada passage in the *Iliad*, A. T. Murray cites additional examples of "the adjective 'lily-like' applied to the voice" in Hesiod's *Theogony* (line 41) and the *Argonautica* of Apollonius of Rhodes (4:903). In Hesiod's poem the Muses of Olympus delight their father Zeus with their "lily-like voice" (*opi leirioessēi*); and in *The Argonauts* the Sirens also send forth "a lily-like voice" (*opa leirion*).[17]

17. See Homer, *The Iliad*, trans. A.T. Murray (London and New York, 1924), 1:128, 128n; *Lucian* 1:64–67; *Hesiod*, trans. Hugh G. Evelyn-White (London and New York, 1929), pp. 80–81; Apollonious Rhodius, *Argonautica*, trans. R.C. Seaton (London and New York, 1912), pp. 356–357.

Bibliography

Adolph, Robert. *The Rise of Modern Prose Style*. Cambridge, Mass., and London, 1968.

Allen, Don Cameron. *Doubt's Boundless Sea: Skepticism and Faith in the Renaissance*. Baltimore, 1964.

———. *Mysteriously Meant: The Rediscovery of Pagan Symbolism and Allegorical Interpretation*. Baltimore and London, 1970.

———. "Some Theories of the Growth and Origin of Language in Milton's Age." *Studies in Philology* 28 (1949):5–16

———. "Style and Certitude." *ELH* 15 (1948):167–175.

Allen, Judson B. "The Style and Content of Baptist Sermons in Seventeenth-Century England." *Furman Studies* 15, no. 4 (1968):1–21.

Altman, Joel B. *The Tudor Play of Mind: Rhetorical Inquiry and the Development of Elizabethan Drama*. Berkeley, 1978.

Anderson, Paul R. *Science in Defense of Liberal Religion: A Study of Henry More's Attempt to Link Seventeenth-Century Religion with Science*. New York, 1933.

Anselment, Raymond A. *"Betwixt Jest and Earnest": Marprelate, Milton, Marvell, Swift, and the Decorum of Religious Ridicule*. Toronto, 1979.

———. "Rhetoric and the Dramatic Satire of Martin Marprelate." *SEL: Studies in English Literature, 1500–1900* 10 (1970):103–119.

Aristotle. *The Basic Works of Aristotle*. Ed. Richard McKeon. New York, 1941.

Armstrong, Robert L. "John Locke's 'Doctrine of Signs': A New Metaphysics." *Journal of the History of Ideas* 26 (1965):369–382.

Asals, Heather. "Rhetoric Agonistic in *Samson Agonistes*." *Milton Quarterly* 11 (1977):1–4.

Ashworth, E. J. "The Scholastic Background to Locke's Theory of Language." In *Progress in Linguistic Historiography*, ed. Konrad Koerner. Amsterdam, 1980. Pp. 59–68.

Auerbach, Erich. *Literary Language and Its Public in Late Latin Antiquity and in the Middle Ages*. Trans. Ralph Manheim. New York, 1965.

———. *Mimesis: The Representation of Reality in Western Literature*. Trans. Willard R. Trask. Princeton, 1953; rpt. Garden City, N.Y., 1957.

Auksi, Peter. "Milton's 'Sanctifi'd Bitternesse': Polemical Technique in the Early Prose." *Texas Studies in Language and Literature* 19 (1977): 363–381.

Bacon, Francis. *Selected Writings of Francis Bacon.* Ed. Hugh G. Dick. New York, 1955.

Bailey, Richard W., and Dolores M. Burton. *English Stylistics: A Bibliography.* Cambridge, Mass., 1968.

Baker, Herschel. *The Wars of Truth: Studies in the Decay of Christian Humanism in the Earlier Seventeenth Century.* Cambridge, Mass., 1952.

Barish, Jonas A. *Ben Jonson and the Language of Prose Comedy.* Cambridge, Mass., 1960.

———. "The Prose Style of John Lyly." *ELH* 23 (1956):14–35.

Basney, Lionel. "'*Lucidus Ordo*': Johnson and Generality." *Eighteenth-Century Studies* 5 (1971–72):39–57.

Bate, Walter Jackson. *From Classic to Romantic: Premises of Taste in Eighteenth-Century England.* New York, 1961.

Baxter, Richard. *Gildas Salvianus: The Reformed Pastor.* London, 1656.

Blake, Ralph, C. J. Ducasse, and E. H. Madden. *Theories of Scientific Method: The Renaissance Through the Nineteenth Century.* Seattle, 1960.

Bennett, Joan. "An Aspect of the Evolution of Seventeenth-Century Prose." *Review of English Studies* 17 (1941):281–297.

Berek, Peter. "'Plain' and 'Ornate' Styles and the Structure of *Paradise Lost.*" *PMLA* 85 (1970):237–246.

Berry, Boyd M. *Process of Speech: Puritan Religious Writing and Paradise Lost.* Baltimore and London, 1976.

Bethell, Samuel Leslie. *The Cultural Revolution of the Seventeenth Century.* London, 1951.

Blanchard, J. Marc. "The Tree and the Garden: Pastoral Poetics and Milton's Rhetoric of Desire." *MLN* 91 (1976):1540–1568.

Blench, J. W. *Preaching in England in the Late Fifteenth and Sixteenth Centuries: A Study of English Sermons 1450–c. 1600.* Oxford, 1964.

Blessington, Francis C. "Autotheodicy: The Father as Orator in *Paradise Lost.*" *Cithara* 14, no. 2 (1975):49–60.

Boas, Marie. *The Scientific Renaissance. 1450–1630.* New York, 1962.

Bond, Donald F. "'Distrust' of Imagination in English Neo-Classicism." *Philological Quarterly* 14 (1935):54–69.

Boughner, D. C. "Notes on Hooker's Prose." *Review of English Studies* 15 (1939):195–196.

Bredvold, Louis I. *The Intellectual Milieu of John Dryden.* Ann Arbor, 1934.

Broadbent, J. B. "Milton's Rhetoric." *Modern Philology* 56 (1959):224–242.

Brown, Huntington. *Prose Styles: Five Primary Types.* Minneapolis, 1966.

Brown, John. *Puritan Preaching in England: A Study of Past and Present.* London, 1900.

Browne, Sir Thomas. *The Prose of Sir Thomas Browne.* Ed. Norman J. Endicott. Garden City, N.Y., 1967.

Bryan, William F., and R. S. Crane, eds. *The English Familiar Essay. Representative Texts.* . . . Boston, 1916.

Bryant, Donald C. *Rhetorical Dimensions of Criticism.* Baton Rouge, 1973.

Bundy, Murray. "Bacon's True Opinion of Poetry." *Studies in Philology* (1936):244–264.

Burtt, Edwin A., ed. *The English Philosophers from Bacon to Mill.* New York, 1939.

Bush, Douglas. *English Literature in the Earlier Seventeenth Century.* Oxford, 1945.

——. *Science and English Poetry.* New York, 1950.

Campbell, Gordon. "Words and Things: The Language of Metaphysical Poetry." *Language and Literature* 2, no. 3 (1974):3–15.

Caplan, Harry, and Henry H. King. "Pulpit Eloquence: A List of Doctrinal and Historical Studies in English." *Speech Monographs* 22, no. 4 (1955).

Carruthers, Mary. *The Search for St. Truth: A Study of Meaning in Piers Plowman.* Evanston, Ill., 1973.

Carson, Michael Joseph. "The Moral Use of Rhetoric in *Paradise Regained.*" *Dissertation Abstracts International* 37 (1976):982A.

Child, Clarence Griffin. *John Lyly and Euphuism.* Erlangen and Leipzig, 1894.

Christensen, Francis. "John Wilkins and the Royal Society's Reform of Prose Style." *Modern Language Quarterly* 7 (1946):179–187, 279–290.

Clark, Donald Lemen. *John Milton at St. Paul's School.* New York, 1948.

——. *Rhetoric and Poetry in the Renaissance.* New York, 1922.

Coffin, C. M. *John Donne and the New Philosophy.* New York, 1958.

Cohen, Jacques. *English Rhythmical Prose and the Hebrew Bible.* London, 1936. Rpt. from "*Ye are my Witnesses,*" Dr. Daiches Semi-Jubilee Volume.

Cohen, Jean. *Structure du langage poétique.* Paris, 1966.

Cohen, John Michael. *The Baroque Lyric.* London, 1963.

Cohen, Jonathan. "On the Project of a Universal Character." *Mind* 63 (1954):49–63.

Cohen, Morris Raphael. "Bacon and Inductive Method." *Studies in Philosophy and Science.* New York, 1949, pp. 99–106.

——. *Reason and Nature: An Essay on the Meaning of Scientific Method.* Glencoe, Ill., 1953.

Cohen, Murray. *Sensible Words: Linguistic Practice in England, 1640–1785.* Baltimore, 1977.

——. "Sensible Words: Linguistic Theory in Late Seventeenth-Century England." In *Studies in Eighteenth-Century Culture,* ed. Ronald C. Rosbottom. Madison, 1976. V:229–252.

Colie, Rosalie. *Paradoxia Epidemica: The Renaissance Tradition of Paradox.* Princeton, 1966.

Colish, Marcia L. *The Mirror of Language: A Study in the Medieval Theory of Knowledge*. New Haven and London, 1968.

Colvin, Daniel Lester. "The Function of Epistemology in John Donne's Poetry." *Dissertation Abstracts International* 37 (1977):4364A–65A.

Coolidge, John S. "Martin Marprelate, Marvell, and *Decorum Personae* as a Satirical Theme." *PMLA* 74 (1959):526–532.

Cooper, Lane. *Theories of Style*. New York, 1907.

Cope, Jackson I. *Joseph Glanvill: Anglican Apologist*. St. Louis, 1956.

———. "Modes of Modernity in Seventeenth-Century Prose." *Modern Language Quarterly* 31 (1970):92–111.

———. "Seventeenth-Century Quaker Style." *PMLA* 71 (1956):725–754.

Costa, Prudence Mapes. "Gracián's Aesthetic of Wit in the Poetry of Góngora and Donne." *Dissertation Abstracts International* 37 (1977):4336A–37A.

Crane, Ronald S. "The Relation of Bacon's *Essays* to His Program for the Advancement of Learning." In Vickers, *Essential Articles*, pp. 272–292.

Crane, W. G. *Wit and Rhetoric in the Renaissance*. New York, 1937.

Crashaw, Richard. *The Complete Poetry*. Ed. George Walton Williams. Garden City, N.Y., 1970.

Croll, Morris W. "'Attic Prose' in the Seventeenth Century." *Studies in Philology* 18 (1921):79–128; rpt. Croll, *Style, Rhetoric, and Rhythm*, pp. 51–101.

———. "Attic Prose: Lipsius, Montaigne, Bacon." *Schelling Anniversary Papers.* . . . New York, 1923, pp. 117–150; rpt. Croll, *Style, Rhetoric, and Rhythm*, pp. 167–202.

———. "The Baroque Style in Prose." *Studies in English Philology: A Miscellany in Honor of Frederick Klaeber*. Ed. Kemp Malone and Martin B. Ruud. Minneapolis, 1929; rpt. Croll, *Style, Rhetoric, and Rhythm*, pp. 207–233.

———. "Juste Lipse et le mouvement anticicéronien à la fin du XVIe et au début du XVIIe siècle." *Revue du seizième siècle* 2 (1914):200–242; rpt. Croll, *Style, Rhetoric, and Rhythm*, pp. 7–44.

———. "Muret and the History of 'Attic Prose.'" *PMLA* 39 (1924), 254–309; rpt. Croll, *Style, Rhetoric, and Rhythm*, pp. 107–162.

———. *Style, Rhetoric, and Rhythm: Essays by Morris W. Croll*. Ed. J. Max Patrick et al. Princeton, 1966.

Curet, Peggy Joann. "The Rhetoric of Humor in Milton's *Areopagitica*." *Dissertation Abstracts International* 38 (1977):801A–02A.

D'Alton, J. F. *Roman Literary Theory and Criticism: A Study in Tendencies*. New York, 1962.

Davidson, Clifford. "Style and the Heavenly Ladder." *The Gordon Review* (Wenham, Mass.) 11 (1968):159–167. (On Sibbes, Baxter, and others.)

Davie, Donald. "Berkeley's Style in *Siris*." *Cambridge Journal* 4 (1950): 427–433.

————. *The Language of Science and the Language of Literature, 1700–1740.* London and New York, 1963.

Davies, Horton. *Worship and Theology in England from Cranmer to Hooker, 1534–1603.* Princeton, 1970.

————. *Worship and Theology in England from Andrewes to Baxter and Fox, 1603–1690.* Princeton, 1975.

————. *The Worship of the English Puritans.* Westminster, London, 1948.

Davis, Walter R. "*Urne Buriall*: A Descent into the Underworld." *Studies in the Literary Imagination* 10, no. 2 (1977), 73–87.

DeMott, Benjamin. "Comenius and the Real Character in England." *PMLA* 70 (1955):1068–81.

————. "The Sources and Development of John Wilkins' Philosophical Language." *Journal of English and Germanic Philology* 57 (1958):1–13.

Descartes, [René]. *Discourse on Method and Other Writings.* Trans. Arthur Wollaston. Baltimore, 1960.

————. *Discourse on Method, Optics, Geometry and Meteorology.* Ed. Paul J. Olscamp. Indianapolis, New York, Kansas City, 1965.

————. *The Meditations . . . of René Descartes.* Trans. John Veitch. La Salle, Ill., 1968.

Dewey, John. *The Quest for Certainty: A Study of the Relation of Knowledge and Action.* New York, 1929.

Dictionary of the History of Ideas: Studies of Selected Pivotal Ideas. Ed. Philip P. Wiener. 5 vols. New York, 1973–74.

Donne, John. *Poetical Works.* Ed. Herbert J. C. Grierson. London, Oxford, New York, 1971.

————. *The Satires, Epigrams, and Verse Letters.* Ed. W. Milgate. Oxford, 1967.

Dryden, John. *Of Dramatic Poesy and Other Critical Essays.* Ed. George Watson. London and New York, 1962.

Duhamel, P. Albert. "Milton's Alleged Ramism." *PMLA* 67 (1952):1035–53.

————. "Sidney's *Arcadia* and Elizabethan Rhetoric." *Studies in Philology* 45 (1948):134–150.

Dunn, E. C. "Lipsius and the Art of Letter-Writing." *Sewanee Review* 3 (1956):145–156.

Edelen, George. "Hooker's Style." In *Studies in Richard Hooker: Essays Preliminary to an Edition of His Works,* ed. W. Speed Hill. Cleveland, 1972. Pp. 241–277.

Edwards, Karen Leigh. "'Various Style': The Poetic Language of *Paradise Lost.*" *Dissertation Abstracts International* 40 (1979):2692A–93A.

Edwards, William F. "Niccolò Leoniceno and the Origins of Humanist Discussions of Method." In *Philosophy and Humanism: Renaissance Essays in Honor of Paul Oskar Kristeller,* ed. Edward P. Mahoney. New York, 1976. Pp. 283–305.

Egan, James. *The Inward Teacher: Milton's Rhetoric of Christian Liberty.* University Park, Pa., 1980.

————. "Milton and the Marprelate Tradition." *Milton Studies* 8 (1975): 103–121.

————. "The Satiric Wit of Milton's Prose Controversies." *Studies in the Literary Imagination* 10, no. 2 (1977):97–104.

Ekfelt, Fred Emil. "The Graphic Diction of Milton's English Prose." *Philological Quarterly* 25 (1946):46-69.

————. "Latinate Diction in Milton's English Prose." *Studies in Philology* 28 (1949):53–71.

Ellis, Katherine. "Rhetoric and Ideology: A Study of Seventeenth-Century Prose Style." *Dissertation Abstracts International* 34 (1973):271A. (On Donne, Andrewes, Laud, and others.)

Ellrodt, Robert. "Scientific Curiosity and Metaphysical Poetry in the Seventeenth Century." *Modern Philology* 61 (1964):180–197.

Elsky, Martin. "History, Liturgy, and Point of View in Protestant Meditative Poetry." *Studies in Philology* 77 (1980):67–83. (On Donne, Herbert, Vaughan, and others.)

Emery, Clark. "John Wilkins' 'Universal Language.'" *Isis* 38 (1948): 174–185.

Endicott, Norman J. "Some Aspects of Self-Revelation and Self-Portraiture in *Religio Medici.*" In *Essays in English Literature . . . ,* ed. Millar MacLure and F. W. Watt. Toronto, 1964. Pp. 85–102.

Enkvist, Nils. "On Defining Style." In *Linguistics and Style,* ed. N. E. Enkvist, J. Spence, and M. Gregory. London, 1964. Pp. 1–56.

Farrington, Benjamin. *The Philosophy of Francis Bacon.* Chicago, 1966.

Feuer, Lewis Samuel. *The Scientific Intellectuals: The Psychological and Sociological Origins of Modern Science.* New York, 1963.

Fisch, Harold. "The Puritans and the Reform of Prose Style." *ELH* 19 (1952):229–248.

———— and H. W. Jones. "Bacon's Influence on Sprat's *History of the Royal Society.*" *Modern Language Quarterly* 12 (1951):399–406.

Fish, Stanley Eugene. *Self-Consuming Artifacts: The Experience of Seventeenth-Century Literature.* Berkeley, Los Angeles, London, 1972.

————, ed. *Seventeenth-Century Prose: Modern Essays in Criticism.* New York, 1971.

————. *Surprised by Sin: The Reader in "Paradise Lost."* London and New York, 1967.

Fleischauer, John F. "A Plaine and Sensible Utterance: The Prose Style of Roger Ascham." *Dissertation Abstracts International* 31 (1971):3501A–02A.

Formigari, Lia. *Linguistica ed empirismo nel Seicento inglese.* Bari, Italy, 1970.

————. "Linguistic Theories in British Seventeenth-Century Philosophy." In *Dictionary of the History of Ideas* 3:73–76.

Fowler, Roger, ed. *Essays on Style and Language: Linguistic and Critical Approaches to Literary Style.* London, 1966.

———, ed. *Style and Structure in Literature: Essays in the New Stylistics.* Ithaca, 1975.

France, Peter. *Rhetoric and Truth in France: Descartes to Diderot.* Oxford, 1972.

Friedman, Lester David. "Bold Inquirers: A Study of the Political Prose of Milton and Shelley." *Dissertation Abstracts International* 36 (1976): 6701A.

From Donne to Marvell. Ed. Boris Ford. *The Pelican Guide to English Literature,* vol. III. Harmondsworth, Middlesex, and Baltimore, Md., 1970.

Funke, Otto. "On the Sources of John Wilkins' Philosophical Language (1668)." *English Studies* 40 (1959):208–214.

———. "Sprachphilosophische Probleme bei Francis Bacon." *Gesammelte Aufsätze zur Anglistike und zur Sprachphilosophie.* Bern, 1965.

———. *Zum Weltsprachenproblem in England im 17. Jahrhundert: G. Dalgarnos "Ars Signorum" (1661) und J. Wilkins "Essay Towards a Real Character and a Philosophical Language" (1668).* Anglistische Forschungen 69 (1929):5ff.

Gallagher, Mary. "Dryden's Translation of Lucretius." *Huntington Library Quarterly* 28 (1974):19–29.

Gilbert, Neal W. *Renaissance Concepts of Method.* New York, 1960.

Gilman, Wilbur Elwyn. *Milton's Rhetoric: Studies in His Defense of Liberty.* Columbia, Mo., 1939.

Givner, D. A. "Scientific Preconceptions in Locke's Philosophy of Language." *Journal of the History of Ideas* 23 (1962):340–354.

Gordon, Ian. *The Movement of English Prose.* Bloomington, Ind., 1966.

Grant, Patrick. *The Transformation of Sin: Studies in Donne, Herbert, Vaughan, and Traherne.* Montreal and London, 1974.

Gray, Hanna H. "Renaissance Humanism: The Pursuit of Eloquence." In *Renaissance Essays,* ed. Paul O. Kristeller and Philip P. Wiener. New York and Evanston, Ill., 1968.

Greene, Thomas M. "Roger Ascham: The Perfect End of Shooting." *ELH* 36 (1969):609–625.

Greenslet, Ferris. *Joseph Glanvill: English Thought and Letters of the Seventeenth Century.* New York, 1900.

Gregory, Donna Uthus. "Articulate Wisdom: Rhetorical Technique in John Donne's Satires." *Dissertation Abstracts International* 38 (1977):2806A.

Grundy, Dominick. "Skepticism in Two Essays by Montaigne and Sir Thomas Browne." *Journal of the History of Ideas* 34 (1973):529–542.

Guerlac, Henry. "Newton and the Method of Analysis." *Dictionary of the History of Ideas* 3:378–391.

Hall, A. Rupert. *The Scientific Revolution, 1500–1800: The Formation of the Modern Scientific Attitude.* 2nd ed. Boston, 1962.

Hall, Anne Drury. "Tudor Prose Style: English Humanists and the Problem of a Standard." *English Literary Renaissance* 7 (1977):267–296.

Hall, Michael L. "Searching the Scriptures: Meditation and Discovery in Donne's Sermons." In *New Essays on Donne*, ed. Gary A. Stringer. Salzburg, 1977. Pp. 211–238.

Haller, William. *The Rise of Puritanism; or, The Way to the New Jerusalem as Set Forth in Pulpit and Press from Thomas Cartwright to John Lilburne and John Milton, 1570–1643.* New York, 1938.

Halley, Janet Elizabeth. "Voice and Sign in Seventeenth-Century Literature: Studies in Donne, Vaughan, Browne, and Milton." *Dissertation Abstracts International* 41 (1980):1609A–10A.

Hamilton, K. G. "The Structure of Milton's Prose." In *Language and Style in Milton*, ed. Ronald D. Emma and John T. Shawcross. New York, 1968. Pp. 304–332.

_____. *The Two Harmonies: Poetry and Prose in the Seventeenth Century.* Oxford, 1963.

Hannah, Robert. *Francis Bacon: The Political Orator, with a Short Study of His Rhetorical Theory and Practice.* New York, 1926. Rpt. from *Studies in Rhetoric and Public Speaking in Honor of James A. Winans.* New York, 1925. Pp. 91–132.

Hansen, David A. "Redefinitions of *Style*: 1600–1800." In *New Aspects of Lexicography . . .*, ed. Howard D. Weinbrot. Carbondale and Edwardsville, London and Amsterdam, 1972. Pp. 95–116.

Hardison, O. B. "The Orator and the Poet: The Dilemma of Humanist Literature." *Journal of Medieval and Renaissance Studies* 1 (1970):33–44.

Hardwick, Lillian Beth. "Identification and Adaptation in Satan's Rhetoric in *Paradise Regained.*" *Dissertation Abstracts International* 39 (1978): 2290A.

Harris, Victor. *All Coherence Gone.* Chicago, 1949.

Harrison, C. T. "Bacon, Hobbes, Boyle, and the Ancient Atomists." *Harvard Studies and Notes, Philological and Literary* 15 (1933):191–218.

Harrison, John L. "Bacon's View of Rhetoric, Poetry, and the Imagination." In Vickers, *Essential Articles*, pp. 253–271.

Hauser, Arnold. *The Social History of Art.* Vol. 2, *Renaissance, Mannerism, Baroque.* 1951. Trans. Stanley Godman. Rpt. New York, n.d.

Hendrickson, G. L. "Horace, *Sermones*, i. 4, A Protest and a Program." *American Journal of Philology* 21 (1900):121ff.

_____. "The Origin and Meaning of the Ancient Characters of Style." *American Journal of Philology* 26 (1905):249–290.

_____. "Satura—The Genesis of a Literary Form." *Classical Philology* 6 (1911):129ff.

Herrick, Marvin T. "The Early History of Aristotle's *Rhetoric* in England." *Philological Quarterly* 5 (1926):242–257.

Hester, M. Thomas. "Donne's Apologia." *Papers on Language and Literature* 15 (1979):137–158.

Hill, Christopher. *The Intellectual Origins of the English Revolution.* Oxford, 1965.

_____. *Some Intellectual Consequences of the English Revolution.* Madison, Wis., 1980.

Hirsch, E. D., Jr. "Stylistics and Synonymity." *Critical Inquiry* 1 (1975):559–579.

Hobbes, Thomas. *Body, Man, and Citizen.* Ed. Richard S. Peters. New York and London, 1962.

_____. *Leviathan, Parts One and Two.* Ed. Herbert W. Schneider. Indianapolis and New York, 1958.

Hoopes, Robert. *Right Reason in the English Renaissance.* Cambridge, Mass., 1962.

Hornbeak, Katherine Gee. *The Complete Letter-Writer in English, 1568–1800.* Northampton, Mass., 1934.

Hornsby, S. G., Jr. "'Ambiguous Words': Debate in *Paradise Lost.*" *Milton Quarterly* 14 (1980):60–62.

Hornstein, Lillian. "Analysis of Imagery: A Critique of Literary Method." *PMLA* 57 (1942):638–653.

Hoskins, John. *Directions for Speech and Style.* Ed. Hoyt H. Hudson. Princeton, 1935.

Howell, A. C. "*Res et Verba*: Words and Things." *ELH* 13 (1946):131–142.

Howell, Wilbur S. *Logic and Rhetoric in England, 1500–1700.* Princeton, 1956.

_____. "Poetics, Rhetoric, and Logic in Renaissance Criticism." In *Classical Influences on European Culture, A.D. 1500–1700*, ed. R. R. Bolgar. Cambridge, 1976. Pp. 155–162.

_____. *Poetics, Rhetoric, and Logic: Studies in the Basic Disciplines of Criticism.* Ithaca, 1975.

Howes, Raymond F., ed. *Historical Studies of Rhetoric and Rhetoricians.* Ithaca, 1961.

Hudson, Hoyt H. "Jewel's Oration Against Rhetoric." *Quarterly Journal of Speech* 14 (1928):374–392.

Hughes, Merritt Y., gen. ed. *A Variorum Commentary on the Poems of John Milton.* Vol. 2, ed. A. S. P. Woodhouse and Douglas Bush. New York, 1972. Vol. 4, ed. Walter MacKellar. New York, 1975.

Hunt, Everett Lee. "Plato and Aristotle on Rhetoric and Rhetoricians." In *Historical Studies of Rhetoric and Rhetoricians*, ed. Raymond F. Howes. Ithaca, 1961. Pp. 21–50.

Hunter, G. K. *John Lyly.* London, 1962.

Hunter, J. Paul. *The Reluctant Pilgrim: Emblematic Method and Quest for Form in "Robinson Crusoe."* Baltimore, 1966.

164 *Bibliography*

Huntley, Frank Livingstone. "Bishop Joseph Hall and Protestant Meditation." *Studies in the Literary Imagination* 10, no. 2 (1977):57–71.
_____. *Sir Thomas Browne: A Biographical and Critical Study.* Ann Arbor, 1962.
Hurt, Ellen Louise. "The Prose Style of Robert Burton: The Fruits of Knowledge." *Dissertation Abstracts International* 25 (1965): 5908.
Hyma, Albert. *The Christian Renaissance: A History of the "Devotio Moderna."* 2nd ed. Hamden, 1965.
Irwin, Franklin. "Ramistic Logic in Milton's Prose Works." Diss. Princeton, 1941.
Jacobus, Lee A. *Sudden Apprehension: Aspects of Knowledge in "Paradise Lost."* The Hague, 1976.
Jaffe, Samuel. "Rhetoric and Ideology in a New History of German Literature." *Modern Philology* 71 (1974):304–324.
Jardine, Lisa. *Francis Bacon: Discovery and the Art of Discourse.* Cambridge, 1974.
Jebb., R. C. *The Attic Orators.* 2 vols. London, 1893.
Johnson, Oliver. *Skepticism and Cognitivism: A Study in the Foundations of Knowledge.* Berkeley and Los Angeles, 1979.
Jones, H. W. Introduction to *The History of the Royal-Society of London*, by Thomas Sprat. St. Louis, 1958. Pp. xxix–xxxi.
Jones, Mansell. *French Introspectives from Montaigne to André Gide.* Cambridge, 1937.
Jones, Richard Foster. *Ancients and Moderns: A Study of the Rise of the Scientific Movement in Seventeenth-Century England.* 2nd ed. Berkeley and Los Angeles, 1965.
_____. "The Attack on Pulpit Eloquence in the Restoration: An Episode in the Development of the Neo-Classical Standard for Prose." *Journal of English and Germanic Philology* 30 (1931):188–217; rpt. Jones, *The Seventeenth Century*, pp. 111–142.
_____. "The Moral Sense of Simplicity." *Studies in Honor of Frederick W. Shipley.* Washington University Studies in Language and Literature, n.s., 14 (1942):265–287.
_____. "Science and Criticism in the Neo-Classical Age of English Literature." *Journal of the History of Ideas* 1 (1940):381–412; rpt. Jones, *The Seventeenth Century*, pp. 41–74.
_____. "Science and English Prose Style in the Third Quarter of the Seventeenth Century." *PMLA* 45 (1930):977–1009; rpt. Jones, *The Seventeenth Century*, pp. 75–110.
_____. "Science and Language in England of the Mid-Seventeenth Century." *Journal of English and Germanic Philology* 31 (1932):315–31; rpt. Jones, *The Seventeenth Century*, pp. 143–160.

———. *The Seventeenth Century: Studies in the History of English Thought and Literature from Bacon to Pope*. Stanford and London, 1969.

———. *The Triumph of the English Language*. Stanford, 1966.

Jones, William Powell. *The Rhetoric of Science: A Study of Scientific Ideas and Imagery in Eighteenth-Century Poetry*. Berkeley and Los Angeles, 1966.

Jonson, Ben. *The Complete Poetry of Ben Jonson*. Ed. William B. Hunter, Jr. New York, 1968.

Kaufmann, U. Milo. *"The Pilgrim's Progress" and Traditions in Puritan Meditation*. New Haven, 1966.

Kearney, Hugh F., ed. *Origins of the Scientific Revolution*. New York, 1964.

Keeling, S. V. *Descartes*. London, Oxford, New York, 1968.

Kennedy, William John. *Rhetorical Norms in Renaissance Literature*. New Haven, 1978.

King, Walter N. "John Lyly and Elizabethan Rhetoric." *Studies in Philology* 52 (1955):149–61.

Knights, L. C. "Bacon and the Seventeenth-Century Dissociation of Sensibility." *Scrutiny* 11 (1943):268–285; rpt. Knights, *Explorations: Essays in Criticism*. London, 1946. Pp. 92–111.

Knott, John R., Jr. "Sir Thomas Browne and the Labyrinth of Truth." In *Approaches to Sir Thomas Browne*, ed. C. A. Patrides. Columbia, Mo., 1982.

Knowlson, James. *Universal Language Schemes in England and France, 1600–1800*. Toronto, 1975.

Kocher, Paul H. *Science and Religion in Elizabethan England*. San Marino, 1953.

Korach, Alice Florence. "The Dialectic Structure of English Renaissance Literature." *Dissertation Abstracts International* 41 (1980):1612A.

Krailsheimer, A. J. *Studies in Self-Interest from Descartes to La Bruyère*. Oxford, 1962.

Kranidas, Thomas. "'Decorum' and the Style of Milton's Antiprelatical Tracts." *Studies in Philology* 62 (1965):176–187.

———. "Milton and the Rhetoric of Zeal." *Texas Studies in Language and Literature* 6 (1965):423–432.

———. "Milton's *Of Reformation*: The Politics of Vision." *ELH* 49 (1982):497–513.

Krapp, George Philip. *The Rise of English Literary Prose*. New York, 1915.

Lanham, Richard A. *The Motives of Eloquence: Literary Rhetoric in the Renaissance*. New Haven, 1976.

Larsen, R. E. "The Aristotelianism of Bacon's *Novum Organum*." *Journal of the History of Ideas* 23 (1962):435–450.

Laughton, Eric. "Cicero and the Greek Orators." *American Journal of Philology* 82 (1961):27–49.

Lausberg, Heinrich. *Handbuch der literarischen Rhetorik: Eine Grundlegung der Literaturwissenschaft.* 2 vols. 1960; rpt. Munich, 1973.

Lechner, Joan Marie. *Renaissance Concepts of the Commonplaces: An Historical Investigation of the General and Universal Ideas Used in All Argumentation and Persuasion.* . . . New York, 1962.

Leeman, Anton Daniël. *Orationis Ratio: The Stylistic Theories and Practice of the Orators, Historians, and Philosophers.* 2 vols. Amsterdam, 1963.

Leibnitz, [Gottfried Wilhelm von]. *Selections.* Ed. Philip P. Wiener. New York, 1951.

Lerch-Davis, Genie S. "Rebellion Against Public Prose: The Letters of Dorothy Osborne to William Temple (1652–54)." *Texas Studies in Language and Literature* 20 (1978):386–415.

Lewalski, Barbara Kiefer. *Donne's "Anniversaries" and the Poetry of Praise: The Creation of a Symbolic Mode.* Princeton, 1973.

———. "Milton: Political Beliefs and Polemical Methods, 1659–60." *PMLA* 74 (1959):191–202.

———. *Protestant Poetics and the Seventeenth-Century Religious Lyric.* Princeton, 1979.

Leyden, W. von. *Seventeenth-Century Metaphysics: An Examination of Some Main Concepts and Theories.* New York, 1968.

Lieb, Michael. "Milton and the Organicist Polemic." *Milton Studies* 4 (1972):79–99.

———. "Milton's *Of Reformation* and the Dynamics of Controversy." In Lieb and Shawcross, *Achievements of the Left Hand* . . . , pp. 55–82.

———, and John T. Shawcross, eds. *Achievements of the Left Hand: Essays on the Prose of John Milton.* Amherst, 1974.

Literary Criticism: Plato to Dryden. Ed. Allan H. Gilbert. New York, 1940; rpt. Detroit, 1962.

Locke, John. *An Essay Concerning Human Understanding.* Ed. Russell Kirk. Chicago, 1956.

Long, Anne B. "'She May Have More Shapes Than One': Milton and the Modern Idea That Truth Changes." *Milton Studies* 6 (1974): 85–99.

McCarron, William E. "The 'Persuasive Rhetoric' of *Paradise Regained.*" *Milton Quarterly* 10 (1976): 15–21.

MacDonald, Hugh. "Another Aspect of Seventeenth-Century Prose." *Review of English Studies* 19 (1943): 33–43.

McGuire, Mary Ann. "'A Most Just Vituperation': Milton's Christian Orator in *Pro Se Defensio.*" *Studies in the Literary Imagination* 10, no. 2 (1977): 105–114.

McKeon, Richard. "Literary Criticism and the Concept of Imitation in Antiquity." In *Critics and Criticism, Ancient and Modern,* ed. R. S. Crane. Chicago, 1952. Pp. 141–175.

———. "Rhetoric in the Middle Ages." In *Critics and Criticism, Ancient and Modern,* ed. R. S. Crane. Chicago, 1952. Pp. 260–296.

McLean, Antonia. *Humanism and the Rise of Science in Tudor England.* New York, 1972.

McRae, Robert. "The Unity of the Sciences: Bacon, Descartes, Leibniz." *Journal of the History of Ideas* 18 (1957): 27–48.

McNamee, Maurice B., S.J. "Bacon's Inductive Method and Humanistic Grammar." *Studies in the Literary Imagination* 4, no. 1 (1971): 81–106.

————. *Literary Decorum in Francis Bacon.* St. Louis University Studies, Series A, Humanities, vol. 1, no. 3. St. Louis, 1950. 1–52.

Major, John M. "Milton's View of Rhetoric." *Studies in Philosophy* 64 (1967): 685–711.

Martz, Louis L. *The Paradise Within: Studies in Vaughan, Traherne, and Milton.* New Haven, 1964.

————. *The Poetry of Meditation.* Rev. ed. New Haven and London, 1962.

Mazzeo, Joseph Anthony. "A Critique of Some Modern Theories of Metaphysical Poetry. *Modern Philology* 50 (1952): 88–96.

————. "St. Augustine's Rhetoric of Silence: Truth vs. Eloquence and Things vs. Signs." *Renaissance and Seventeenth-Century Studies.* New York and London, 1964. Pp. 1–28.

————. "Seventeenth-Century English Prose Style: The Quest for a Natural Style." *Mosaic* 6, no. 3 (1973): 104–144.

Merton, Egon Stephen. *Science and Imagination in Sir Thomas Browne.* New York, 1949.

————. "Sir Thomas Browne's Scientific Quest." *Journal of the History of Medicine and Allied Science* 3, no. 2 (1948): 214–228.

Merton, R.K. "Science, Technology, and Society in Seventeenth-Century England." *Osiris* 4 (1938): 360–632.

Metaphysical Poetry. Ed. Malcolm Bradbury and David Palmer. Bloomington and London, 1971.

The Metaphysical Poets: Key Essays on Metaphysical Poetry and the Major Metaphysical Poets. Ed. Frank Kermode. Greenwich, Conn., 1969.

Metz, Rudolf. "Bacon's Part in the Intellectual Movement of His Time." In *Seventeenth Century Studies Presented to Sir Herbert Grierson.* Oxford, 1938. Pp. 21–32.

Miller, George E. "Stylistic Rhetoric and the Language of God in *Paradise Lost*, Book III." *Language and Style* 8 (1975): 111–126.

Miller, Perry. *The New England Mind: The Seventeenth Century.* New York, 1939; rpt. Boston, 1961.

Miller, William E. "Double Translation in English Humanistic Education." *Sewanee Review* 10 (1963): 163–174.

Milton, John. *Complete Poetry and Major Prose.* Ed. Merritt Y. Hughes. New York, 1957.

Miner, Earl. "Patterns of Stoicism in Thought and Prose Styles, 1530–1700." *PMLA* 85 (1970): 1023–34.

Mintz, Samuel I. "The Motion of Thought: Intellectual and Philosophical

Backgrounds." In *The Age of Milton: Backgrounds to Seventeenth-Century Literature*, ed. C. A. Patrides and Raymond B. Waddington. Manchester, England, and Totowa, N.J., 1980 Pp. 138–69. (On Milton, Bacon, Browne, Hobbes, and others.)

Miriam, Joseph, Sister. *Rhetoric in Shakespeare's Time*. New York, 1962.

―――. *Shakespeare's Use of the Arts of Language*. New York, 1947.

Mitchell, W. Fraser. *English Pulpit Oratory from Andrewes to Tillotson: A Study of Its Literary Aspects*. New York and Toronto, 1932.

Montaigne. *The Complete Essays of Montaigne*. Trans. Donald M. Frame. Stanford, 1965.

Morrissey, Thomas P. "The Self and the Meditative Tradition in Donne's *Devotions*." *Notre Dame English Journal* 13 (1980): 29–49.

Moss, Leonard. "The Rhetorical Style of *Samson Agonistes*. *Modern Philology* 62 (1965): 296–301.

Mourgues, Odette de. *Metaphysical, Baroque, and Précieux Poetry*. Oxford, 1953.

Mueller, William R. *John Donne: Preacher*. Princeton, 1962.

Mulder, John R. "Literary Scepticism: Montaigne and Sir Thomas Browne." *Dissertation Abstracts International* 24 (1964): 5389.

Murphy, James J. *Rhetoric in the Middle Ages: A History of Rhetorical Theory from St. Augustine to the Renaissance*. Berkeley, 1974.

―――, ed. *Renaissance Eloquence: Studies in the Theory and Practice of Renaissance Rhetoric*. Berkeley and Los Angeles, 1983.

―――. *Renaissance Rhetoric: A Short Title Catalogue*. New York, 1981.

Murrin, Michael. "The Language of Milton's Heaven." *Modern Philology* 74 (1977): 350–365.

Nathanson, Leonard. *The Strategy of Truth: A Study of Sir Thomas Browne*. Chicago and London, 1967.

Nauert, Charles G., Jr. *Agrippa and the Crisis of Renaissance Thought*. Urbana, 1955.

Nelson, Norman E. *Peter Ramus and the Confusion of Logic, Rhetoric, and Poetry*. University of Michigan Contributions in Modern Philology no. 2. Ann Arbor, 1947.

Neumann, Joshua H. "Milton's Prose Vocabulary." *PMLA* 60 (1945): 102–112.

Nicolson, Majorie Hope. *The Breaking of the Circle: Studies in the Effect of the "New Science" upon Seventeenth Century Poetry*. Evanston, 1950; rev. ed., New York, 1960.

―――. "The Early Stage of Cartesianism in England." *Studies in Philology* 26 (1929): 356–374.

―――. *Newton Demands the Muse*. Princeton, 1946.

―――. *Science and Imagination*. Ithaca, 1962.

Norden, Eduard. *Die antike Kunstprosa vom VI. Jahrhundert v. Chr. bis in die Zeit der Renaissance*. 2 vols. Leipzig, 1898; 5th ed., Stuttgart, 1958.

Ong, Walter J., ed. and trans. *A Fuller Course in the Art of Logic ... Complete Prose Works of John Milton*, vol. VIII. New Haven, 1982.

———. "Logic and the Epic Muse: Reflections on Noetic Structures in Milton's Milieu." In Lieb and Shawcross, eds., *Achievements of the Left Hand ...*, pp. 239–268.

———. "Milton's Logical Epic and Evolving Consciousness." *Proceedings of the American Philosophical Society* 120 (1976): 295–305.

———. "Oral Residue in Tudor Prose Style." *PMLA* 80 (1965), 145–54.

———. "Ramism." In *Dictionary of the History of Ideas* 4:42–45.

———. *Ramus, Method, and the Decay of Dialogue: From the Art of Discourse to the Art of Reason*. Cambridge, Mass., 1958.

———. *Rhetoric, Romance, and Technology: Studies in the Interaction of Expression and Culture*. Ithaca, 1971.

Orgel, Stephen, ed. *The Renaissance and the Gods*. New York and London, 1976.

Patrick, J. Max, et al., eds. *Style, Rhetoric, and Rhythm: Essays by Morris W. Croll*. Princeton, 1966.

Patrick, Mary. *Sextus Empiricus and Greek Scepticism*. Cambridge, 1899.

Patrides, C. A., ed. *Approaches to Sir Thomas Browne: The Ann Arbor Tercentenary Lectures and Essays*. Columbia, Mo., 1982.

———. and Raymond B. Waddington, eds. *The Age of Milton: Backgrounds to Seventeenth-Century Literature*. Manchester, England, and Totowa, N.J., 1980.

Patterson, Annabel M. *Hermogenes and the Renaissance: Seven Ideas of Style*. Princeton, 1970.

Pebworth, Ted-Larry. "Johnson's *Timber* and the Essay Tradition." In *Essays in Honor of Esmond Linworth Marilla*, ed. Thomas A. Kirby and William J. Olive. Baton Rouge, 1970. Pp. 115–126.

———. "Not Being, but Passing: Defining the Early English Essay." *Studies in the Literary Imagination* 10, no. 2 (1977): 17–27.

———. "'Real English Evidence': Stoicism and the English Essay Tradition." *PMLA* 87 (1972): 101–102.

———. "Wandering in the America of Truth: *Pseudodoxia Epidemica* and the Essay Tradition." In *Approaches to Sir Thomas Browne ...*, ed. C. A. Patrides. Columbia, Mo., and London, 1982.

Perkins, William. *Prophetica, sive de sacra et unica ratione concionandi (1592)*. Trans. as *The Arte of Prophecying*. London, 1631.

Perlette, John M. "Milton, Ascham, and the Rhetoric of the Divorce Controversy." *Milton Studies* 10 (1977): 195–215.

Peterson, Douglas L. *The English Lyric from Wyatt to Donne: A History of the Plain and Eloquent Styles*. Princeton, 1967.

Pigman, G. W., III. "Imitation and the Renaissance Sense of the Past: The Reception of Erasmus' *Ciceronianus*." *The Journal of Medieval and Renaissance Studies* 9 (1979): 155–177.

―――. "Versions of Imitation in the Renaissance." *Renaissance Quarterly* 33 (1980): 1–32.

Plato. *The Works of Plato*. Trans. B. Jowett. New York, [1937].

Plett, Heinrich F. *Rhetorik der Affekte: Englische Wirkungsästhetik im Zeitalter der Renaissance*. Tübingen, 1975.

Pooley, Roger. "Language and Loyalty: Plain Style at the Restoration." *Literature and History* 6 (1980): 2–18.

Popkin, Richard H. *The History of Scepticism from Erasmus to Descartes*. Assen, Netherlands, 1960. [Rev. ed., *The History of Scepticism from Erasmus to Spinoza*. Berkeley, 1979.]

―――. "Skepticism in Modern Thought." In *Dictionary of the History of Ideas* 4:240–251.

―――. "Skepticism, Theology, and the Scientific Revolution in the Seventeenth Century." In *Problems in the Philosophy of Science*. ed. Imre Lakatos and Alan Musgrave. Proceedings of the International Colloquium in the Philosophy of Science. Amsterdam, 1968. 3:1–39.

Preus, James Samuel. *From Shadow to Promise: Old Testament Interpretation from Augustine to the Young Luther*. Cambridge, Mass., 1969.

Prior, Moody E. "Eighteenth-Century Bibliography." *Philological Quarterly* 11 (1932): 179–180. (Critique of R. F. Jones's essay "The attack on pulpit eloquence in the Restoration. . . .")

Purver, Margery. *The Royal Society: Concept and Creation*. London, 1967.

―――, and Edmund John Bowen. *The Beginnings of the Royal Society*. London, 1960.

Quinn, Dennis. "Donne's Christian Eloquence." *ELH* 27 (1960): 276–297. Rpt. in Fish, ed., *Seventeenth-Century Prose*, pp. 353–374.

Randall, John Herman, Jr. "The Development of Scientific Method in the School of Padua." In *Renaissance Essays*, ed. Paul O. Kristeller and Philip P. Wiener. New York and Evanston, 1968. Pp. 217–251.

Randall, Steven. "The Rhetoric of Montaigne's Self-Portrait: Speaker and Subject." *Studies in Philology* 73 (1976): 285–301.

Regosin, Richard L. *The Matter of My Book: Montaigne's Essais as the Book of the Self*. Berkeley, 1977.

Riffaterre, Michael. "The Stylistic Approach to Literary History." *New Literary History* 2 (1970): 39–55.

Righter, Anne. "Francis Bacon." In Vickers, *Essential Articles*, pp. 300–321.

Robertson, Jean. *The Art of Letter Writing: An Essay on the Handbooks Published in England During the Sixteenth and Seventeenth Centuries*. Liverpool and London, 1942.

Rollin, Roger B. "Milton's 'I's': The Narrator and the Reader in *Paradise Lost*." In *Renaissance and Modern Essays in Honor of Edwin M. Moseley*, ed. Murray J. Levith. Saratoga Springs, N.Y., 1976. Pp. 33–35.

Rossi, Paolo. "Baconianism." *Dictionary of the History of Ideas* 1:172–179.

———. *Francis Bacon: From Magic to Science.* Trans. Sacha Rabinovitch. Chicago, 1968.

Rubel, Veré. *Poetic Diction in the English Renaissance from Skelton through Spenser.* New York and London, 1941.

Ryan, Lawrence. *Roger Ascham.* Stanford, 1963.

Sackton, Alexander. "Donne and the Privacy of Verse." *SEL:Studies in English Literature, 1500–1900* 7 (1967): 67–82.

———. *Rhetoric as a Dramatic Language in Ben Jonson.* New York, 1948.

Safer, Elaine B. "The Socratic Dialogue and 'Knowledge in the Making' in *Paradise Regained." Milton Studies* 6 (1974): 215–226.

Salmon, Vivian. *The Study of Language in Seventeenth-Century England.* Amsterdam, 1979.

Sammons, Todd Hunter. "Stylistic Variation in Milton's *Paradise Lost." Dissertation Abstracts International* 40 (1980): 5879A.

Samuel, Irene. "Milton on the Province of Rhetoric." *Milton Studies* 10 (1977): 177–193.

Sasek, Lawrence A. *The Literary Temper of the English Puritans.* Baton Rouge, 1961.

Saveson, J. E. "Differing Reactions to Descartes Among the Cambridge Platonists." *Journal of the History of Ideas* 31 (1960): 560–567.

Sayce, R. A. *The Essays of Montaigne: A Critical Exploration.* London, 1972.

———. "Montaigne et la peinture du passage." *Saggi e Ricerche di Letteratura Francese* 4 (Torino, 1963): 9–59.

———. *Style in French Prose.* Oxford, 1953.

———. "Style in Literature." *Dictionary of the History of Ideas* 4: 330–333.

Schapiro, Meyer. "Style." In *Anthropology Today,* ed. A. L. Kroeber. Chicago, 1953. Pp. 387–412.

Schouls, Peter A. *The Imposition of Method: A Study of Descartes and Locke.* Oxford, 1980.

Scott, Izora. *Controversies over the Imitation of Cicero as a Model for Style, and Some Phases of Their Influence on the Schools of the Renaissance.* New York, 1910.

Segel, Harold B. *The Baroque Poem: A Comparative Survey.* New York, 1974.

Seigel, Jerrold E. *Rhetoric and Philosophy in Renaissance Humanism: The Union of Eloquence and Wisdom, Petrarch to Valla.* Princeton, 1968.

Sellin, Paul. "The Proper Dating of Donne's 'Satyre III'." *Huntington Library Quarterly* 43 (1980): 275–312.

Seventeenth-Century English Poetry. Ed. John T. Shawcross and Ronald David Emma. Philadelphia and New York, 1969.

Shapiro, Barbara J. "History and Natural History in Sixteenth- and Seventeenth-Century England: An Essay on the Relationship between Humanism and Science." In *English Scientific Virtuosi of the Sixteenth and Seventeenth Centuries*, ed. Barbara Shapiro and Robert G. Frank, Jr. Los Angeles, 1979. Pp. 1–55.

———. *John Wilkins, 1614–1672: An Intellectual Biography*. Berkeley, 1969.

———. *Probability and Certainty in Seventeenth-Century England: A Study of the Relationships Between Natural Science, Religion, History, Law and Literature*. Princeton, 1983.

Shawcross, John T. "The Poet as Orator: One Phase of His Judicial Pose." In *The Rhetoric of Renaissance Poetry from Wyatt to Milton*, ed. Thomas O. Sloan and Raymond B. Waddington. Berkeley, 1974. Pp. 5–36.

———. "The Rhetor as Creator in *Paradise Lost*." *Milton Studies* 8 (1975): 209–219.

Sherry, Beverly. "Speech in *Paradise Lost*. *Milton Studies* 8 (1975): 247–266.

Simon, Irène. "Dryden's Prose Style." *Revue des langues vivantes* 31 (1965): 505–530. Rpt. in Fish, ed., *Seventeenth-Century Prose*, pp. 543–572.

———. *Three Restoration Divines: Barrow, South, Tillotson*. Paris, 1967.

Skinner, Quentin. "Motives, Intentions, and the Interpretation of Texts." *New Literary History* 3 (1971–72): 393–408.

Sloan, Thomas O. "Rhetoric and Meditation: Three Case Studies." *Journal of Medieval and Renaissance Studies* 1 (1971): 45–58.

———. "Rhetoric, 'Logic,' and Poetry: The Formal Cause." In C. A. Patrides and Raymond B. Waddington, eds., *The Age of Milton . . .*, pp. 307–337.

Smallenburg, Harry R. "Continguities and Moving Limbs: Style as Argument in *Areopagitica*." *Milton Studies* 9 (1976): 169–184.

———. "Government of the Spirit: Style, Structure, and Theme in *Treatise of Civil Power*." In Lieb and Shawcross, eds., *Achievements of the Left Hand . . .*, pp. 219–238.

———. "Milton's Cosmic Sentences." *Language and Style* 5 (1972): 108–114. (On *Tenure of Kings. . . .*)

Smith, A. J. "An Examination of Some Claims Made for Ramism." *Review of English Studies* n.s., 7 (1956): 348–359.

Smith, G. C. Moore. "A Note on Milton's *Art of Logic*." *Review of English Studies* 13 (1937): 335–340.

Smith, George William, Jr. "Iterative Rhetoric in *Paradise Lost*." *Modern Philology* 74 (1976): 1–19.

———. "Milton's 'Prompt Eloquence,' Debate and Rhetoric." *Dissertation Abstracts International* 36 (1975): 2225A.

Smith, John. *The Mysterie of Rhetorique Unveiled*. London, 1657 [1656].

Sonnino, Lee A. *A Handbook to Sixteenth-Century Rhetoric*. London, 1968.

Spitzer, Leo. *Linguistics and Literary History*. Princeton, 1948.

———. "Notes on the Poetic and the Empirical 'I' in Medieval Authors." *Traditio* 4 (1946): 414–422.

Sprat, Thomas. *History of the Royal Society*. Ed. Jackson I. Cope and Harold Whitmore Jones. St. Louis, 1958.

Starr, G. A. *Defoe and Spiritual Autobiography*. Princeton, 1965.

————. "Defoe's Prose Style: 1. The Language of Interpretation." *Modern Philology* 71 (1974): 274–294.

Staton, Walter F., Jr. "The Characters of Style in Elizabethan Prose." *Journal of English and Germanic Philology* 57 (1958): 197–207.

Stavely, Keith W. *The Politics of Milton's Prose Style*. New Haven and London, 1975.

Steadman, John M. "Beyond Hercules: Bacon and the Scientist as Hero." *Studies in the Literary Imagination* 4 (1971): 3–47.

————. *Milton's Epic Characters: Image and Idol*. Chapel Hill, 1968. Pp. 139–173. ("Logic and the Argument"); pp. 227–277 ("The Devil as Rhetorician").

————. "'Passions Well Imitated': Rhetoric and Poetic in the Preface to *Samson Agonistes*." In *Calm of Mind . . .*, ed. Joseph Anthony Wittreich, Jr. Cleveland, 1971. Pp. 175–207.

Stein, Arnold. *George Herbert's Lyrics*. Baltimore, 1968.

Stephens, James. *Francis Bacon and the Style of Science*. Chicago and London, 1975.

————. "Rhetorical Problems in Renaissance Science." *Philosophy and Rhetoric* 8 (1975): 213–229.

————. "Science and the Aphorism: Bacon's Theory of the Philosophical Style." *Speech Monographs* 37 (1970): 157–171.

Steward, Stanley. *The Expanded Voice: The Art of Thomas Traherne*. San Marino, Calif., 1970.

Stimson, Dorothy L. "Comenius and the Invisible College." *Isis* 23 (1935): 383–388.

————. "Dr. Wilkins and the Royal Society." *Journal of Modern History* 3 (1931): 539–563.

————. "Puritanism and the 'New Philosophy' in Seventeenth Century England." *Bulletin of the Institute of the History of Medicine* 3 (1935): 321–334.

————. *Scientists and Amateurs: A History of the Royal Society*. New York, 1948.

Strauss, Leo. *The Political Philosophy of Hobbes: Its Basis and Its Genesis*. Trans. Elsa M. Sinclair. Chicago and London, 1963.

Strong, E. W. "Newton's 'Mathematical Way.'" In *Roots of Scientific Thought*, ed. Philip P. Wiener and Aaron Noland. New York, 1957.

Struever, Nancy S. *The Language of History in the Renaissance: Rhetoric and Historical Consciousness in Florentine Humanism*. Princeton, 1970.

Summers, Joseph H. *George Herbert, His Religion and Art*. London and Cambridge, Mass., 1954.

————. "Stanley Fish's Reading of Seventeenth-Century Literature." *Modern Language Quarterly* 35 (1934): 403–417.

Sutherland, James. *Restoration and Augustan Prose.* . . . Los Angeles, 1956.

————. "Restoration Prose." In *Stuart and Georgian Moments.* Berkeley, 1972. Pp. 109–126.

Syme, Sir Ronald. *Tacitus.* 2 vols. Oxford, 1958; rpt. 1967.

Sypher, Wylie. *Four Stages of Renaissance Style: Transformations in Art and Literature, 1400–1700.* Garden City, N.Y., 1955.

Szenher, Phillip John. "'Poetry, Both in Divine and Human Things': A Rhetorical Reading of *Paradise Regained.*" *Dissertation Abstracts International* 36 (1975): 1539A–40A.

Takács, Ferenc. "Seventeenth Century English Philosophy on the Poetic Use of Language." In *Studies in English and American,* ed. Erzsébet Perényi and Tibor Frank. Budapest, 1975. 2: 57–89.

Tarselino, R. "'All colours will agree in the dark': A Note on a Feature of the Style of Francis Bacon." In Vickers, *Essential Articles,* pp. 293–299.

Taylor, Warren. *Tudor Figures of Rhetoric.* Whitewater, Wisc., 1972.

Thompson, Elbert N. S. "Milton's Prose Style." *Philological Quarterly* 14 (1935): 1–15.

————. *The Seventeenth Century Essay.* Iowa City, 1926.

Tillman, James S. "The Satirist Satirized: Burton's Democritus, Jr." *Studies in the Literary Imagination* 10, no. 2 (1977): 89–96.

Tindall, William York. *John Bunyan, Mechanick Preacher.* New York, 1934.

Tricomi, A. H. "Milton and the Jonsonian Plain Style." *Milton Studies* 13 (1979): 129–144.

Trimpi, Wesley. *Ben Jonson's Poems: A Study of the Plain Style.* Stanford, 1962.

Trousdale, Marion. "Recurrence and Renascence: Rhetorical Imitation in Ascham and Sturm." *English Literary Renaissance* 6 (1976): 156–179.

Tulloch, John. *Rational Theology and Christian Philosophy in England in the Seventeenth Century.* Edinburgh and London, 1872.

Tuve, Rosemond. "Baroque and Mannerist Milton?" *Milton Studies in Honor of Harris Francis Fletcher.* Urbana, Ill., 1961. Pp. 209–225.

————. *Elizabethan and Metaphysical Imagery: Renaissance Poetic and Twentieth-Century Critics.* Chicago, 1947.

————. "Imagery and Logic: Ramus and Metaphysical Poetics." *Journal of the History of Ideas* 3 (1942): 365–400.

Van Leeuwen, Henry G. "Certainty in Seventeenth-Century Thought." *Dictionary of the History of Ideas* 1: 304–311.

————. *The Problem of Certainty in English Thought, 1630–1690.* 2nd ed. The Hague, 1970.

Vickers, Brian. *Classical Rhetoric in English Poetry.* London, 1968; New York, 1970.

———, ed. *Essential Articles for the Study of Francis Bacon*. Hamden, Conn., 1968.

———. *Francis Bacon and Renaissance Prose*. Cambridge, 1968.

———, ed. *Rhetoric Revalued: Papers from the International Society for the History of Rhetoric*. New York, 1982.

———. "Swift and the Baconian Idol." In *The World of Jonathan Swift*, ed. Brian Vickers. Oxford, 1968. Pp. 87–128.

Vico, Giambattista. *On the Study Methods of Our Time*. Trans. Elio Gianturco. Indianapolis, New York, Kansas City, 1965.

Villey, Pierre. *Montaigne et François Bacon*. Paris, 1913.

———. *Les Sources et l'évolution des Essais de Montaigne*. Paris, 1908; 2nd ed., Paris, 1933.

Vos, Alvin. "Form and Function in Roger Ascham's Prose." *Philological Quarterly* 55 (1976): 305–322.

———. "'Good Matter and Good Utterance': The Character of English Ciceronianism." *SEL: Studies in English Literature, 1500–1900* 19 (1979): 3–18.

———. "Humanistic Standards of Diction in the Inkhorn Controversy." *Studies in Philology* 73 (1976): 376–396.

———. "Models and Methodologies in Renaissance Prose Stylistics." *Studies in the Literary Imagination* 10 no. 2 (1977): 1–15.

———. Review of James Stephens, *Francis Bacon and the Style of Science* (1975). *Modern Philology* 76 (1979): 401–403.

Wallace, Karl R. "Aspects of Modern Rhetoric in Francis Bacon." *Quarterly Journal of Speech* 42 (1956): 398–406.

———. "Bacon's Conception of Rhetoric." In *Historical Studies of Rhetoric and Rhetoricians*, ed. Raymond F. Howes. Ithaca, 1961.

———. "Chief Guides for the Study of Bacon's Speeches." *Studies in the Literary Imagination* 4 (1971): 173–188.

———. "Francis Bacon and Method: Theory and Practice." *Speech Monographs* 40 (1973): 243–272.

———. *Francis Bacon and the Nature of Man* . . . . Urbana, Chicago, London, 1967.

———. *Francis Bacon on Communication and Rhetoric*. Chapel Hill, 1943.

———. "Francis Bacon on Understanding, Reason, and Rhetoric." *Speech Monographs* 38 (1971): 79–91.

———. "Imagination and Bacon's View of Rhetoric." In *Dimensions of Rhetorical Scholarship*, ed. Roger E. Nebergall. Norman, Okla., 1963. Pp. 65–81.

Wallerstein, Ruth. *Studies in Seventeenth Century Poetic*. Madison, 1950; rpt. Madison and Milwaukee, 1965.

Walzer, Michael. *The Revolution of the Saints: A Study in the Origin of Radical Politics*. Cambridge, Mass., 1965.

Wanning, Andrews. "Some Changes in the Prose Style of the Seventeenth Century." Diss., Cambridge, 1936.

Warren, Austin. "The Style of Sir Thomas Browne." *Kenyon Review* 13 (1951): 674–687.

Watson, Richard A. *The Downfall of Cartesianism, 1673–1712: A Study of Epistemological Issues in Late Seventeenth-Century Cartesianism.* The Hague, 1966.

Weaver, Richard. *The Ethics of Rhetoric.* Chicago, 1953.

Webber, Joan. "Celebration of Word and World in Lancelot Andrewes' Style." *Journal of English and Germanic Philology* 64 (1965): 255–269.

———. *Contrary Music: The Prose Style of John Donne.* Madison, Wis., 1963.

———. *The Eloquent "I": Style and Self in Seventeenth-Century Prose.* Madison, Milwaukee, London, 1968.

———. "Stylistics: A Bridging of Life and Art in Seventeenth-Century Studies." *New Literary History* 2 (1971): 283–296.

Weber, Henri. *La Création poétique au XVIe siècle en France.* Paris, 1955.

Webster, Charles. *The Great Instauration: Science, Medicine, and Reform, 1626–1660.* New York, 1976.

———, ed. *The Intellectual Revolution of the Seventeenth Century.* London and Boston, 1974.

Webster, John. "'The Method of a Poete': An Inquiry into Tudor Conceptions of Poetic Sequence." *English Literary Renaissance* 11 (1981): 22–43.

———. "Oration and Method in Sidney's *Apology*: A Contemporary's Account." *Modern Philology* 79 (1981): 1–15.

Weinberg, Bernard. "Rhetoric After Plato." *Dictionary of the History of Ideas* 4: 167–173.

———, ed. *Trattati di poetica e retorica del Cinquecento.* 3 vols. Bari, Italy, 1970–72.

Weinbrot, Howard D. "The Reader, the General and the Particular." *Eighteenth-Century Studies* 5 (1971–72): 80–96.

Weiss, Brian. "Milton's Use of Ramist Method in His Scholarly Writings." *Dissertation Abstracts International* 35 (1975): 4569A.

Weitzel, Roy L. "Eloquence and Truth in Milton's Prose." *Dissertation Abstracts International* 34 (1974): 7724A–25A.

Wellek, René. "Concept of Baroque in Literary Scholarship." *Journal of Aesthetics and Art Criticism* 5 (1946): 77–100.

Westby, Selmer N. "The Puritan Funeral Sermon in Seventeenth Century England." *Dissertation Abstracts International* 31 (1972): 6076A.

Westfall, Richard S. *Science and Religion in Seventeenth-Century England.* New Haven, 1958.

Whelan, Edward J. "The Rhetoric of Early Renaissance Meditation." *Dissertation Abstracts International* 34 (1974): 5935A–36A.

Whitaker, Juanita. "'The Wars of Truth': Wisdom and Strength in *Areopagitica.*" *Milton Studies* 9 (1976): 185–201.

Wiley, Margaret L. "Francis Bacon: Induction and/or Rhetoric." *Studies in the Literary Imagination* 4, no. 1 (1971): 65–79.

_____. *The Subtle Knot: Creative Scepticism in Seventeenth-Century England.*London, 1952.

Wilkinson, L.P. *Golden Latin Artistry.* Cambridge, 1963.

Willey, Basil. *The Seventeenth Century Background: Studies in the Thought of the Age in Relation to Poetry and Religion.* London, 1934; rpt. 1949.

Williams, George Walton, ed. *The Complete Poetry of Richard Crashaw.* Garden City, N.Y., 1970.

Williamson, George. *The Senecan Amble: A Study of Prose Form from Bacon to Collier.* Chicago, 1966.

_____. "Strong Lines." *English Studies* 18 (1936): 152–159.

Wilson, F. P. *Seventeenth Century Prose: Five Lectures.* Berkeley and Los Angeles, 1960.

Wimsatt, W. K. *The Prose Style of Samuel Johnson.* New Haven, 1941.

Wittreich, Joseph Anthony, Jr. "'The Crown of Eloquence': The Figure of the Orator in Milton's Prose Works." In Lieb and Shawcross, ed., *Achievements of the Left Hand . . .* , pp. 3–54.

Wölfflin, Heinrich. *Renaissance and Baroque.* Trans. Kathrin Simon. Ithaca, 1966.

Wright, Abraham. *Five Sermons, in Five Several Styles: or Waies of Preaching.* London, 1656.

Wurtele, Douglas. "Milton, Satan, and the Sophists." *Renaissance and Reformation* 3 (1979): 189–200.

_____. "'Persuasive Rhetoric': The Techniques of Milton's Archetypal Sophist." *English Studies in Canada* (Toronto) 3 (1977): 18–33.

Youngren, William H. "Conceptualism and Neoclassic Generality." *ELH* 47 (1980): 705–740.

_____. "Dr. Johnson, Joseph Warton, and the 'Theory of Particularity'." *Dispositio* 4 (1979): 163–188.

_____. "Generality in Augustan Satire." In *In Defense of Reading*, ed. Reuben A. Brower and Richard Poirier. New York, 1962. Pp. 206–234.

_____. "Generality, Science and Poetic Language in the Restoration." *ELH* 35 (1968): 158–187.

_____. *Semantics, Linguistics, and Criticism.* New York, 1972.

Zarov, Herbert. "Milton and the Rhetoric of Rebellion." *Milton Quarterly* 7 (1973): 47–50.

Zeitlin, Jacob. "The Development of Bacon's Essays, with Special Reference to Montaigne's Influence on Them." *Journal of English and Germanic Philology* 27 (1928): 496–519.

Index

Adams, Thomas, 38
Addison, Joseph, 130, 134
Adolph, Robert, 34, 48*n*26, 49*n*28, 50*n*29, 133*n*16
Aeschylus, 12–13*n*9, 140
Agrippa von Nettesheim, Henry Cornelius, 13
Alberti, Leon Battista, 115*n*3, 119*n*8
Alciati, Andreas, 138, 139, 141, 146, 150
Aletheia, 138
Allegories, 112. *See also* Figures of speech
America: symbolic, 9
Ammianus Marcellinus, 13*n*9
Amphion, 146
Analogy, universal, 123–24
Andrewes, Lancelot, 38
Anguillara, Giovanni Andrea dell', 146
Animals: symbolic, 146. *See also* Chimaera; Cicada; Dog; Dragon; Frog; Goat; Lion; Parakeet; Parrot; Pegasus; Serpent; Sphynx
Anti-Ciceronian movement, 25–29, 31, 32, 47*n*25, 62. *See also* Ciceronianism
Aphorisms, proverbs, and adages, 84–85; Bacon on, 28–29, 43*n*21, 48*n*26
Apollonius of Rhodes, 153
Apuleius, 151
Archimedes, 87
Ariosto, Ludovico, 113*n*1, 116*n*4
Aristotle and Aristotelians, 42, 111; on rhetoric, 30, 58, 61*n*6, 67, 90, 124; Paduan, 87; mentioned, 51*n*30, 93, 96, 134, 142. *See also* Scholasticism
Armor: symbolic, 143

Arrow: symbolic, 149
Art history and literary history, 125. *See also* Precedents
Ascham, Roger, 35*n*14, 46–47, 66
Athena, 147
Attic style, 31, 62
Augustine, St., 41, 41*n*20, 74–75*n*4; and Milton, 79; on truth, 13*n*9, 54*n*1; mentioned, 49, 59, 113*n*1, 131

Bacon, Sir Francis: on education, 75*n*5; essays of, 48, 48*n*26, 129, 130; and idols of the marketplace, 20; on language, 20, 67–68, 79; on method, 43*n*21, 47–48, 102, 119*n*9, 134; on rhetoric, 90–91; style of, 19, 49*n*28, 104; on style of writing, 25–29, 35*n*14, 86, 106; on truth, 3–5, 4*n*3, 6–8, 13*n*9, 14, 15; mentioned, 100, 103, 110, 133
Baker, Herschel, 3*n*2
Balzac, Jean Louis Guez, sieur de, 32
Barish, Jonas, 35, 35*n*14, 50
Baroque style, 27, 31, 50–51, 88, 112, 115, 115*n*3, 4, 116–117, 120–23
Barptolemaeus Anulus, 147
Baudoin, Jean, 143–44
Baxter, Richard, 35–36 and *n*15
Bernini, Giovanni Lorenzo, 139
Bible: interpretation of, 44*n*22, 75*n*4; as source of truth, 54*n*1; as stylistic model, 34*n*13, 40–41 and *n*20, 46*n*23, 56–58, 63, 79, 81. *See also* Christ's life as model of style
Bie, Jacques de, 143
Bland, Robert, 13*n*9
Blount, Thomas, 24

Designer: Barbara Llewellyn
Compositor: Innovative Media
Printer: Braun-Brumfield, Inc.
Binder: Braun-Brumfield, Inc.
Text: 10/12 Sabon
Display: Sabon